Studying the Holocaust Through Film and Literature

Human Rights and Social Responsibility

Studying the Holocaust Through Film and Literature

Human Rights and Social Responsibility

Miriam Klein Kassenoff and Anita Meyer Meinbach

With a Foreword by
Dr. Michael Berenbaum

Christopher-Gordon Publishers, Inc.
Norwood, Massachusetts

Copyright Acknowledgments

Every effort has been made to contact copyright holders for permission to reproduce borrowed material where necessary. We apologize for any oversights and would be happy to rectify them in future printings.

Christopher~Gordon Publishers, Inc.
Bridging Theory and Practice

1502 Providence Highway, Suite 12
Norwood, Massachusetts 02062

800-934-8322
781-762-5577
www.Christopher-Gordon.com

Printed in Canada
10 9 8 7 6 5 4 3 2   08 07
ISBN-10 : 1-929024-76-2
ISBN-13 : 978-1-929024-76-6
Library of Congress Catalogue Number: 2004100014

Sara and Lili

She is one of two,
she is half of one,
and the other has vanished
and keeps vanishing.
She has outlived everything
except that vanishing.

She is one of two,
half of one;
she is less than half
and more than all,
for she contains all those
who did not come with her.
Her memory follows their hands
waving and shrinking faces
and helplessly chases them,
screaming warnings,
along that other road
that leads to trains;
she is still imploring them,
and they never stop dying.

She is one of two,
half of one.
The one who could not possibly
survive,
who bolted recklessly
from safety, with toddler and infant
and fugitive husband,
                    walked
from Hungary to Portugal,
lived—
and in Nashville, Cleveland, and Miami
lived. And Tibor became Teddy,
Marika was Miriam,
and the new one was just Hank, "our little Yankee."

One of two and half of one
and less than half and more than all.

Two stylish girls, identical,
in a very old photo,
arms around each other's waists,
inseparable.
Their eyes look into the camera
with such calm openness,
such clear understanding
that the camera's eternal moment
merely indicates the truth.

Everything except that separation
she has outlived.
Everything except that divergence
she has buried.

Millions have been born and have died,
entire spans of lives unfolded and expired,
since that photo was taken.

Ninety-one years old,
she holds the picture, and implores
the one, the half, the nothing, the all
who stands beside her:
"I told you, we have to go—now,
now, we have to go now!
We can't stay here.
Why didn't you
believe me?"

—James Berger

James Berger teaches English at Hofstra University. He is the author of *After the End: Representations of Post-Apocalypse* and the editor of Helen Keller's *The Story of My Life: The Restored Edition*. James Berger is married to Jennifer Klein, niece of Miriam Klein Kassenoff (Marika), co-author of this book.

On the Run and in Hiding:
Miriam Klein Family's Escape
From the Holocaust

The previous poem, "Sara and Lili," was written as a tribute to my mother, Sara, and her twin sister, Lili.

In December, 1940, my father, of blessed memory, Rabbi Maurice Klein, had managed to escape from the Hungarian Nazi Fascist Labor Battalion Work Camp, Saraspatek, where he had been a prisoner for a few months. When he rushed home to his family in Kosice, Slovakia, he convinced my mother Sara to embark on an escape route to Lisbon, Portugal, where he knew of ships that were waiting to take Jews to safety in America—that is, if one could make the journey in such perilous times.

Reluctantly and with much fear, Sara agreed to leave Kosice, and all she dearly loved, knowing that if she did not, my father would be recaptured and taken back to the Labor Camp.

She tried to convince her twin sister, Lili, and her family to come with us, but Lili refused, saying, "Sara, what will happen to us here will happen to you on the run. I am staying."

My mother took me (Marika), a small child of 4 years, and my new infant brother, Ted (Tibor), and we fled with my Dad. After 3 months of hiding and running throughout Eastern Europe, "running between the raindrops," with the Nazis always at our heels, we arrived in Lisbon, Portugal.

Our visa entry papers to the United States had expired, so we could not leave on The Nyassa for which we had transport reservations on April 15. After all those months of anticipation, we had made it alive and safely—only to miss the ship!

The Portuguese government housed us and other Jewish refugees in pensiones while our families waited in long, unbearable lines trying to get paperwork and permission to embark on other ships. The government gave us limited time to do this or we would be sent back to our countries of origin, which would certainly have meant death for all of us, as history would prove.

In May 1941, my father finally obtained the necessary papers and we boarded the ship *Ciudad Da Sevilla,* which brought us to the shore of the United States in June 1941, safe at last.

Soon after we arrived in the United States, my mother gave birth to my brother Hank. They chose an American name to celebrate our becoming American citizens.

The remaining Jews of Kosice, Czechoslovakia, and Hungary were transported to Auschwitz in 1944. Out of the 15,000 Jews of Kosice, 12,000 were immediately gassed on their arrival in Auschwitz. My father's family, the Kleins, had hidden in the ghetto attics of Kosice when the residents were transported to Auschwitz. The entire Klein family survived the Holocaust.

My mother's twin sister, Lili, and her husband and two small children were never heard from again.

This book was written in memory of Lili, her family, and all those Jewish families who perished from Hungary and Kosice, Czechoslovakia. They are gone but not forgotten.

Personal testimony of Dr. Miriam (Marika) Klein Kassenoff, who fled Nazi Europe in 1941 with her mother Sara, father Maurice, and infant brother Ted. Dr. Miriam Klein Kassenoff is co-author with Dr. Anita Meyer Meinbach of *Memories of the Night: Studies of the Holocaust.*

© 2004 Christopher-Gordon Publishers, Inc.

Once again, for my parents, Sara and Maurice.

M.K.K.

For the children—may the world you build be one of peace.

A.M.M.

Contents

Acknowledgments xi

Foreword xiii

Introduction xvii

Table I-1: Topic Resources xix

Part I. Historical Overview of the Holocaust 1

Part II. Topics: Film and Literature 17

  1. The World of the Persecuted: Into the Darkness 19

  2. The Mind of the Perpetrator: Anatomy of Evil 33

  3. The Mind of the Bystander: Indifference and Apathy 45

  4. Life in the Ghetto: Images of Hope and Despair 59

  5. Fighting Back: Spiritual and Physical Resistance 75

  6. Courage and Compassion: Stories of Rescue 95

  7. The Final Solution: The Camps 111

  8. The Power of Perseverance: Children Surviving the Holocaust ... 129

  9. The Holocaust, Human Rights, and Social Responsibility 151

Appendixes 165

  A. Bibliography 167

  B. Professional Bibliography 173

  C. Videography 177

  D. Webography 193

  E. Resource Centers 197

  F. Teacher Training Institutes, Community Programs, and Seminars ... 199

About the Authors 201

Index 203

Acknowledgments

Thank you to all the authors whose pieces are included in this book for graciously contributing their words and wisdom so that others can learn and remember.

Our deepest appreciation goes to Dr. Michael Berenbaum for his scholarly expertise and assistance.

A special thank you goes to the students of the "Holocaust Through Film and Literature" course at the University of Miami, Miami, Florida, whose enthusiasm, insights, and suggestions proved we were on the right course in using film and literature to teach the Holocaust.

To Sue Canavan, our editor, for her insight, sensitivity, patience, and creative suggestions whose patience and fortitude kept us inspired to keep going—keep writing—there aren't enough words in any text to thank her.

Finally, we also dedicate the book to the memory of Judith Doneson, who made us aware of the power of film in teaching the Holocaust.

Foreword

by

Dr. Michael Berenbaum

The systematic state-sponsored murder of six million Jews, which Americans commonly call the Holocaust (Israelis the "Shoah" and Germans the "Final Solution to the Jewish Question") is an enormously large event that darkens the landscape of 20th-century humanity and continues to haunt us in the first decade of the new millennium. Auschwitz redefined the moral landscape of our common humanity.

The history of this event can be written in many ways and in many disciplines and genres: history—Jewish history, German history, American history, European history—and sociology, religion, psychology, political science, art, music, literature, film, and theater, to name but a few.

It can be outlined in stages and processes. The great historian Raul Hilberg spoke of *definition, expropriation, concentration, deportation, mobile killing units* and *death camps.*

German law defined the Jews in 1935, declaring that all those of Jewish ancestry, even two generations back, were Jews, no matter what religion they practiced, what traditions they embraced, or the identity they maintained. This held true throughout, even in the territories the Germans later conquered.

From 1933 onward, German law and society expropriated Jewish property and business, possessions and holdings, reversing a 150-year process of emancipation that saw the Jews gain rights as citizens of the country, denying them civil liberties and rights, introducing apartheid. Over the past decade we learned that even neutral powers such as Switzerland and supposedly neutral industries such as banking and insurance—even distinguished museums and trend-setting art collectors—participated in the processes of expropriation and enjoyed its fruits. All of these decrees were designed to get the Jews to leave, to make Germany and its conquered lands *judenrein*—free of Jews.

These laws and decrees, business practices, and social norms were designed to give an incentive and to provide a reward for discrimination. Expropriation did not end in 1945 but continues even in our time.

Jews were concentrated first in ghettos and later in concentration and slave labor camps, kept together pending a decision on what to do about the "Jewish question," what to do about these Jews. They were deported from small communities to larger ghettos in the East and from cities to transit camps in Western Europe. All the while, the German Reich expanded, and more and more Jews came under its control.

Then the decision was taken.

It was large and bold. It was truthfully, albeit euphemistically, called "the Final Solution to the Jewish Question"; in simple terms, the murder of all Jews the Germans could get their hands on. At first, mobile troops were sent to stationary victims; Jews were shot one by one in the towns and villages of captured Soviet territory in 1941.

Later, when this process proved cumbersome both for the killers and the bystanders—no consideration was given to their victims—a new method was developed. The victims would be made mobile and the killing would be conducted in killing centers, where an economy of scale could be achieved and an assembly-line process introduced. Bullets would no longer be required. Gas chambers—first developed by the German, to kill mentally retarded, physically handicapped and emotionally disturbed Germans who were an embarrassment to the claim of Aryan supremacy—were employed. Gassing was followed by cremation so that the bodies of the murdered would disappear. Deportation was again employed, taking the Jews from the ghettos and transit camps of their incarceration to the death camps of their annihilation.

Although historians may talk about processes, times, and dates, history is shaped by—and imposed upon—real people, people like you and me.

Who were these people? Who were the victims and what was their story? Who were the killers and what was their story? Who were the bystanders and what was their story?

If only it were that simple.

Within each category of participant—yes, even the bystanders were participants—there were a wide variety of people whose age, background, and experience differed so widely and so greatly, even within the same community and even within the same family.

What was their story and how are we to learn of it?

Ancient people told stories, transmitted from one generation to another to recount their history. The Hebrew Bible's books of Genesis, Exodus, Deuteronomy, and Kings are a prime example; the New Testament another; so too *The Iliad* and *The Odyssey,* classic works of Greek literature. Preachers would tell their stories, ballads would be used, so too drawings. This process continues in our time.

There are two major ways of telling stories in our time that engage the public—books and movies. In books, words dominate, and in movies, including television, visual images are combined with words to tell a story that engages the eyes, the ears, and the mind.

Miriam Klein Kassenoff and Anita Meyer Meinbach have offered these two most popularly used tools as entry points into an understanding of the Holocaust. They have chosen, wisely and widely, masterful films and classical works of literature, insightful and powerful poems, works that have withstood the test of time and that are outstanding—standing out from—the very many works that have appeared over the past 60 years in an effort to understand the Holocaust.

The literary choices include memoirs, novels, and poetry. Each is accessible to students. To this the authors have added documents carefully culled from the tens of millions of documents relating to the Holocaust—letters and diaries—all in an effort to bring us inside the minds and the souls of those who went through this event.

We enter into this darkness with eyewitnesses as our guide, and we travel between that world and our world through the choice of works and also through the carefully chosen questions posed for critical thinking. The authors insist that we not become passive recipients of this learning but active researchers, guided in our research but given the freedom to explore individually as well as to work jointly, collectively. We are given room to reflect and the opportunity, if taken, will lead us to many important places.

Anyone who has taught the Holocaust knows that students—and their teachers—are reflective about this material. They speak of it at home and in the classrooms, when they are walking with their friends and talking with their parents. They inquire of their grandparents, and they sit and listen with rapt and unusually respectful attention to survivors.

The organization of the material is wise. The topics are comprehensive, reflecting clearly how large the subject is, how profound the questions are, and knowing full well how meager and inadequate are our answers. Questions can be pursued together, and after each reading our questions become deeper, more intense and we rightfully reject the all too facile answers. Premature answers are usually immature answers. There is room for creativity in this book, space for reflection and an opportunity to learn.

There is so much here—perhaps too much—but don't be put off by the depth of the material. Read it bit by bit; see the movies alone and with others. Some movies should be seen with others. They recommend *Into the Arms of Strangers,* which describes the *kindertransport.* It is a powerful, Academy Award–winning film. The film is set in the Holocaust, but its subtext is the bond between parents and children. This is a film that children should see with their parents and parents with their children. They wisely use *Conspiracy,* a reenactment of the Wannsee Conference, to explore the motivations of the killers, their ideology, and even their feeble struggles with conscience. It is a film that should also be seen with adults, who will note an eerie resemblance between meetings they have attended and a meeting at which genocide became the announced policy of Nazi Germany.

The authors have given us an important means by which to enter the inner world of those who were there, to enter it with those who were there as our guides or to enter it with those who have used the tools of the imagination to bridge our world and that world, to bridge, to enter, to transmit. They have asked important questions and given us a way to begin the discussion that confronts us with unanswerable—but not unaskable—questions.

Remember, we can only approximate that world, approach its outer perimeters, but even from our safe vantage point, the questions it raises, the challenges it poses, are critical to 21st-century humanity.

You are about to begin a journey of learning and teaching, of teaching for the sake of learning. Begin it with confidence but also with humility. At the other end of the journey, something within you will have changed, for one does not approach this material easily, and one does not emerge unscathed. Still, almost all of us who have begun this journey regard it as essential to our moral development and critical thinking as well as to our common humanity.

Dr. Michael Berenbaum
Founding Project Director
United States Holocaust Memorial Museum, Washington, DC

Sigi Ziering Institute
Exploring the Ethical and Religious Implications of the Holocaust
Professor of Theology
Los Angeles, California

Introduction

The Ashes of Auschwitz are everywhere.

— *Elie Wiesel*

Why teach the past? Why teach about something that happened in the last century? Why teach about the Nazi Holocaust in the 21st century?

After the devastating events of September 11, 2001, the lessons of the past are even more compelling. The lessons of the past will help us to deal with the tragedies of today and inspire us as we build tomorrow. The lessons of the past offer hope as we invite a new generation to guide their lives with a deep regard for humanity, a commitment to the values of caring and respect for others, and the development of a strong moral and ethical fiber that will enable them to stand up for what they believe in and speak out against injustice.

At the cornerstone of education is history. Only as we become aware of how the past has shaped the present can we build a more positive future. Today more than ever, the study of the events of the Holocaust and its lessons are vital. As the Holocaust is studied, students discover significant truths about human nature and the importance of compassion and the courage of the human spirit.

At the core of Holocaust education are lessons for life, lessons that will guide generations of students as they establish goals and take responsibility for themselves and one another in building a community that celebrates the diversity that exists among us. Every day the news is filled with accounts of racial hatred and genocide. Yet these acts of prejudice and persecution continue, and the world watches. Students must become aware of the devastating effects of prejudice, indifference, and apathy. Students must be guided in the ideals of human decency and moral courage.

Through a study of the Holocaust, students are inspired to take a stand for what they believe in and to recognize that certain universal values of right and wrong must be upheld. Most important, they need to recognize that each individual has the potential to effect change.

Studying the Holocaust Through Film and Literature: Human Rights and Social Responsibility bridges the past, present, and future. We must teach the history and events of the Holocaust first. Students must know what occurred during the years 1933–1945 that almost destroyed an entire culture, the Jewish people of Eastern Europe, as well as millions of other innocent people. Yehuda Bauer, the esteemed Holocaust scholar, has said, "The Holocaust can either be a precedent or a warning." It is the intention of this book to teach the events of the Holocaust as a warning. However, as we have entered a new century, a knowledge of the history is not enough. We must teach the moral and ethical lessons that have evolved from the Holocaust so that students can connect these with the moral dilemmas they face in their own lives.

Yad Vashem, the Center for World Holocaust Studies in Jerusalem, Israel, teaches three main lessons to be learned from the Holocaust that address moral and ethical issues. These three lessons can be connected to any aspect of life and are the threads that run through the issues explored in this book. These three lessons must be considered as we reflect on the choices we make in our daily lives:

1. Thou shalt not be a victim.

2. Thou shalt not be a perpetrator.

3. Thou shalt not be a bystander.

Character Education and Core Values

In addition to dealing with major ethical and moral issues of human rights and social responsibility, this book will address the issues of courage, compassion, character, and civility that determine an individual's behavior on a daily basis and include the core values of *citizenship, cooperation, fairness, honesty, integrity, kindness, empathy, respect,* and *responsibility.*

Components and Framework: An Overview

This book contains a wide variety of film and literature that invites students to explore all aspects of the Holocaust. Each piece is developed to encourage students to think critically, explore choices, and make decisions based on a code of conduct that reflects a commitment to humanity.

The film and literature highlighted in this book were selected based on the following specific criteria for each:

• It provides a framework for exploring various aspects of the Holocaust.

• It is thought-provoking, enabling the reader or viewer to reach deeper levels of understanding.

• It helps students to consider the ramifications of the Holocaust in terms of who they are and how they will conduct their lives.

• It encourages discussion on human rights and social responsibility for today's world.

• It is easily accessible.

• It has the ability to motivate, enrich, and illuminate.

Studying the Holocaust Through Film and Literature is divided into nine specific topics, each based on the Holocaust and society's attempt today to learn from the past. Each topic is addressed through the reading of literature and the viewing of the films listed in Table I-1. Although suggested grade levels are given, *it is highly recommended that teachers preview all films and literature* to ensure that they are appropriate for individual classrooms and students. Literature indicated with an asterisk (*) denotes that the piece or an excerpt of the piece is included.

When preparing your lessons, it is important to note the section "Select Appropriate Learning Activities" recommended by The United States Holocaust Memorial Museum (see part I, p. 14).

Table I-1.   Topic Resources

Topics	Film	Literature
1. The World of the Persecuted: Into the Darkness	1. *The Camera of My Family: Four Generations in Germany 1845–1945* 2. *One Survivor Remembers*	1. *I Have Lived a Thousand Years* (Livia Bitton-Jackson) 2. "We Were Children Just Like You" (poem) (Yaffa Eliach)* 3. *All the Rivers Run to the Sea* (Elie Wiesel) 4. *Night* (Elie Wiesel)—excerpt*
2. The Mind of the Perpetrator: Anatomy of Evil	1. *Heil Hitler: Confessions of a Hitler Youth* 2. *Conspiracy*	1. *Nazi Olympics* (Susan D. Bachrach) 2. *Parallel Journeys* (Eleanor Ayer) 3. "Words" (poem) (Ursula Duba)*
3. The Mind of the Bystander: Indifference and Apathy	1. *The Hangman* 2. *The Voyage of the St. Louis*	1. "The Hangman" (poem) (Maurice Ogden)* 2. *Friedrich* (Hans Peter Richter) 3. *In the Shadow of the Swastika* (Hermann Wygoda)—excerpt*
4. Life in the Ghetto: Images of Hope and Despair	1. *Korczak* 2. *Kovno Ghetto* 3. *The Pianist*	1. *The King of the Children: The Life and Death of Januscz Korczak:* "The Last March—August 1942" (Betty Lifton)—excerpt* 2. *The Pianist* (Wladyslaw Szpilman) 3. *Images of the Holocaust*—"Lodz Ghetto" (Elaine C. Stephens et al.)
5. Fighting Back: Spiritual and Physical Resistance	1. *Daring to Resist* 2. *Uprising*	1. *Anne Frank: The Diary of a Young Girl* (Anne Frank) 2. *I Never Saw Another Butterfly* (Hana Volavkova, ed.) 3. "Terezin" (Survivor Memoir) (Arno Erban)* 4. *On Both Sides of the Wall*—(Vladka Meed)—excerpt* 5. *Images of the Holocaust*—"Volunteers" (Elaine C. Stephens et al.)—excerpt*
6. Courage and Compassion: Stories of Rescue	1. *Diplomats for the Damned* 2. *Rescuers: Stories of Courage—Two Couples* 3. *The Courage to Care*	1. *Into the Arms of Strangers: Stories of the Kindertransport* (Mark Jonathan Harris & Deborah Oppenheimer) 2. *Rescue: The Stories of How Gentiles Saved the Jews During the Holocaust* (Milton Meltzer) 3. *Dry Tears* (Nechama Tec) 4. *Hasidic Tales of the Holocaust:* "The Merit of a Young Priest" (Yaffa Eliach)—excerpt* *(Continued)*

Table I-1. Topic Resources *(Continued)*

Topics	Film	Literature
7. The Final Solution: The Camps	1. *Genocide—1941–1945* 2. *Schindler's List*	1. "Auschwitz" (Survivor Memoir) (Arno Erban)* 2. *Night* (Elie Wiesel) 3. *Hasidic Tales of the Holocaust* "Stars" (Yaffa Eliach)—excerpt* 4. *The Cage* (Ruth M. Sender)
8. The Power of Perseverance: Children Surviving the Holocaust	1. *Let Memory Speak* 2. *Marion's Triumph* 3. *The Power of Good*	1. *The Hidden Children* (Jane Marks) 2. *Revealing Evidence: Witnesses In and Out of Hiding* (Ellen Fine)— excerpt* 3. *A Scrap of Time:* "The Tenth Man" (Ida Fink)—excerpt* 4. *My Bridges of Hope: Searching for Life and Love After Auschwitz* (Livia Bitton-Jackson) 5. *The Children of Buchenwald:* "Elie Wiesel" (Judith Hemmendinger & Robert Krell)—excerpt*
9. The Holocaust, Human Rights, and Social Responsibility	1. *Judgment at Nuremberg* (TNT version) 2. *Not in Our Town*	1. *The Sunflower* (Simon Wiesenthal) 2. *The United Nations Universal Declaration of Human Rights, 1948**

The main objectives of this book are twofold: (a) to teach the Holocaust and its lessons about human behavior and to try and understand why such events occur, and (b) to clarify and strengthen students' conviction about the code of conduct they will adopt as they face life's decisions and help them to envision their place in the world.

To achieve these goals, activities are included based on each selection (a memoir or a video) to involve students in a dynamic exploration of not only what was but also what is and, most important, what can be. These activities include the following:

1. *Symposium: Critical Thinking and Discussion:* Socratic questions invite students to clarify their own understandings and judgments, strengthen their moral courage, and develop a strategy for problem solving and decision making. A core question that will be repeatedly asked in this section is "What lesson(s) did you learn from this memoir or film that will influence your life today and choices you make?" Questions can be used as a basis for group discussion and either formal or informal debate.

2. *Reflections in Writing:* Writing topics encourage students to analyze and synthesize what they have learned and address specific issues as they strive for deeper meaning and understanding.

3. *Researching the History:* Individual and group projects stimulate further research and understanding about the Holocaust and connect ideas presented with current events affecting their lives.

In addition, a culminating section, *Lessons for Today,* follows the development of the various films and pieces of literature within a specific topic and acts as a bridge among the past, present, and future. Inviting students to make connections, activities included in this section promote character development and core values. They have been designed to encourage students to analyze the information and understandings gained from the films and literature so that students might determine how these ideas and insights will impact their lives, the choices they make, and the paths they choose.

Finally, a comprehensive list of resources that offer additional information for each topic is included as appendixes:

- Bibliography
- Webography
- Videography
- Holocaust Resource Centers
- Teacher Training Institutes, Community Programs, and Seminars on Holocaust Studies

Getting Started

The guidelines that follow will help educators to easily implement the material presented in this book. The material can be adapted to most classroom settings grades 8–12 and, in many cases, college level.

Enhancing Teacher Knowledge

Holocaust education is a fairly recent addition to the curriculum of schools throughout the country. Therefore, many teachers have had little training, if any, on the subject. There are a great many resources available that will augment your understanding (see appendixes). Web sites such as the one prepared by the United States Holocaust Memorial Museum (www.ushmm.org) also provide a wealth of information, as do videos related to the history of the Holocaust.

Enhancing Student Knowledge

The following films, historical texts, and Web sites are highly recommended for the instructor to review and select appropriate pieces for classroom introduction to the history and study of the Holocaust through film and literature (see appendixes for more information):

Films:	*Heritage: Civilization and the Jews*
	The Longest Hatred
	There Once Was a Town
Historical texts:	*The World Must Know* by Michael Berenbaum (1993)
	A History of the Holocaust by Yehuda Bauer and Nili Keren (1982)
	Holocaust: A History by Deborah Dwork and Robert Van Pelt (2002)
Web sites:	The United States Holocaust Memorial Museum Web site, www.ushmm.org, includes "Education Resources for Teachers." This site provides links to a com-

plete and comprehensive summary of the Holocaust, timelines, maps, photographs, and a glossary as well as survivor testimony.

The History Place, www.historyplace.com, also provides historical information and a comprehensive timeline of the Holocaust.

The *Holocaust Chronicle* Web site, www.holocaustchronicle.org, includes more than 800 pages of Holocaust history on-line.

Setting Up the Classroom and Finding the Right Resources

Fill your room with appropriate maps, news articles, encyclopedias, and reference books to help students in their research. Additional resources that correlate to the history as well as to each of the issues developed in Part II are listed in the appendixes.

Organizing the Lessons

Introduce your students first to the material in Part I, "Historical Overview of the Holocaust," which is reprinted with permission directly from the United States Holocaust Memorial Museum Resource *Guide for Educators*. Supplement this information with selections from the various films, literature, and Web sites listed in the appendixes. Select questions, writing prompts, and activities that best fit student levels and abilities to help them extend their understanding. Once students have a basic knowledge of the Holocaust, introduce the topics developed in Part II. These topics can be presented in any order. Within each topic there are several literature and film selections from which to choose. Be careful to select materials and related activities that best meet student needs, interests, and abilities.

Survivor Visitation

A study of the Holocaust is incomplete without first-person testimony. Survivors provide a rich and powerful experience and bring history to life. The best time to have a survivor speak with your class is after students have studied the history of the Holocaust and have a basis for understanding. You can arrange to have a speaker visit your classroom by calling the local Holocaust center in your area (see Appendix E). If it is not possible to arrange for a speaker, you may wish to show one or more of the videos listed in the Videography (Appendix C), which includes survivor testimony such *as Survivors of the Shoah* (Visual History Foundation). This is also available on CD-ROM.

If students wish to write to a survivor, they can send their letters to the following e-mail site, which will, in turn, forward it to a survivor who will respond to student questions: holocaustchild@comcast.net.

Journal Writing

All students should keep a journal to record their reactions and reflections as they take part in the study of the Holocaust and the moral and ethical issues involved. Journal writing is often cathartic, allowing students to sort out their feelings and express their emotions. In addition, it gives them the opportunity to search for their own meanings and draw conclusions.

Film Critique

Have students analyze various movie critiques from newspapers and magazines so that they are aware of the way in which such critiques are written. As students view the various films suggested in this book, have them write critiques and then select a few to be distributed to the rest of the school through e-mail or closed-circuit TV.

Book Reviews

Have students analyze various book reviews from newspapers and magazines so that they are aware of the way in which such reviews are written. As students read the literature suggested in this book, have them write book reviews and then select a few to be distributed to the rest of the school through e-mail or closed-circuit TV.

Interdisciplinary Teaching

Because of the nature of this book and its features, teachers representing various disciplines may wish to plan the unit together. When possible, involve teachers in the humanities departments.

Guidelines for Teaching the Holocaust Through Film and Literature

1. Review this book. Although it is organized chronologically according to the history of the Holocaust, depending upon your time limitations you can choose specific topics to cover. For example, if you have 3 weeks to dedicate to Holocaust study, along with a summarized history of the Holocaust you might choose Topic 1 "The World of the Persecuted"; Topic 6, "Courage and Compassion"; and Topic 9, "The Holocaust, Human Rights, and Social Responsibility."

2. Once you have determined which topics you wish to focus on, select the related literature and film most appropriate for your students' abilities.

3. For each topic in the book, valuable literature selections are included, whether it be Holocaust survivor testimony, a primary document, an essay, a poem, or a short story. These pieces are perfect for enhancing literature analysis, critical thinking skills, and reading and writing skills.

4. Always preview the film and literature before introducing them to students.

5. Excerpts, excerpts, excerpts!!! In almost every instance, the films and literature do not have to be used in their entirety. In fact, we encourage using selected excerpts from films and literature to augment your study of specific topics. For example, the film *Conspiracy* has an excellent 3- to 5-minute scene which clearly portrays the 15 Nazi perpetrators who made the decision to murder all the Jews of Europe. The entire film need not be shown.

6. Character education is mandated in many states today. A study of the Holocaust is a perfect vehicle for lessons in character development and values. We encourage you to use the films and literature to discuss the moral and ethical issues included at the end of each topic in this book.

7. Many of the videos suggested in this book can be borrowed through the lending library services of the **Facing History and Ourselves National Foundation,** www.facinghistory.org (click on "resources"), and from the **National Center for Jewish Film,** Brandeis University, www.jewishfilm.org. In addition, although each film highlighted and listed in the videography includes a source, many of the films are available at your local video stores, the **United States Holocaust Memorial Museum Bookstore** (www.ushmm.org), and **Social Studies School Service** (www.socialstudies.com).

As a final note on *Guidelines,* we re-emphasize the importance of sensitivity to appropriate visual images for teaching purposes by the following from the United States Holocaust Memorial Museum "Methodological Considerations" see p. 13 (Part 1). Reprinted with permission from the United States Holocaust Memorial Museum.

Be sensitive to appropriate written and audiovisual content.

One of the primary concerns of educators teaching the history of the Holocaust is how to present horrific images in a sensitive and appropriate manner. Graphic material should be used judiciously and only to the extent necessary to achieve the objective of the lesson. You should remind yourself that each student and each class is different and that what seems appropriate for one may not be appropriate for all.

Students are essentially a "captive audience." When you assault them with images of horror for which they are unprepared, you violate a basic trust: the obligation of a teacher to provide a "safe" learning environment. The assumption that all students will seek to understand human behavior after being exposed to horrible images is fallacious. Some students may be so appalled by images of brutality and mass murder that they are discouraged from studying the subject further. Others may become fascinated in a more voyeuristic fashion, subordinating further critical analysis of the history to the superficial titillation of looking at images of starvation, disfigurement, and death. Though they can be powerful tools, shocking images of mass killings and barbarisms should not overwhelm a student's awareness of the broader scope of events within Holocaust history. Try to select images and texts that do not exploit the students' emotional vulnerability or that might be construed as disrespectful of the victims themselves.

Part I

Historical Overview
of the Holocaust

> *Only guard yourself and guard your soul*
> *carefully, lest you forget the things your eyes saw*
> *and lest these things depart your heart all the*
> *days of your life, and you shall make them known*
> *to your children and your children's children.*
>
> — Deuteronomy 4:9

The following is an excerpt from *Teaching About the Holocaust: A Resource Book for Educators.* Reprinted with permission from the United States Holocaust Memorial Museum, Washington, DC.

HISTORY OF THE HOLOCAUST: AN OVERVIEW

On January 20, 1942, an extraordinary 90-minute meeting took place in a lakeside villa in the wealthy Wannsee district of Berlin. Fifteen high-ranking Nazi party and German government leaders gathered to coordinate logistics for carrying out "the final solution of the Jewish question." Chairing the meeting was SS Lieutenant General Reinhard Heydrich, head of the powerful Reich Security Main Office, a central police agency that included the Secret State Police (the Gestapo). Heydrich convened the meeting on the basis of a memorandum he had received six months earlier from Adolf Hitler's deputy, Hermann Göring, confirming his authorization to implement the "Final Solution."

The "Final Solution" was the Nazi regime's code name for the deliberate, planned mass murder of all European Jews. During the Wannsee meeting German government officials discussed "extermination" without hesitation or qualm. Heydrich calculated that 11 million European Jews from more than 20 countries would be killed under this heinous plan.

During the months before the Wannsee Conference, special units made up of SS, the elite guard of the Nazi state, and police personnel, known as *Einsatzgruppen,* slaughtered Jews in mass shootings on the territory of the Soviet Union that the Germans had occupied. Six weeks before the Wannsee meeting, the Nazis began to murder Jews at Chelmno, an agricultural estate located in that part of Poland annexed to Germany. Here SS and police personnel used sealed vans into which they pumped carbon monoxide gas to suffocate their victims. The Wannsee meeting served to sanction, coordinate, and expand the implementation of the "Final Solution" as state policy.

During 1942, trainload after trainload of Jewish men, women, and children were transported from countries all over Europe to Auschwitz, Treblinka, and four other major killing centers in German-occupied Poland. By year's end, about 4 million Jews were dead. During World War II (1939–1945), the Germans and their collaborators killed or caused the deaths of up to 6 million Jews. Hundreds of Jewish communities in Europe, some centuries old, disappeared forever. To convey the unimaginable, devastating scale of destruction, postwar writers referred to the murder of the European Jews as the "Holocaust."

Centuries of religious prejudice against Jews in Christian Europe, reinforced by modern political antisemitism developing from a complex mixture of extreme nationalism, financial insecurity, fear of communism, and so-called race science, provide the backdrop for the Holocaust. Hitler and other Nazi ideologues regarded Jews as a dangerous "race" whose very existence threatened the biological purity and strength of the "superior Aryan race." To secure the assistance of thousands of individuals to implement the "Final Solution," the Nazi regime could and did exploit existing prejudice against Jews in Germany and the other countries that were conquered by or allied with Germany during World War II.

"While not all victims were Jews, all Jews were victims," Holocaust survivor Elie Wiesel has written. "Jews were destined for annihilation solely because they were born Jewish. They were doomed not because of something they had done or proclaimed or acquired but because of who they were, sons and daughters of Jewish people. As such they were sentenced to death collectively and individually. . . ."

SUMMARY OF THE HISTORY OF THE HOLOCAUST IN TWO MAIN SECTIONS: 1933–1939 AND 1939–1945

1933–1939

On January 30, 1933, Adolf Hitler was named chancellor, the most powerful position in the German government, by the aged President Hindenburg, who hoped Hitler could lead the nation out of its grave political and economic crisis. Hitler was the leader of the right-wing National Socialist German Workers Party (called the "Nazi party" for short). It was, by 1933, one of the strongest parties in Germany, even though—reflecting the country's multiparty system—the Nazis had won only a plurality of 33 percent of the votes in the 1932 elections to the German parliament (Reichstag).

Once in power, Hitler moved quickly to end German democracy. He convinced his cabinet to invoke emergency clauses of the constitution that permitted the suspension of individual freedoms of press, speech, and assembly. Special security forces—the Gestapo, the Storm Troopers (SA), and the SS—murdered or arrested leaders of opposition political parties (Communists, socialists, and liberals). The Enabling Act of March 23, 1933—forced through a Reichstag already purged of many political opponents—gave dictatorial powers to Hitler.

Also in 1933, the Nazis began to put into practice their racial ideology. The Nazis believed that the Germans were "racially superior" and that there was a struggle for survival between them and "inferior races." They saw Jews, Roma (Gypsies), and the handicapped as a serious biological threat to the purity of the "German (Aryan[1]) Race," what they called the "master race."

Jews, who numbered about 525,000 in Germany (less than one percent of the total population in 1933), were the principal target of Nazi hatred. The Nazis identified Jews as a race and defined this race as "inferior." They also spewed hate-mongering propaganda that unfairly blamed Jews for Germany's economic depression and the country's defeat in World War I (1914–18).

In 1933, new German laws forced Jews out of their civil service jobs, university and law court positions, and other areas of public life. In April 1933, a boycott of Jewish businesses was instituted. In 1935, laws proclaimed at Nuremberg made Jews second-class citizens. These Nuremberg Laws defined Jews not by their religion or by how they wanted to identify themselves, but by the religious affiliation of their grandparents. Between 1937 and 1939, new anti-Jewish regulations segregated Jews further and made daily life very difficult for them: Jews could not attend public schools; go to theaters, cinemas, or vacation resorts; or reside or even walk in certain sections of German cities.

Also between 1937 and 1939, Jews increasingly were forced from Germany's economic life: The Nazis either seized Jewish businesses and properties outright or forced Jews to sell them at bargain prices. In November 1938, the Nazis organized a riot (pogrom), known as *Kristallnacht* (the "Night of Broken Glass"). This attack against German and Austrian Jews included the physical destruction of synagogues and Jewish-owned stores, the arrest of Jewish men, the vandalization of homes, and the murder of individuals.

Although Jews were the main target of Nazi hatred, the Nazis persecuted other groups they viewed as racially or genetically "inferior." Nazi racial ideology was buttressed by scientists

---

1   The term "Aryan" originally referred to peoples speaking Indo-European languages. The Nazis perverted its meaning to support racist ideas by viewing those of Germanic background as prime examples of Aryan stock, which they considered racially superior. For the Nazis, the typical Aryan was blond, blue-eyed, and tall.

who advocated "selective breeding" (eugenics) to "improve" the human race. Laws passed between 1933 and 1935 aimed to reduce the future number of genetic "inferiors" through involuntary sterilization programs: 320,000 to 350,000 individuals judged physically or mentally handicapped were subjected to surgical or radiation procedures so they could not have children. Supporters of sterilization also argued that the handicapped burdened the community with the costs of their care. Many of Germany's 30,000 Roma (Gypsies) were also eventually sterilized and prohibited, along with Blacks, from intermarrying with Germans. About 500 children of mixed African-German backgrounds were also sterilized.[2] New laws combined traditional prejudices with the racism of the Nazis, which defined Roma, by "race," as "criminal and asocial."

Another consequence of Hitler's ruthless dictatorship in the 1930s was the arrest of political opponents and trade unionists and others the Nazis labeled "undesirables" and "enemies of the state." Some 5,000 to 15,000 homosexuals were imprisoned in concentration camps; under the 1935 Nazi-revised criminal code, the mere denunciation of a man as "homosexual" could result in arrest, trial, and conviction. Jehovah's Witnesses, who numbered at least 25,000 in Germany, were banned as an organization as early as April 1933, because the beliefs of this religious group prohibited them from swearing any oath to the state or serving in the German military. Their literature was confiscated, and they lost jobs, unemployment benefits, pensions, and all social welfare benefits. Many Witnesses were sent to prisons and concentration camps in Nazi Germany, and their children were sent to juvenile detention homes and orphanages.

Between 1933 and 1936, thousands of people, mostly political prisoners, were imprisoned in concentration camps, while several thousand German Roma (Gypsies) were confined in special municipal camps. The first systematic roundups of German and Austrian' Jews occurred after *Kristallnacht,* when approximately 30,000 Jewish men were deported to Dachau and other concentration camps, and several hundred Jewish women were sent to local jails. The wave of arrests in 1938 also included several thousand German and Austrian Roma (Gypsies).

Between 1933 and 1939, about half the German-Jewish population and more than two-thirds of Austrian Jews (1938–40) fled Nazi persecution. They emigrated mainly to the United States, Palestine, elsewhere in Europe (where many would be later trapped by Nazi conquests during the war), Latin America, and Japanese-occupied Shanghai (which required no visas for entry). Jews who remained under Nazi rule were either unwilling to uproot themselves or unable to obtain visas, sponsors in host countries, or funds for emigration. Most foreign countries, including the United States, Canada, Britain, and France, were unwilling to admit very large numbers of refugees.

1939–1945

On September 1, 1939, Germany invaded Poland and World War II began. Within weeks, the Polish army was defeated, and the Nazis began their campaign to destroy Polish culture and enslave the Polish people, whom they viewed as "subhuman." Killing Polish leaders was the first step: German soldiers carried out massacres of university professors, artists, writers, politicians, and many Catholic priests. To create new living space for the "superior Germanic race," large segments of the Polish population were resettled, and German families moved

---

2   These children, called "the Rhineland bastards" by Germans, were the offspring of German women and African soldiers from French colonies who were stationed in the 1920s in the Rhineland, a demilitarized zone the Allies established after World War I as a buffer between German and western Europe.

into the emptied lands. Other Poles, including many Jews, were imprisoned in concentration camps. The Nazis also "kidnapped" as many as 50,000 "Aryan-looking" Polish children from their parents and took them to Germany to be adopted by German families. Many of these children were later rejected as not capable of Germanization and were sent to special children's camps where some died of starvation, lethal injection, and disease.

As the war began in 1939, Hitler initialed an order to kill institutionalized, handicapped patients deemed "incurable." Special commissions of physicians reviewed questionnaires filled out by all state hospitals and then decided if a patient should be killed. The doomed were then transferred to six institutions in Germany and Austria where specially constructed gas chambers were used to kill them. After public protests in 1941, the Nazi leadership continued this "euthanasia" program in secret. Babies, small children, and other victims were thereafter killed by lethal injection and pills and by forced starvation.[3]

The "euthanasia" program contained all the elements later required for 'mass murder of European Jews and Roma (Gypsies): a decision to kill, specially trained personnel, the apparatus for killing by gas, and the use of euphemistic language like "euthanasia" that psychologically distanced the murderers from their victims and hid the criminal character of the killings from the public.

In 1940 German forces continued their conquest of much of Europe, easily defeating Denmark, Norway, the Netherlands, Belgium, Luxembourg, France, Yugoslavia, and Greece. On June 22, 1941, the German army invaded the Soviet Union and by late November was approaching Moscow. In the meantime, Italy, Romania, and Hungary had joined the Axis powers led by Germany and were opposed by the main Allied powers (British Commonwealth, Free France, the United States, and the Soviet Union).

In the months following Germany's invasion of the Soviet Union, Jews, political leaders, Communists, and many Roma (Gypsies) were killed in mass shootings. Most of those killed were Jews. These murders were carried out at improvised sites throughout the Soviet Union by members of mobile killing squads *(Einsatzgruppen)* who followed in the wake of the invading German army. The most famous of these sites was Babi Yar, near Kiev, where an estimated 33,000 persons, mostly Jews, were murdered over two days. German terror extended to institutionalized handicapped and psychiatric patients in the Soviet Union; it also resulted in the death of more than 3 million Soviet prisoners of war.

World War II brought major changes to the concentration camp system. Large numbers of new prisoners, deported from all German-occupied countries, now flooded the camps. Often entire groups were committed to the camps, such as members of underground resistance organizations who were rounded up in a sweep across western Europe under the 1941 Night and Fog decree. To accommodate the massive increase in the number of prisoners, hundreds of new camps were established in occupied territories of eastern and western Europe.

During the war, ghettos, transit camps, and forced-labor camps, in addition to the concentration camps, were created by the Germans and their collaborators to imprison Jews, Roma (Gypsies), and other victims of racial and ethnic hatred as well as political opponents and resistance fighters. Following the invasion of Poland, 3 million Polish Jews were forced into approximately 400 newly established ghettos where they were segregated from the rest of the

---

3 On March 11, 1938. Hitler sent his army into Austria, and on March 13, the incorporation (Anschluss) of Austria with the German empire (Reich) was proclaimed in Vienna. Most of the population welcomed the Anschluss and expressed their fervor in widespread riots and attacks against the Austrian Jews, numbering 180,000 (90 percent of whom lived in Vienna).

population. Large numbers of Jews also were deported from other cities and countries, including Germany, to ghettos and camps in Poland and German-occupied territories further east.

In Polish cities under Nazi occupation, like Warsaw and Lodz, Jews were confined in sealed ghettos where starvation, overcrowding, exposure to cold, and contagious diseases killed tens of thousands of people. In Warsaw and elsewhere, ghettoized Jews made every effort, often at great risk, to maintain their cultural, communal, and religious lives. The ghettos also provided a forced-labor pool for the Germans, and many forced laborers (who worked on road gangs, in construction, or at other hard labor related to the German war effort) died from exhaustion or maltreatment.

Between 1942 and 1944, the Germans moved to eliminate the ghettos in occupied Poland and elsewhere, deporting ghetto residents to "extermination camps"—killing centers equipped with gassing facilities—located in Poland. After the meeting of senior German government officials in late January 1942 at a villa in the Berlin suburb of Wannsee, Jews from western Europe also were sent to killing centers in the East.

The six killing sites, chosen because of their closeness to rail lines and their location in semirural areas, were at Belzec, Sobibor, Treblinka, Chelmno, Majdanek,[4] and Auschwitz-Birkenau. Chelmno was the first camp in which mass executions were carried out by gas piped into mobile gas vans; at least 152,000 persons were killed there between December 1941 and March 1943, and between June and July 1944. A killing center using gas chambers operated at Belzec, where about 600,000 persons were killed between May 1942 and August 1943. Sobibor opened in May 1942 and closed following a rebellion of the prisoners on October 14, 1943; about 250,000 persons had already been killed by gassing at Sobibor. Treblinka opened in July 1942 and closed in November 1943; a revolt by the prisoners in early August 1943 destroyed much of that facility. At least 750,000 persons were killed at Treblinka, physically the largest of the killing centers. Almost all of the victims at Chelmno, Belzec, Sobibor, and Treblinka were Jews; a few were Roma (Gypsies), Poles, and Soviet POWs. Very few individuals survived these four killing centers, where most victims were murdered immediately upon arrival.

Auschwitz-Birkenau, which also served as a concentration camp and slave labor camp, became the killing center where the largest numbers of European Jews and Roma (Gypsies) were killed. After an experimental gassing there in September 1941—of 250 malnourished and ill Polish prisoners and 600 Soviet POWs—mass murder became a daily routine; more than 1 million people were killed at Auschwitz-Birkenau, 9 out of 10 of them Jews. In addition, Roma, Soviet POWs, and ill prisoners of all nationalities died in the gas chambers there. Between May 15 and July 9, 1944, nearly 440,000 Jews were deported from Hungary in more than 140 trains, overwhelmingly to Auschwitz. This was probably the largest single mass deportation during the Holocaust. A similar system was implemented at Majdanek, which also doubled as a concentration camp, and where between 170,000 and 235,000 persons were killed in the gas chambers or died from malnutrition, brutality, and disease.

The methods of murder were similar in the killing centers, which were operated by the SS. Jewish victims arrived in railroad freight cars and passenger trains, mostly from ghettos and camps in occupied Poland, but also from almost every other eastern and western European

---

4 Despite concerns among some historians that, operationally, Majdanek resembled a concentration camp more than it did a killing center, most scholars include it among the killing centers because of the large number of prisoners who died there and the use of poison gas in the killing process.

country. On arrival, men were separated from women and children. Prisoners were forced to undress and hand over all valuables. They were then forced naked into the gas chambers, which were disguised as shower rooms, and either carbon monoxide or Zyklon B (a form of crystalline prussic acid, also used as an insecticide in some camps) was used to asphyxiate them. The minority selected for forced labor were, after initial quarantine, vulnerable to malnutrition, exposure, epidemics, medical experiments, and brutality; many perished as a result.

The Germans carried out their systematic murderous activities with the active help of local collaborators in many countries and the acquiescence or indifference of millions of bystanders. However, there were instances of organized resistance. For example, in the fall of 1943, the Danish resistance, with the support of the local population, rescued nearly the entire Jewish community in Denmark by smuggling them via a dramatic boatlift to safety in neutral Sweden. Individuals in many other countries also risked their lives to save Jews and other individuals subject to Nazi persecution. One of the most famous was Raoul Wallenberg, a Swedish diplomat who played a significant role in some of the rescue efforts that saved the lives of tens of thousands of Hungarian Jews in 1944.

Resistance existed in almost every concentration camp and ghetto of Europe. In addition to the armed revolts at Sobibor and Treblinka, Jewish resistance in the Warsaw ghetto led to a courageous uprising in April and May 1943, despite a predictable doomed outcome because of superior German force. In general, rescue or aid to Holocaust victims was not a priority of resistance organizations, whose principal goal was to fight the war against the Germans. Nonetheless, such groups and Jewish partisans (resistance fighters) sometimes cooperated with each other to save Jews. On April 19, 1943, for instance, members of the National Committee for the Defense of Jews, in cooperation with Christian railroad workers and the general underground in Belgium, attacked a train leaving the Belgian transit camp of Malines headed for Auschwitz and succeeded in assisting Jewish deportees to escape.

The U.S. government did not pursue a policy of rescue for victims of Nazism during World War II. Like their British counterparts, U.S. political and military leaders argued that winning the war was the top priority and would bring an end to Nazi terror. Once the war began, security concerns, reinforced in part by antisemitism, influenced the U.S. State Department (led by Secretary of State Cordell Hull) and the U.S. government to do little to ease restrictions on entry visas. In January 1944, President Roosevelt established the War Refugee Board within the U.S. Treasury Department to facilitate the rescue of imperiled refugees. Fort Ontario in Oswego, New York, began to serve as an ostensibly free port for refugees from the territories liberated by the Allies.

After the war turned against Germany, and the Allied armies approached German soil in late 1944, the SS decided to evacuate outlying concentration camps. The Germans tried to cover up the evidence of genocide and deported prisoners to camps inside Germany to prevent their liberation. Many inmates died during the long journeys on foot known as "death marches." During the final days, in the spring of 1945, conditions in the remaining concentration camps exacted a terrible toll in human lives. Even concentration camps such as Bergen-Belsen, never intended for extermination, became death traps for thousands, including Anne Frank, who died there of typhus in March 1945. In May 1945, Nazi Germany collapsed, the SS guards fled, and the camps ceased to exist.

AFTERMATH OF THE HOLOCAUST

The Allied victors of World War II (Great Britain, France, the United States, and the Soviet Union) faced two immediate problems following the surrender of Nazi Germany in May 1945: to bring Nazi war criminals to justice and to provide for displaced persons (DPs) and refugees stranded in Allied-occupied Germany and Austria.

Following the war, the best-known war crimes trial was the trial of "major" war criminals, held at the Palace of Justice in Nuremberg, Germany, between November 1945 and August 1946. Under the auspices of the International Military Tribunal (IMT), which consisted of prosecutors and judges from the four occupying powers (Great Britain, France, the Soviet Union, and the United States), leading officials of the Nazi regime were prosecuted for war crimes. The IMT sentenced 13 of those convicted to death. Seven more defendants were sentenced to life imprisonment or to prison terms ranging from 10 to 20 years. One defendant committed suicide before the trial began. Three of the defendants were acquitted. The judges also found three of six Nazi organizations (the SS, the Gestapo-SD, and the Leadership Corps of the Nazi Party) to be criminal organizations.

In the three years following this major trial, 12 subsequent trials were conducted under the auspices of the IMT but before U.S. military tribunals. The proceedings were directed at the prosecution of second- and third-ranking officials of the Nazi regime. They included concentration camp administrators; commanders of the *Einsatzgruppen* (mobile killing units); physicians and public health officials; the SS leadership; German army field commanders and staff officers; officials in the justice, interior, and foreign ministries; and senior administrators of industrial concerns that used concentration camp laborers, including I. G. Farben and the Flick concern.

In addition, each occupying power (Great Britain, France, the United States, and the Soviet Union) conducted trials of Nazi offenders captured in its respective zone of occupation or accused of crimes perpetrated in that zone of occupation. The U.S. military authorities conducted the trials in the American zone at the site of the Nazi concentration camp Dachau. In general, the defendants in these trials were the staff and guard units at concentration camps and other camps located in the zone and people accused of crimes against Allied military and civilian personnel.

Those German officials and collaborators who committed crimes within a specific location or country were generally returned to the nation on whose territory the crimes were committed and were tried by national tribunals. Perhaps the most famous of these cases was the trial in 1947, in Cracow, Poland, of Rudolf Höss, the commandant of Auschwitz. Trials of German war criminals and their collaborators were conducted during the late 1940s and early 1950s in Poland, Hungary, Romania, Bulgaria, Yugoslavia, and the Soviet Union. After the establishment of West Germany in 1949, many former Nazis received relatively lenient treatment by the courts. Courts in West Germany ruled the offenders were not guilty because they were obeying orders from their superior officers. Some Nazi criminals were acquitted and returned to normal lives in German society, a number of them taking jobs in the business world. Many war criminals, however, were never brought to trial or punished. In 1958, the Federal Republic of Germany established a Central Agency for the Investigation of National Socialist Violent Crimes to streamline the investigation of Nazi offenders living in West Germany. These efforts, which continue to this day, led to some significant proceedings such as the Frankfurt Trial of Auschwitz camp personnel in the 1960s. The investigation of Nazi offenders residing in the United States began in earnest during the late 1970s and continues to this day.

Even as the Allies moved to bring Nazi offenders to justice, the looming refugee crisis threatened to overwhelm the resources of the Allied powers. During World War II, the Nazis uprooted millions of people. Within months of Germany's surrender in May 1945, the Allies repatriated more than 6 million (DPs) to their home countries.

Some 250,000 Jewish DPs, including most of the Jewish survivors of concentration camps, were unable or unwilling to return to Eastern Europe because of postwar antisemitism and the destruction of their communities during the Holocaust. Many of those who did return feared for their lives. Many Holocaust survivors found themselves in territory liberated by the Anglo-American armies and were housed in DP camps that the Allies established in Germany, Austria, and Italy. They were joined by a flow of refugees, including Holocaust survivors, migrating from points of liberation in eastern Europe and the Soviet-occupied zones of Germany and Austria.

Most Jewish DPs hoped to leave Europe for Palestine or the United States, but the United States was still governed by severely restrictive immigration legislation, and the British, who administered Palestine under a mandate from the defunct League of Nations, severely restricted Jewish immigration for fear of antagonizing the Arab residents of the Mandate. Other countries had closed their borders to immigration during the Depression and during the war. Despite these obstacles, many Jewish DPs were eager to leave Europe as soon as possible.

The Jewish Brigade Group, formed as a unit within the British army in late 1944, worked with former partisans to help organize the Beriha (literally, "escape"), the exodus of Jewish refugees across closed borders from inside Europe to the coast in an attempt to sail for Palestine. However, the British intercepted most of the ships. In 1947, for example, the British stopped the *Exodus* 1947 at the port of Haifa. The ship had 4,500 Holocaust survivors on board, who were forcibly returned on British vessels to Germany.

In the following years, the postwar Jewish refugee crisis eased. In 1948, the U.S. Congress passed the Displaced Persons Act, which provided up to 400,000 special visas for DPs uprooted by the Nazi or Soviet regimes. Some 63,000 of these visas were issued to Jews under the DP Act. When the DP Act expired in 1952, it was followed by a Refugee Relief Act that remained in force until the end of 1956. Moreover, in May 1948, the State of Israel became an independent nation after the United Nations voted to partition Palestine into a Jewish state and an Arab state. Israel quickly moved to legalize the flow of Jewish immigrants into the new state, passing legislation providing for unlimited Jewish immigration to the Jewish homeland. The last DP camp closed in Germany in 1957.

From: *Teaching About the Holocaust: A Resource Book for Educators.* Reprinted with permission from the United States Holocaust Memorial Museum, Washington, DC.

METHODOLOGICAL CONSIDERATIONS

The teaching of Holocaust history demands of educators a high level of sensitivity and a keen awareness of the complexity of the subject matter. The recommendations that follow, while reflecting methodological approaches that would be appropriate to effective teaching in general, are particularly relevant in the context of Holocaust education.

1. Define the term "Holocaust."

The Holocaust refers to a specific genocidal event in twentieth-century history: the state-sponsored, systematic persecution and annihilation of European Jewry by Nazi Germany and its collaborators between 1933 and 1945. Jews were the primary victims—6 million were murdered; Gypsies, the handicapped, and Poles were also targeted for destruction or decimation for racial, ethnic, or national reasons. Millions more, including homosexuals, Jehovah's Witnesses, Soviet prisoners of war, and political dissidents, also suffered grievous oppression and death under Nazi tyranny.

2. Avoid comparisons of pain.

A study of the Holocaust should always highlight the different policies carried out by the Nazi regime toward various groups of people; however, these distinctions should not be presented as a basis for comparison of suffering between those groups. Similarly, one cannot presume that the horror of an individual, family, or community destroyed by the Nazis was any greater than that experienced by victims of other genocides. Avoid generalizations that suggest exclusivity, such as "the victims of the Holocaust suffered the most cruelty ever faced by a people in the history of humanity."

3. Avoid simple answers to complex history.

A study of the Holocaust raises difficult questions about human behavior, and it often involves complicated answers as to why events occurred. Be wary of oversimplifications. Allow students to contemplate the various factors that contributed to the Holocaust; do not attempt to reduce Holocaust history to one or two catalysts in isolation from the other factors that came into play. For example, the Holocaust was not simply the logical and inevitable consequence of unbridled racism.

Rather, racism combined with centuries-old bigotry and antisemitism; renewed by a nationalistic fervor that emerged in Europe in the latter half of the nineteenth century; fueled by Germany's defeat in World War I and its national humiliation following the Treaty of Versailles; exacerbated by worldwide economic hard times, the ineffectiveness of the Weimar Republic, and international indifference; and catalyzed by the political charisma and manipulative propaganda of Adolf Hitler's Nazi regime contributed to the occurrence of the Holocaust.

4. Just because it happened does not mean it was inevitable.

Too often students have the simplistic impression that the Holocaust was inevitable. Just because a historical event took place, and it was documented in textbooks and on film, does not mean that it had to happen. This seemingly obvious concept is often overlooked by students and teachers alike. The Holocaust took place because individuals, groups, and nations made decisions to act or not to act. By focusing on those decisions, you gain insight into history and human nature and can better help your students to become critical thinkers.

5. Strive for precision of language.

Any study of the Holocaust touches upon nuances of human behavior. Because of the complexity of the history, there is a temptation to overgeneralize and thus to distort the facts (e.g., "all concentration camps were killing centers" or "all Germans were collaborators"). Rather, you must strive to help your students clarify the information presented and encourage them to distinguish the differences between prejudice and discrimination, collaborators and bystanders, armed and spiritual resistance, direct orders and assumed orders, concentration camps and killing centers, and guilt and responsibility.

Words that describe human behavior often have multiple meanings. Resistance, for example, usually refers to a physical act of armed revolt. During the Holocaust, it also encompassed partisan activity; the smuggling of messages, food, and weapons; and actual military engagement. But resistance also embraced willful disobedience such as continuing to practice religious and cultural traditions in defiance of the rules or creating fine art, music, and poetry inside ghettos and concentration camps. For many, simply maintaining the will to remain alive in the face of abject brutality was an act of spiritual resistance.

6. Make careful distinctions about sources of information.

Students need practice in distinguishing among fact, opinion, and fiction; between primary and secondary sources; and among types of evidence such as court testimonies, oral histories, and other written documents. Hermeneutics—the science of interpretation—should be called into play to help guide your students in their analysis of sources. Students should be encouraged to consider why a particular text was written, who wrote it, who the intended audience was, whether there were any biases inherent in the information, whether any gaps occurred in discussion, whether omissions in certain passages were inadvertent or not, and how the information has been used to interpret various events.

Because scholars often base their research on different bodies of information, varying interpretations of history can emerge. Consequently, all interpretations are subject to analytical evaluation. Only by refining their own "hermeneutic of suspicion" can students mature into readers who discern the difference between legitimate scholars who present competing historical interpretations and those who distort or deny historical fact for personal or political gain.

7. Try to avoid stereotypical descriptions.

Though all Jews were targeted for destruction by the Nazis, the experiences of all Jews were not the same. Simplistic views and stereotyping take place when groups of people are viewed as monolithic in attitudes and actions. How ethnic groups or social clusters are labeled and portrayed in school curricula has a direct impact on how students perceive groups in their daily lives. Remind your students that although members of a group may share common experiences and beliefs, generalizations about them, without benefit of modifying or qualifying terms (e.g., "sometimes," "usually," "in many cases but not all") tend to stereotype group behavior and distort historical reality. Thus, all Germans cannot be characterized as Nazis nor should any nationality be reduced to a singular or one-dimensional description.

8. Do not romanticize history to engage students' interest.

People who risked their lives to rescue victims of Nazi oppression provide useful, important, and compelling role models for students. However, given that only a small fraction of non-Jews under Nazi occupation helped to rescue Jews, an overemphasis on heroic tales in a unit on the Holocaust can result in an inaccurate and unbalanced account of the history. Similarly, in exposing students to the worst aspects of human nature as revealed in the history of the Holocaust, you run the risk of fostering cynicism in your students. Accuracy of fact along with a balanced perspective on the history must be priorities for any teacher.

9. Contextualize the history you are teaching.

Events of the Holocaust and, particularly, how individuals and organizations behaved at that time, should be placed in historical context. The occurrence of the Holocaust must be studied in the context of European history as a whole to give students a perspective on the precedents and circumstances that may have contributed to it.

Similarly, study of the Holocaust should be viewed within a contemporaneous context, so students can begin to comprehend the circumstances that encouraged or discouraged particular actions or events. Frame your approach to specific events and acts of complicity or defiance by considering when and where an act took place; the immediate consequences to oneself and one's family of one's actions; the impact of contemporaneous events; the degree of control the Nazis had on a country or local population; the cultural attitudes of particular native populations historically toward different victim groups; and the availability, effectiveness, and risk of potential hiding places.

Students should be reminded that individuals and groups do not always fit neatly into categories of behavior. The very same people did not always act consistently as "bystanders," "collaborators," "perpetrators," or "rescuers." Individuals and groups often behaved differently depending upon changing events and circumstances. The same person who in 1933 might have stood by and remained uninvolved while witnessing social discrimination of Jews might later have joined up with the SA and become a collaborator or have been moved to dissent vocally or act in defense of Jewish friends and neighbors.

Encourage your students not to categorize groups of people only on the basis of their experiences during the Holocaust: contextualization is critical so that victims are not perceived only as victims. The fact that Jews were the central victims of the Nazi regime should not obscure the vibrant culture and long history of Jews in Europe prior to the Nazi era. By exposing students to some of the cultural contributions and achievements of 2,000 years of European Jewish life, you help them to balance their perception of Jews as victims and to better appreciate the traumatic disruption in Jewish history caused by the Holocaust.

Similarly, students may know very little about Gypsies (Roma and Sinti) except for the negative images and derogatory descriptions promulgated by the Nazis. Students would benefit from a broader viewpoint, learning something about Gypsy history and culture as well as understanding the diverse ways of life among different Gypsy groups.

10. Translate statistics into people.

In any study of the Holocaust, the sheer number of victims challenges easy comprehension. You need to show that individual people—families of grandparents, parents, and children—are behind the statistics and to emphasize that within the larger historical narrative is a diversity of personal experience. Precisely because they portray people in the fullness of their lives and not just as victims, first-person accounts and memoir literature provide students with a way of making meaning out of collective numbers and give individual voices to a collective experience. Although students should be careful about overgeneralizing from first-person accounts, such as those from survivors, journalists, relief workers, bystanders, and liberators, personal accounts help students get beyond statistics and make historical events of the Holocaust more immediate and more personal.

11. Be sensitive to appropriate written and audiovisual content.

One of the primary concerns of educators teaching the history of the Holocaust is how to present horrific images in a sensitive and appropriate manner. Graphic material should be used judiciously and only to the extent necessary to achieve the objective of the lesson. You should remind yourself that each student and each class is different and that what seems appropriate for one may not be appropriate for all.

Students are essentially a "captive audience." When you assault them with images of horror for which they are unprepared, you violate a basic trust: the obligation of a teacher to provide a "safe" learning environment. The assumption that all students will seek to understand human behavior after being exposed to horrible images is fallacious. Some students may be so appalled by images of brutality and mass murder that they are discouraged from studying the subject further. Others may become fascinated in a more voyeuristic fashion, subordinating further critical analysis of the history to the superficial titillation of looking at images of starvation, disfigurement, and death. Though they can be powerful tools, shocking images of mass killings and barbarisms should not overwhelm a student's awareness of the broader scope of events within Holocaust history. Try to select images and texts that do not exploit the students' emotional vulnerability or that might be construed as disrespectful of the victims themselves.

12. Strive for balance in establishing whose perspective informs your study of the Holocaust.

Often, too great an emphasis is placed on the victims of Nazi aggression rather than on the victimizers who forced people to make impossible choices or simply left them with no choice to make. Most students express empathy for victims of mass murder. But it is not uncommon for students to assume that the victims may have done something to justify the actions against them and, thus, to place inappropriate blame on the victims themselves.

There is also a tendency among students to glorify power, even when it is used to kill innocent people. Many teachers indicate that their students are intrigued and, in some cases, intellectually seduced by the symbols of power that pervaded Nazi propaganda (e.g., the swastika and/or Nazi flags, regalia, slogans, rituals, and music). Rather than highlight the trappings of Nazi power, you should ask your students to evaluate how such elements are used by governments (including our own) to build, protect, and mobilize a society. Students should also be encouraged to contemplate how such elements can be abused and manipulated by governments to implement and legitimize acts of terror and even genocide.

In any review of the propaganda used to promote Nazi ideology—Nazi stereotypes of targeted victim groups and the Hitler regime's justifications for persecution and murder—you need to remind your students that just because such policies and beliefs are under discussion in class does not mean they are acceptable. Furthermore, any study of the Holocaust should attempt to portray all individuals, especially the victims and the perpetrators of violence, as human beings who are capable of moral judgment and independent decision making.

13. Select appropriate learning activities.

Word scrambles, crossword puzzles, and other gimmicky exercises tend not to encourage critical analysis but lead instead to low-level types of thinking and, in the case of Holocaust curricula, trivialize the history. When the effects of a particular activity, even when popular with you and your students, run counter to the rationale for studying the history, then that activity should not be used.

Similarly, activities that encourage students to construct models of killing centers should also be reconsidered because any assignment along this line will almost inevitably end up being simplistic, time-consuming, and tangential to the educational objectives for studying the history of the Holocaust.

Thought-provoking learning activities are preferred, but even here, there are pitfalls to avoid. In studying complex human behavior, many teachers rely upon simulation exercises meant to help students "experience" unfamiliar situations. Even when great care is taken to prepare a class for such an activity, simulating experiences from the Holocaust remains pedagogically unsound. The activity may engage students, but they often forget the purpose of the lesson and, even worse, they are left with the impression at the conclusion of the activity that they now know what it was like during the Holocaust. Holocaust survivors and eyewitnesses are among the first to indicate the grave difficulty of finding words to describe their experiences. It is virtually impossible to simulate accurately what it was like to live on a daily basis with fear, hunger, disease, unfathomable loss, and the unrelenting threat of abject brutality and death.

An additional problem with trying to simulate situations from the Holocaust is that complex events and actions are oversimplified, and students are left with a skewed view of history. Because there are numerous primary source accounts, both written and visual, as well as survivors and eyewitnesses who can describe actual choices faced and made by individuals, groups, and nations during this period, you should draw upon these resources and refrain from simulation games that lead to a trivialization of the subject matter.

Rather than use simulation activities that attempt to re-create situations from the Holocaust, teachers can, through the use of reflective writing assignments or in-class discussion, ask students to empathize with the experiences of those who lived through the Holocaust era. Students can be encouraged to explore varying aspects of human behavior such as fear, scapegoating, conflict resolution, and difficult decision making or to consider various perspectives on a particular event or historical experience.

14. Reinforce the objectives of your lesson plan.

As in all teaching situations, the opening and closing lessons are critically important. A strong opening should serve to dispel misinformation students may have prior to studying the Holocaust. It should set a reflective tone, move students from passive to active learning, indicate to students that their ideas and opinions matter, and establish that this history has multiple ramifications for them as individuals and as members of society as a whole.

Your closing lesson should encourage further examination of Holocaust history, literature, and art. A strong closing should emphasize synthesis by encouraging students to connect this history to other world events and to the world they live in today. Students should be encouraged to reflect on what they have learned and to consider what this study means to them personally and as citizens of a democracy.

Part II

Topics

Film and Literature

Topic 1

The World of the Persecuted: Into the Darkness

How can you know what we lost, if you don't know what we had?

— Abba Kovner

They were somebody's mother, somebody's father, somebody's sister or brother. They were the six million Jewish men, women, and children murdered during the Holocaust in the Nazis' systematic plan to annihilate an entire group of people; they were the millions killed who did not fit into the master plan; and they were the millions more who survived, against all odds, to give testimony to the atrocities that were committed. Who were these individuals? What happened to them? What might they have accomplished had their lives not been cut short or their childhoods stolen? What roads might they have traveled and what dreams might have come true?

Before delving into the moral and ethical issues associated with the Holocaust, before attempting to strip away the layers of what was to help guide us through what is and perhaps might be, it is important to become acquainted with the victims of the Holocaust, the millions consumed by the flames of hate, ignorance, and apathy. Through their words, their testimony, survivors take us "into the darkness" and allow us to enter the world of the persecuted. Yet we are given only a small glimpse of this nightmare past, for it is impossible to perceive, no less comprehend, the evil that was perpetuated.

The selections in this topic chapter relive a life before the Holocaust and recount the experiences of those persecuted during the Holocaust. Through their pain we learn of the deepest kinds of love and the deepest kinds of grief as families are torn apart and forced into ghettos and concentration camps. Their words remind us of the despair, the terror, and the suffering that human beings were forced to endure. Their words are a testament to hope, courage, and the indomitable human spirit. In the end, it is the words of the survivors of the Holocaust that must inspire us—their words must remind us what it means to be human, to respect life and hold it sacred.

Film: *The Camera of My Family:*
Four Generations in Germany, 1845–1945

Sources: United States Holocaust Memorial Museum Shop
100 Raoul Wallenberg Place SW
Washington, DC 20024-2150
(800) 259-9998

Social Studies School Service
10200 Jefferson Boulevard
P.O. Box 802
Culver City, CA 90232-0802
(800) 421-4246

Recommended for: Middle school, high school, and college

Summary

Catherine Hanf Noren, an author and photographer, began researching the history of her Jewish family's roots in Germany. The result is a beautiful and moving documentary film that uses a collection of family photographs found after the war to describe the historical events that led to Noren's family's fate before and during the early years of the Nazi Holocaust. The power of this visually gentle informative film is that it shows the Jewish people of Germany in their everyday lives—innocent, trusting, loving people—until the Nazis began their reign of discrimination and terror. It is 18 minutes long.

Symposium: Critical Thinking and Discussion

1. In what ways is the title of this film an appropriate one? If you were the producer, what title might you select? Explain.

2. Review the image of the Nazis in the streets arresting Jews and the image of Hitler in a prison cell writing *Mein Kampf*. How are the two connected?

3. Select an image from the film that best personifies how the Jewish people were typical families before "the darkness descended." Compare this image to the usual ones we see of a people who have been dehumanized in the ghettos and camps.

4. Why didn't most of the German Jews flee when they could?

5. How was immigration to the United States possible and impossible for Jewish families in Germany in 1936–1939?

Reflections in Writing

1. In the film, the narrator says, "These are the images that unlocked the past for me." Images are powerful tools and can say far more than words. Research the history of the Jewish people in

Europe in the years before the Holocaust and select one image that unlocks the past for you in some way. Write a descriptive paper that would enable the reader to "see" and "feel" the image.

2. What did you learn from this film that will influence your life today? What did you learn about our responsibilities to others as human beings?

3. "The past must be linked to the present if there is to be a future," the narrator explains. Explore the meaning of this quote and use examples from the film and from other events in history.

4. The narrator in the film became familiar with members of her family only through photographs. Select one or more photographs of a family member you have never met. Write a descriptive piece based only on the photograph(s).

5. Create a PowerPoint presentation, "Camera of My Family," using photographs of your family. Write the narration for this PowerPoint presentation and incorporate information about your family's roots, culture, and traditions.

Researching the History

1. Research World War I and the Treaty of Versailles. Explain how much of the socioeconomic and political conditions that resulted from that war might have led to the rise of Nazism, Hitler's power, and the ultimate tragedy of the Holocaust.

2. Research the term *Kristallnacht* and discuss how and why this has been called the first stage or precursor of the Holocaust. Create a collage of images of Kristallnacht. (Include a caption for each image that reflects your thoughts, feelings, and reflections.)

3. The Germans passed 42 anti-Jewish measures in 1933, 19 more in 1934, and more than 400 additional laws between 1935 and 1945. In 1935, Hitler announced new laws that had far-reaching effects, including the "Nuremberg Law for the Protection of German Blood and German Honor" and the "First Regulation of the Reich Citizenship Law." Read the documents in Table 1-1. What do they say? For each law, think of three effects and design a poster to illustrate them. Further research the German's anti-Jewish measures from 1933–1945. Which policy do you believe had the most dramatic effect upon the Jewish people? Which policy do you believe impacted the non-Jewish community most? Explain.

4. Research segregation laws passed in the 1800s and early 1900s in the United States. Discuss your findings in a panel discussion on discrimination and exclusion.

5. Research the response of the average German citizen to the anti-Jewish laws that were being introduced. (Several laws passed between 1933 and 1942 are included in the Table 1-2.) Write a paper that summarizes your findings and comes to some conclusions about human rights and social responsibility.

Table 1-1

NUREMBERG LAW FOR THE PROTECTION OF GERMAN BLOOD AND GERMAN HONOR, SEPTEMBER 15, 1935

Moved by the understanding that purity of the German Blood is the essential condition for the continued existence of the German people, and inspired by the inflexible determination to ensure the existence of the German Nation for all time, the Reichstag has unanimously adopted the following Law, which is promulgated herewith:

§1

1) Marriages between Jews and subjects of the state of German or related blood are forbidden. Marriages nevertheless concluded are invalid, even if concluded abroad to circumvent this law.

2) Annulment proceedings can be initiated only by the State Prosecutor.

§2

Extramarital intercourse between Jews and subjects of the state of German or related blood is forbidden.

§3

Jews may not employ in their households female subjects of the state of German or related blood who are under 45 years old.

§4

1) Jews are forbidden to fly the Reich or National flag or to display the Reich colors.

2) They are, on the other hand, permitted to display the Jewish colors. The exercise of this right is protected by the State.

1) Any person who violates the prohibition under §1 will be punished by a prison sentence with hard labor. 2) A male who violates the prohibition under §2 will be punished with a prison sentence with or without hard labor. 3) Any person violating the provisions under §3 or §4 will he punished with a prison sentence of up to one year and a fine, or with one or the other of these penalties.

The Reich Minister of the Interior, in coordination with the Deputy of the Führer and the Reich Minister of Justice, will issue the Legal and Administrative regulations required to implement and complete this Law.

The Law takes effect on the day following promulgations except for §3, which goes into force on January 1, 1936.

Nuremberg, September 15, 1935, at the Reich Party Congress of Freedom

The Führer and Reich Chancellor
Adolf Hitler
The Reich Minister of the Interior
Frick
The Reich Minister of Justice
Dr. Gürtner
The Deputy of the Führer
R. Hess

Reichsgesetzblatt, I, *1935, pp.* 1146-1147.

Source: Arad, Y. et al., Eds. *Documents on the Holocaust:* Jerusalem: KTAV Publishing House, 1981.

First Regulation to the Reich Citizenship Law
November 14, 1935

1) A Jew cannot be a Reich citizen. He has no voting rights in political matters; he cannot occupy a public office.
2) Jewish officials will retire as of December 31, 1935 . . .

1) A Jew is a person descended from at least three grandparents who are full Jews by race . . .
2) A Mischling who is a subject of the state is also considered a Jew if he is descended from two full Jewish grandparents
   a) who was a member of the Jewish Religious Community at the time of the promulgation of this Law, or was admitted to it subsequently;
   b) who was married to a Jew at the time of the promulgation of this Law, or subsequently married to a Jew
   c) who was born from a marriage with a Jew in accordance with paragraph 1, contracted subsequently to the promulgation of the Law for the Protection of German Blood and German Honor of September 15, 1935 (Reichsgesetzblatt, I, p. 1146);
   d) who was born as the result of extramarital intercourse with a Jew in accordance with Paragraph 1, and was born illegitimately after July 31, 1936 . . .

Source: Arad, Y. et al., Eds. *Documents on the Holocaust:* Jerusalem: KTAV Publishing House, 1981.

Table 1-2. Dates of Decrees

Dates given for laws, decrees, and regulations are dates of public announcement.

April 7, 1933   All non-Aryan civil servants, with the exception of soldiers, are forcibly retired.

Sept. 16, 1935   The Nuremberg Laws deprive Jews of German citizenship and reduce them to the status of "subject."

March 7, 1936   Jews no longer have the right to participate in parliamentary elections.

July 2, 1937   More Jewish students are removed from German schools and universities.

July 23, 1938   As of January 1, 1939, all Jews must carry identification cards.

June 19, 1942   Jews must hand over all electrical and optical equipment, as well as typewriters and bicycles.

Source: Arad, Y. et al., Eds. *Documents on the Holocaust:* Jerusalem: KTAV Publishing House, 1981.

Film: *One Survivor Remembers*

Source: United States Holocaust Memorial Museum Shop
100 Raoul Wallenberg Place SW
Washington, DC 20024-2150
(800) 259-9998

Recommended for: High school and college

Summary

In this Academy Award winning documentary, Holocaust survivor Gerda Weissmann Klein recounts the personal story of her life before the war in Poland, her Holocaust experiences, and the suffering she endured on a final death march. Her autobiography, *All But My Life* (Klein, 1995), recounts her experiences in even greater detail. Gerda Weissmann Klein and her husband, Kurt, spent many years together educating students about the Holocaust. Sadly, Kurt died in the summer of 2002, yet Gerda continues to write, travel, and lecture on the Holocaust. The film is 39 minutes long.

Symposium: Critical Thinking and Discussion

1. Describe the first scenes Gerda witnesses of the German occupation. What happened to the able-bodied Jewish men? What happened to Gerda's brother?

2. Gerda says that June 28, 1942, was the "worst day" of her life. Why? What happened on that date?

3. What were Gerda's mother's last words to her? What effect do you think her words had on Gerda throughout the Holocaust and after?

4. Gerda believes that she owes her life to the Nazi German woman who oversaw the labor camps. What did this woman do that made Gerda feel so indebted?

5. Describe the conditions in the labor camp in which Gerda was found. What do you think enabled her to survive under these conditions (e.g., books, and her promise to her father)?

Reflections in Writing

1. Write a journal entry that one of the liberators might have written when he found the survivors of the death march.

2. Write a human interest newspaper article that describes the meeting of Kurt Klein and Gerda Weissman.

3. Of the 2,000 women who started the death march, most died, but 95 of them survived, including Gerda Weissman. Write an essay that speaks to the subject of surviving under such horrific conditions and the strength of the women in the Holocaust.

4. Create an album of Gerda Weissman Klein's life. Use photos (from the Internet and books) along with informative captions to tell the story of her life.

5. Some survivors have said, "To die was easy." What, then, motivated survivors to not give in but resist and struggle to survive? Explain this phenomenon.

Researching the History

1. Research the topic *death march*. What was a death march? Why was it carried out?

2. Read Gerda Weissman Klein's autobiography, *All But My Life*. What is one impression or fact that you learned from the book that you didn't gain from the documentary? Share this with the rest of your classmates in a discussion of the strength of Gerda.

3. After reading Gerda Weissman Klein's autobiography, *All But My Life*, write a letter to the author (in care of the publisher) to express your thoughts and feelings about the memoir.

Memoir: *I Have Lived a Thousand Years*

Author: Livia Bitton-Jackson (1997)

Recommended for: Middle school and high school

Summary

Livia Bitton-Jackson was 13 when her mother, her brother, and she were taken to Auschwitz from Czechoslovakia. *I Have Lived a Thousand Years* chronicles her life from 1943–1951, when she came to the United States. She received a Ph.D. in Hebrew culture and Jewish history from New York University. Her book *My Bridges of Hope* (Bitton-Jackson, 2002) traces her search for life and love after Auschwitz (see Topic 8).

Symposium: Critical Thinking and Discussion

1. Why did the Germans establish a law to force the Jewish people to identify themselves and their homes with a yellow star? Why did most people comply?

2. Why did the author find the law regarding the yellow star humiliating? Compare her attitude with the attitudes of the other members of the family. How do you think you would feel if you were ordered to wear a badge that identified you by race or religion?

3. What might the rest of the population have done to show their distaste with the various anti-Jewish policies established by the Nazis? What effect might this have had on Nazi policy?

4. Discuss the concept of "resettlement." How did this and other euphemisms aid the Nazis in their objective to murder the Jewish people?

5. Describe your impression of Livia Bitton-Jackson. What did she say or do to suggest this impression you have?

Reflections in Writing

1. With a small group or individually, create a headline for a story that would reflect an event in the book that you find especially meaningful. Write an article to accompany the headline and include photograph(s) and caption(s).

2. Throughout her experiences in the ghetto and in the concentration camps, the author experienced times of hope and times of terror. If she were to address your class, what do you think she would say to you? What advice would she give? Write and deliver a 1-minute speech from the perspective of Livia Bitton-Jackson.

3. Read the poem "We Were Children Just Like You" by Yaffa Eliach (1990). Yaffa Eliach is a foremost scholar in Holocaust studies and a professor of history and literature in the department of Judaic Studies at Brooklyn College. Her books *Hasidic Tales of the Holocaust* (1982) and *There Once Was a World* are international bestselling classics. As you read the poem, connect it with the information you gleaned from Jackson's *I Have Lived a Thousand Years* to respond to the writing activities that follow.

We Were Children Just Like You

by Yaffa Eliach

We were children just like you,
a million and a half young innocents
among the Six Million souls
martyred during the Holocaust.

We were children just like you,
the pride and promise of
flourishing Jewish communities
throughout Europe and North Africa,
our parents' joy, our people's future
and gift to mankind.

We were children just like you,
the children of wealth
and the children of poverty.
We laughed, we played,
we went to school and summer camp,
we sang and danced and dreamed;
but we never grew up.
Our world was suddenly engulfed
in flames of hatred so vicious that it
demanded our deaths –
only because we were Jews.

Just like you, we wanted to live.
We clung to life and faith and
we fought, body and spirit,
for physical survival and Jewish identity,
with partisan and resistance groups,
in ghetto and camp uprisings,
participating in clandestine
schools and prayers.
We were smugglers and couriers,
and many of us died
at the sides of our adult comrades.

We suffered the hunger and misery
of the ghettos, the fear of betrayal of
our hiding places and false identities,
and the barbarism and the horror of
the concentration camps, dying alone
or in the trembling arms of mothers
in gas chambers and mass graves.

We were the children of smoke and
ash and flame.

Some of us were fortunate.
We, young survivors, brands plucked
from the consuming fire, are links
in the chain of Jewish continuity.

We built new lives, in Israel, America
and many other countries.
we overcame the burden of
our experiences to enrich the world
with our talents and achievements.

We are all the children of yesterday.
But one and a half million of us
live only in the images of memory –
lorever children – a million and a half
promises never to be fulfilled.

Remember us!

By Yaffa Eliach, author of *We Were Children Just Like You*, and *Hasidic Tales of the Holocaust*. Re-printed with permission.

- In what ways were the children of the Holocaust just like you? In what ways were they different? Explain.

- In the second stanza of the poem, the author writes, "We never grew up." Describe how this supports the testimony of child survivors who said they never had a childhood.

- Consider the lines and verses in the poem and book. Which one(s) make(s) you most uncomfortable? Sad? Hopeful? Write three journal entries in which you react to the line(s) selected.

- In the poem, the author writes, "Just like you we wanted to live." What did children do to fight back, both physically and spiritually?

4. Based on your knowledge of the Holocaust and from the understandings you gained from *I Have Lived a Thousand Years,* add a stanza to the poem above beginning with, "We were children just like you." Select a picture from various resources on the Holocaust to illustrate your stanza. Combine your stanza with others in the class to form an original version dedicated to the children of the Holocaust.

5. The poem above ends with the line "a million and a half promises never filled." Write a journal entry to explain how a specific act of hatred can change the world. Give specifics from not only the Holocaust but from current times.

Researching the History

1. Much has been written about the world of the Jewish people, their strong cultural and traditional ties, and their contributions of 2000 years to society before the Holocaust. Select one city or area of Eastern Europe. Research the life of the Jewish people in that area in the years before Hitler and the Nazi Party came into power (1933). What generalizations can you make concerning their assimilation into the general population? What did you discover concerning the way in which they lived with their non-Jewish neighbors? Locate photographs that capture the insights you gained. How does this help you understand the traumatic disruption of Jewish history caused by the Holocaust?

2. During the Holocaust, other groups such as political dissidents and Gypsies were also identified with assigned badges. Research this identification process and write a brief paper to explain what groups were singled out and why. Describe the badges each group had to wear.

3. What is a ghetto? How does your definition of the term *ghetto* differ from the types of ghettos established during the Holocaust? Research some of the larger ghettos established during the Holocaust such as the Warsaw Ghetto, Vilna Ghetto, and Lodz Ghetto to learn the realities of life in the ghettos during the Holocaust. Use this information to create a diary that might have been written by someone your age living in one of the ghettos.

4. Research laws that were passed between 1933 and 1936 that discriminated against the Jewish people and took away their rights. Create an illustrated timeline that describes these policies and reflects how the Jewish people became excluded from mainstream society in their own communities.

5. In the remains of several of the death camps today are rooms filled with the shoes of the victims, hundreds of thousands of pairs of shoes. Look at the photograph below. Research the victims of the Holocaust and select one specific individual. Write a short biography of this person.

Memoirs: *Night* (excerpt) and *All the Rivers Run to the Sea*

Author: Elie Wiesel (1982, 1995)

Recommended for: High school and college

Summary

Elie Wiesel was born in Sighet, Rumania, in 1928, one of four children. In 1940, Sighet was turned over to Hungary as a reward for its alliance with Germany. In 1944 Elie Wiesel and his family were transported to Auschwitz, where his mother and younger sister were immediately murdered in the gas chamber. His father and he remained together throughout their internment and were on a death march together near the end of the war. His father died in Buchenwald. Wiesel shares the experiences that have haunted him throughout his lifetime in *Night*, a moving account of a young boy robbed of his childhood and the love of his family. In *All the Rivers Run to the Sea: Memoirs,* Wiesel takes us from his childhood memories of life in Sighet through the horrors of Auschwitz and his spiritual struggle to his emergence as a voice for the survivors and for humanity. Both books express some of his deepest and most profound feelings and the memories that will haunt him all his life.

Night (an excerpt)

Never shall I forget that night, the first night in camp, which has turned my life into one long night, seven times cursed and seven times sealed. Never shall I forget that smoke. Never shall I forget the little faces of the children, whose bodies I saw turned into wreaths of smoke beneath a silent blue sky.

Never shall I forget those flames which consumed my faith forever.

Never shall I forget that nocturnal silence which deprived me, for all eternity, of the desire to live. Never shall I forget those moments which murdered my God and my soul and turned my dreams to dust. Never shall I forget these things, even if I am condemned to live as long as God Himself. Never.

Symposium: Critical Thinking and Discussion

1. In both books, Wiesel uses images such as *night, darkness,* and *silence.* Discuss the uses of these images.

2. Wiesel often ponders the fact that he survived the camps. Often he attributes his survival to the need to testify and bear witness. Discuss the importance of this testimony to us and to future generations.

---

3. Explore Wiesel's meaning when he wrote, "Meanwhile, our world contracted steadily. The country became a city, the city a street, the street a house, the house a room, the room a sealed cattle car, the cattle car a concrete cellar." Explain how Wiesel's world was so contracted. What policies were enacted by the Nazis that took away his freedom, his home, his world?

4. In *All the Rivers Run to the Sea,* Wiesel struggles to understand what has happened to his family, the Jewish people, and humanity. He concludes, "Perhaps there was nothing to understand." Discuss this observation. Explain in your own words.

5. Elie Wiesel is considered a "spokesman for humanity." After reading one or more of his works, discuss how his writings benefit all humanity.

Reflections in Writing

1. In *All the Rivers Run to the Sea,* Wiesel writes, "the Germans' psychological methods often failed. They tried to get the inmates to think only of themselves, to forget relatives and friends, to tend only to their own needs. But what happened was just the reverse. Those who retreated to a universe limited to their own bodies had less chance of getting out alive, while to live for a brother, a friend, an ideal, helped you hold out longer." React to this statement in a journal entry.

2. Locate photographs of Auschwitz. Select one photograph that affects you deeply and describe what you see.

3. In *Night* Wiesel discusses Moche the Beadle who escaped death at the hand of the Nazis and returned to Sighet to warn the Jewish people there of the true intentions of the Nazis. In *All the Rivers Run to the Sea,* Wiesel relates that two "veterans" (men who had been there for a longer period of time) of the camps asked why he was there. At first he didn't understand the question, but later he learned that two of their companions, Vrba and Wetzler, had managed to escape from Birkenau to warn Hungarian Jews of what was awaiting them. Write a journal entry to explain why people such as Moche the Beadle or Vrba and Wetzler were unable to convince their friends and neighbors of the truth.

4. Both *Night* and *All the Rivers Run to the Sea* affect the reader in profound ways. Write an essay in which you discuss one or more of the concepts that continue to plague Wiesel, concepts such as *human ideals,* the *beauty of innocence, the weight of justice* and *faith.* Use information from your readings to support your position.

5. Read the excerpt from *Night.* Then write a brief piece, "Never Shall I Forget" based on an experience Wiesel relates in either *Night* or *All the Rivers Run to the Sea.*

Researching the History

1. Do further research about Elie Wiesel. What did you learn that coincided with what you inferred about him from his writing? What were you surprised to learn?

2. Elie Wiesel returned to his hometown of Sighet, Romania, in July 2002. Research this homecoming and write a news article that summarizes this trip.

3. "Why the Jews?" This question is often asked by students. Research the history of the Jewish people and the history of anti-Semitism. You will find many rationalizations that attempt to answer this question. With other members of your group, select one rationalization and discuss how this is an example of prejudice and stereotype that leads to hatred and misunderstanding of other cultures.

4. The six death camps were all located in eastern Poland. Research the significance of this. Select one of the death camps and research it to understand how the Nazis were able to systematically murder and torture such enormous numbers of people. Write a paper that explains your findings.

5. Use the Internet to locate reactions to and reviews of either of these two books by Wiesel. From the ideas expressed by others, what new insights or new ideas did you gain? Share this with members of your class.

Lessons for Today

Moral or Ethical Dilemma

In the selection from *All the Rivers Run to the Sea*, Wiesel asks, "Why were those trains allowed to roll unhindered into Poland? Why were the tracks leading to Birkenau never bombed?" He writes that he asked this question of American presidents and generals. Based on your knowledge of the Holocaust and additional research, how do you think the questions were answered? What do you believe was the real reason nothing was officially done to slow down the train or destroy the tracks leading to Auschwitz-Birkenau? Set up panel discussions in which each group presents findings from the research.

*   Discuss whether the official decision of the United States not to bomb the tracks and the trains violated a code of morality. Research the newest information there is on the whole issue of bombing Aushwitz and report on it for a basis of discussion.

*   Assume that you were part of the government of the United States at the time the decision to do nothing was made. What would you have suggested they do, perhaps being the only dissenter in the group?

Making Connections

1. Research other groups in your community who have been targets of prejudice. Discuss how these prejudices are based on stereotypes, myths, and racism.

2. "We are all the Children of Yesterday—remember us!" wrote Elie Wiesel, the author of *Night* and *All the Rivers Run to the Sea*. Furthermore, he wrote, "Memory is the link that fights indifference." Using the theme of Remembrance, create a program or a project in your classroom in memory of those who have suffered from prejudice and indifference. Ideas include the following: a wall mosaic made of tiles depicting messages of peace in a land where there was no peace, or a book of original poetry dedicated to those who lost their lives.

3. Read the poem "Written in Pencil in the Sealed Railway-Car" by Dan Pagis, a Holocaust survivor (from *Points of Departure*, 1982, Jewish Publication Society), and complete the questions that follow.

Written in pencil in the sealed railway car (reprinted with permission).

Here in this carload
I am Eve
With Abel my son
If you see my other son
Cain son of man
Tell him that I . . .

written by Dan Pagis

Read the poem and discuss its meaning in terms of the context and history of the Holocaust. (The references to Eve, Cain, and Abel are from the Bible—see explanation below.) What unwritten words and thoughts are there? Complete the poem yourself.

1. Who is the speaker of the poem?

2. What message does Eve want you, the reader, as part of humanity to understand? What message is she conveying to Cain?

3. Why did the message never end?

4. Cain, in the Bible killed his own brother. Relate to the Holocaust.

5. What does "son of man" mean?

6. Pagis has been called a "poet of the unspeakable." Explain.

7. Complete the poem yourself. Discuss with others your reasons for your final ending.

Notes on the poem

[These notes reprinted with permission from Yad Vashem, Jerusalem, Israel.]

- Pagis uses the first murder as a metaphor for the Holocaust. The question raised by the biblical reference returns us to the question of the human capacity for murder: The first murder occurs at humanity's very outset.

- The reference to Cain and Abel recalls the common origin of all of humanity: Eve, the victim in the poem, is the mother of both brothers—the murderer and the murdered.

The Story of Cain and Abel in the Bible: Genesis, Chapter 4: 2–11

And Abel was a keeper of the sheep, but Cain was a tiller of the ground. And in process of time, it came to pass that Cain brought of the fruit of the ground an offering unto the Lord. And Abel, he also brought of the firstlings of his flock and of the fat thereof. The Lord had respect unto Abel and to his offering: but unto Cain and to his offering he had no respect. And Cain was very wroth, and his countenance fell. And the Lord said unto Cain, Why art thou wroth? And why is thy countenance fallen? If thou doest well, shalt thou not be accepted? And if thou doest not well, shalt thou not be accepted? And if thou doest not well, sin lieth at the door. And unto thee shall be his desire, and thou shalt rule over him. And Cain talked with Abel his brother: and it came to pass, when they were in the field, that Cain rose up against Abel his brother, and slew him. And the Lord said unto Cain, Where is Abel thy brother? And he said, I know not: Am I my brother's keeper? And He said, What hast thou done? The voice of thy brother's blood crieth unto me from the ground . . .

Topic 2

The Mind of the Perpetrator: Anatomy of Evil

Evil does not prevail until it is given power.

— *The Zohar*

During the International Military Tribunal at Nuremberg, the chief American prosecutor, Justice Robert H. Jackson, wrote:

> These crimes are unprecedented ones because of the shocking numbers of victims. They are even more shocking and unprecedented because of the large number of persons who united to perpetrate them . . . they developed a contest in cruelty and a competition in crime.

The Nazis set out to rid Europe of its Jewish population. The work of murdering Jews was that of ordinary men and women. Although the statistics of the Holocaust are common knowledge, what is not known is the "Why?" How could a civilized population not only follow the dictates of the Nazi leadership but actually wage war on innocent men, women, and children? How could they inflict such death and despair on others and then go home to their families? How could they treat their animals more humanely than they treated human beings?

The behavior of the perpetrators during the Holocaust has been examined and re-examined. Although there is no simple explanation, their behavior could only have occurred because of their failure to recognize the value of each individual human being. Many of the perpetrators of the Holocaust perceived their victims as less than human, "life unworthy of life." What gave birth to this ideology? What nurtured and sustained it?

We may never understand how people let the Holocaust happen, how they not only allowed mass murder but chose to carry it out. They could have made different choices—but the vast majority didn't. This chapter focuses on the evil that men do and the men that do evil—the perpetrator.

Film: *Heil Hitler! Confessions of a Hitler Youth*

Source: Social Studies School Service
10200 Jefferson Boulevard
P.O. Box 802
Culver City, CA 90232-0802
(800) 421-4246

Recommended for: Middle school, high school, and college

Summary

Alfons Heck, the narrator of the film, describes his life as part of the Hitler Youth movement. He explains how he watched as friends were taken away and murdered by the Nazis while caring about nothing but winning the war or dying for Germany and its leader. Graphic archival footage dramatizes the way in which songs, youth camps, speeches, and "education" glorified Hitler and his beliefs. It is important for the student of today to know how perpetrators are made, and today Heck looks back on his participation and fanaticism with regret. He speaks to students to remind them to be on the alert to racism and prejudice in order to ensure that history is not repeated. The film is 30 minutes long.

Symposium: Critical Thinking and Discussion

1. What motivated Alfons Heck to join the Hitler Youth movement before he was ten years of age?

2. What power do the songs, youth camps, speeches, and "education" have on a person's philosophy? What do you believe most influenced Heck's loyalty to Hitler and the Nazis?

3. When Alfons was inducted into the Hitler Youth movement, he said that he felt as if he belonged to something very important. Explain the impact of "belonging." How does the idea of a crowd mentality fit with this phenomenon?

4. In the opening scenes, Alfons Heck explains that when he saw images of the camps he couldn't believe it. How did he rationalize what he saw?

5. In 1943 Alfons was 15 years old. It was then that he realized that Germany might be defeated. How did this realization affect him?

Reflections in Writing

1. Today Alfons Heck, the narrator of the film, speaks with students about his experiences. Write and deliver a brief speech that Heck might make to students your age. Consider the message he would like students to take with them.

2. Select a specific phrase from Hitler's speeches that were delivered to entice the young people to follow without question. Write a rebuttal to this phrase. On what fallacies is it based? What is wrong with the logic behind it?

3. Heck describes Kristallnacht, November 9–10, 1938, as an "exciting event" spurring him forward. Contrast his feelings as a young Nazi to that of a Jewish boy his age. Describe the event from both points of view.

4. It took Alfons a year to accept the truth. During the 1946 Nuremberg trial, one of the 22 Nazis being brought to trial was the former leader of his Nazi youth group. Think about the effect his testimony and arrest had on Alfons. Write a letter from Alfons to his former leader describing his feelings after hearing the testimony.

5. Alfons's last words in the film are, "The story of the Hitler Youth can be repeated because despite Auschwitz, the world has not changed all that much." Contrast this with Anne Frank's famous quote, "It's a wonder I haven't abandoned all my ideals, they seem so absurd and impractical. Yet I cling to them because I still believe, in spite of everything, that people are truly good at heart." Select one of these quotes and write an opinion paper that reflects your reaction to the statement.

Researching the History

1. Research the Hitler Youth movement, its history, objectives, and its effect on Germany's youth.

2. Find political cartoons used during the Nazi era to spread racism and hate. Select one, copy it, and analyze the purpose of the cartoon and how it accomplished its goal.

3. Research the life of Alfons Heck and the work he has been doing since he immigrated to the United States. What do you believe to be the most important thing he has accomplished?

4. Research the life of other children who were part of the Hitler Youth or the League of German Girls. What generalizations can you make about the children who became so fanatical in their belief in Hitler? What does this suggest to educators and parents of today?

5. Research the use of political cartoons. Create a political cartoon that might have been designed at the height of Hitler's power by someone who was attempting to shed light on the truth and undermine Hitler's power.

Film: *Conspiracy*

Source: United States Holocaust Memorial Museum Shop
          100 Raoul Wallenberg Place SW
          Washington, DC 20024-2150
          (800) 259-9998

Recommended for: High school and college

Summary

This extraordinary film is a must for students if they are to understand the way the plans to purposely murder the Jews of Europe came about. The movie is based on the actual protocol of the Wannsee Conference meeting on January 20, 1942, at a lakeside villa in Berlin. Fifteen men gathered, all of them high-ranking and senior representatives of not only the Nazi Party but the Interior Ministry of Germany as well. Gestapo Chief Heinrich Mueller and the now infamous Adolf Eichmann were key people at the meeting. Two out of three attendees were university graduates; half had doctorates, mostly in the law. They were the "best and the brightest," yet on this day they gathered for one purpose only: how to efficiently use their talents and brains to best logistically murder the Jews of Europe. The method was soon selected: gassing—murder by gas. Well documented, this film shows how the plan to implement the Holocaust was initiated by supposedly intelligent human beings following an agenda item as in any other meetings. The film is 96 minutes long.

Symposium: Critical Thinking and Discussion

1. Michael Berenbaum, author, scholar, and historical consultant for the film *Conspiracy*, explains, "This was a meeting unlike any other meeting in recorded history, yet not unlike meetings that you and I have seen on television or have attended." Comment on this observation and what we can learn from it.

2. Reinhard Heydrich convened the meeting of the Wannsee Conference. Since it is apparent that the decision to murder the Jews had already been decided on before this meeting, what was the reason for convening this group of 15 men at that time?

3. Discuss the irony of the detailed, meticulous preparation of the food served at the meeting as well as the beautiful setting.

4. Discuss the language used during the meeting to disguise the plans to murder the Jews (e.g., "evacuation to the east"). What other euphemisms were used during the meeting? Since this was a private meeting of the perpetrators, why do you suppose these disguised phrases were used?

5. Scholars have suggested that Heydrich accomplished three concrete goals at this conference. What do you think they were?

Reflections in Writing

1. Read various film critiques. Create a review of this film that might appear in a local newspaper emphasizing the hidden context of the meeting.

2. Create a dialogue between two of the participants of the Wannsee Conference after the meeting was over. Remember that your dialogue for each must reflect the person's attitudes as reflected in the film. Consider what they might say in a more informal setting.

3. Imagine that you are at the Wannsee Conference. Write and deliver a dissenting argument that could possibly have changed the tone and intention of the conference.

Researching the History

1. Research the Wannsee Conference and its participants. Who were these men? Why were they chosen to attend? What was their area of expertise and educational background? With others, create a "Who's Who" biographical poster that examines the conference participants and what happened to each after the war was over.

2. Where is Wannsee? Why was it chosen for the meeting? Research its history as a famous historic site and how it is utilized today for educational tours in Europe.

3. The film *Conspiracy* is based on an actual protocol of the meeting that survived in only one file. Research where the information came from and how events in history revealed this valuable data.

4. Beginning in 1933, the policy of the German state was to rid itself of its Jewish population by forced migration as the state made it increasingly difficult for Jews to live in Germany. Research the steps the Nazis took to make the Jewish people feel unwelcome in their own country.

5. Read the following "Extract from Written Evidence of Rudolf Höss, commander of the Auschwitz Extermination Camp" and answer the questions below.

EXTRACT FROM WRITTEN EVIDENCE OF RUDOLF HÖSS, COMMANDER OF THE AUSCHWITZ EXTERMINATION CAMP

In the summer of 1941, I cannot remember the exact date, I was suddenly summoned to the Reichsführer SS, directly by his adjutant's office. Contrary to his usual custom, Himmler received me without his adjutant being present and said in effect:

The Führer has ordered that the Jewish question be solved once and for all and that we, the SS, are to implement that order.

The existing extermination centers in the East are not in a position to carry out the large Aktionen which are anticipated. I have therefore earmarked Auschwitz for this purpose, both because of its good position as regards communications and because the area can easily be isolated and camouflaged. At first I thought of calling in a senior SS officer for this job, but I changed my mind in order to avoid difficulties concerning the terms of reference. I have now decided to entrust this task to you. It is difficult and onerous and calls for complete devotion notwithstanding the difficulties that may arise. You will learn further details from Sturmbannführer Eichmann of the Reich Security Main Office who will call on you in the immediate future.

The departments concerned will be notified by me in due course. You will treat this order as absolutely secret, even from your superiors. After your talk with Eichmann you will immediately forward to me the plans for the projected installations.

The Jews are the sworn enemies of the German people and must be eradicated. Every Jew that we can lay our hands on is to be destroyed now during the war, without exception. If we cannot now obliterate the biological basis of Jewry, the Jews will one day destroy the German people.

On receiving these grave instructions, I returned forthwith to Auschwitz, without reporting to my superior at Oranienburg.

Shortly afterwards Eichmann came to Auschwitz and disclosed to me the plans for the operations as they affected the various countries concerned. I cannot remember the exact order in which they were to take place. First was to come the eastern part of Upper Silesia and the neighboring parts of Polish territory under German rule, then, depending on the situation, simultaneously Jews from Germany and Czechoslovakia, and finally the Jews from the West: France, Belgium and Holland. He also told me the approximate number of transports that might be expected, but I can no longer remember these.

Source: Arad, Y. et al., Eds. *Documents on the Holocaust:* Jersulam: KTAV Publishing House, 1981.

- How does Heinrich Himmler justify the Final Solution to Höss?

- In giving this evidence, there are many things Höss seems to have forgotten. What reasons can you think of to explain this lapse in memory?

- From this report, what inferences can you make about the Final Solution and the men behind it?

Document: Historical Information:
The Nazi Olympics

Author: Susan Bachrach (2000).

Recommended for: Middle school, high school, and college

Summary

After 1935 (after the Nuremberg Laws had come into effect), the Jewish people experienced a steady deterioration in their position in Germany. The Nazis committed numerous acts of destruction and sadistic cruelty by looting businesses, burning synagogues, and beating and torturing Jews. Jews were forbidden to go to the cinema, swimming pools, and theaters. It was at this period of hate that Berlin, Germany, was chosen by the International Olympic Committee (IOC) as the host site for the 1936 Summer Olympics. In visual and graphic detail, Susan Bachrach's *The Nazi Olympics* describes how and why the city of Berlin was chosen and chronicles the stories of how both Jewish and Black athletes were discriminated against before, during, and after the games due to Nazi policy.

Bachrach has written probably the only authentic documented history of the Nazi Olympics of 1936, and it is an important piece of literature. Of particular interest to the student of today who participates in sports is the detailed account in Part 2, "The Nazification of German Sport." In addition, the chapter entitled "African-American Voices" is the best selection available on the blatant prejudice shown by the Nazis against Olympic winners such as Jesse Owens.

Symposium: Critical Thinking and Discussion

1. Why did Hitler hold the Olympics in such low regard? What finally convinced him to become a strong supporter?

2. When and who began a public support of the boycott of the games? What organizations agreed with the boycott? How was the boycott defeated?

3. Why did African Americans, knowing the racist policies of the Nazis, continue to support participation in the Olympic games?

4. What is the major political change that took place in Germany 2 years after Berlin was chosen for the 1936 Summer Olympics? How did this change in government leadership affect the tone of the Olympics?

5. Study the photo on page 78 of Hitler with famous ice skater Sonja Henie. What do you find ironic about this photo? What does it say about the duplicitous character of evil?

Reflections in Writing

1. Study the picture on page 25. Consider how this picture and the accompanying note, which explains that it is from a slide lecture on genetics and race in Dresden, Germany, reflect the Nazi view of race discrimination. Write an essay to explain what the term *Rhineland Bastards* refers to and how the term came about.

2. Create an editorial cartoon that helps people to understand the true meaning of "the Nazification of German sport."

3. How and when did the persecution of Jewish athletes in Germany begin? What specific actions were taken? How did the rest of the world react to this discrimination? Study the news clippings on pages 44–45. Develop an outline that highlights the persecution of Jewish athletes in Germany, beginning in 1933, and the reaction of the rest of the world.

4. Read a biography or other bibliographic information on the life of Jesse Owens. Make two lists—one "in favor of" and one "against" his participation in the Olympics. Hold a class debate on the subject.

Researching the History

1. Research the history of the Olympic games from its inception to 1936. How did the Olympic games in Germany support or deny the spirit of the Olympics?

2. The Olympic games opened on Saturday, August 1, 1936. In the first week, 10 of the 66 men competing from the United States were African American. They won 8 of the 12 events and captured a total of 14 gold, silver, and bronze medals in individual and team events. The hero of the Olympics was Ohio track star Jesse Owens, who took home four gold metals. Hitler, however, never posed with Owens for photographs and refused the opportunity to shake hands with him. Trace these events and the follow-up of Jesse Owens when he returned to the United States.

3. Research the participation of Jewish athletes in the Olympic games of 1936. Who were they and why were they allowed to participate? What did American-Jewish athlete Sam Stoller describe it as the most "humiliating episode" of his life?

4. Discrimination against Blacks in Germany and in the United States during the 1930s and 1940s is widely acknowledged. What similarities and differences can be found?

5. Research articles written about the 1936 Olympic games in Germany. In what ways did these articles affect public perception in the United States regarding the government of Germany and its policies? Show how all individuals, especially perpetrators are, after all, human beings capable of moral judgment and independent decision making.

Memoir: *Parallel Journeys*

Source: Helen Ayer & Alfons Heck (1995)

Recommended for: Middle school, high school, and college

Summary

This is the fascinating memoir of Helen (Eleanor Ayer), a young Jewish woman trying to survive the tyranny of the Nazi perpetrators, and Alfons Heck, a young German boy who is part of the Hitler Youth. In alternate chapters, they discuss their "parallel journeys" through the Holocaust years. As we read about their lives, we are astounded to discover how their very dichotomous journeys brought them together in the struggle for human rights. This is a must-read!

Consider using this book with the film *Heil Hitler: Confessions of a Hitler Youth,* which is developed for this topic as well.

Symposium

1. What was the Hitler Youth? Why was this organization so vital to the Nazis? How did Alfons Heck qualify as one of the chosen few for the Hitler Youth?

2. Why did most Germans willingly follow Hitler even though he announced his plan to ultimately wipe out Christianity and its churches and ordered massive book burnings?

3. Why did millions of teens join the Jungvolk, the junior branch of the Hitler Youth? What part did girls play in this organization? How did the training for boys and girls differ?

4. Alfons says that the Hitler Youth never once thought that the Final Solution meant the extermination of the Jews. He said it did, however, approve of slave labor. Comment on this.

5. Do you consider Alfons more of a perpetrator or a bystander? Explain.

6. Alfons and Helen decided to travel together and give lectures on their parallel experiences. The reactions in audiences vary from admiration for both to outright hostility toward Alfons, at which time Helen defends him. Discuss the reaction of Helen and of the audiences they address.

Reflections in Writing

1. German newspapers screamed headlines such as "Jews for sale—who wants them? No one!" (p. 35). Write a theory to explain why people "stood by and let this happen."

2. Compose an open letter that Alfons Heck might have written after the Holocaust to discuss his participation.

3. What might Helen say to audiences to defend Alfons Heck? Write a paper that expresses your attitude toward Helen's stance.

4. Create a headline and an article that might appear in current-day German newspapers on the subject of guilt and responsibility regarding the Holocaust.

Researching the History

1. Are there other former Hitler Youth members who have spoken up about their experiences and involvement during the Holocaust? What are they saying?

2. Helen faced many problems after liberation, including the continuation of anti-Semitism. Research this phenomenon and write a brief report that details one such incident.

3. Research the Hitler Youth. Write five facts that you uncovered that you find particularly unsettling, startling, or significant today.

Lessons for Today

Moral or Ethical Dilemma

In a suburb of Chicago, a group of female juniors were part of a traditional hazing by female seniors. Over the years, the hazing had become more and more outlandish, until finally, in 2003, many girls were seriously injured. There were hundreds of witnesses to the hazing, and many videotaped it. Many others had cell phones. Yet no one called the authorities or any adults for help. In fact, many encouraged the seniors and enjoyed the "entertainment."

The seniors involved were the perpetrators. The audience was the bystanders. This was not a simulation, it was real. What justice would you determine for each of these groups of individuals? What reasons affect your decision?

Debate this issue with classmates, then research this event on the Internet to learn the fate of those involved.

Making Connections

Read the poem below, **"Words"** by Ursula Duba, and then answer these questions: Consider the point Ursula Duba is trying to make about the choice of words used to describe the Holocaust and other tragedies. Find examples in articles in local papers in which euphemisms and other less specific words are used to color the truth. Discuss the way in which euphemisms change our perspectives. Create a stanza about the tragedy of 9-11. Be careful to choose the right words to describe what happened.

Words

by Ursula Duba

bold letters
on top of the page
declare
this newsletter is dedicated
to all those
who perished
in the Holocaust

the German man,
now living in the USA
is proud of his efforts
to pay homage
to the victims of the Shoah
on the anniversary
of kristallnacht

but i am disturbed
by the word perish
in this dedication—
it conjures up images
of people dying in earthquakes
in a storm out on the open sea
in a hurricane or a tornado—

the word perish
does not tell me
about open ditches
rapidly filling up with the corpses
of innocent men women and children
shot by members of the einsatzgruppen and
   the Wehrmacht
it doesn't show me piles of emaciated bodies
deliberately starved to death
it doesn't show me ss guards
using victims for target practice
nor does it display the twisted bodies
of people who died
at the hands of doctors
who performed cruel experiments
in the name of science

there are no gas chambers
crematoria
or perpetrators

weren't Jews Gypsies and non-Aryans
murdered
i ask the German man

yes of course
the victims of the Holocaust
were murdered
he answers
taken aback
by my question
but this word
sounds so aggressive
he says with dismay

after several days
of back and forth
on the telephone
the German man decides to delete the
   entire sentence
on top of the newsletter
rather than using the word murdered
in his dedication to the victims
of the Shoah

while discussing this
with several friends
we take note
that a lengthy article
in a leading magazine
had recently informed us
that most of the victims
of the massacres in Rwanda
had been hacked to death
by their Hutu neighbours—
no euphemisms there
as to how these victims died
and on discussing the

three million Cambodians
who died in the killing fields—
the language is quite clear—
they were starved to death
or brutally murdered
by the Kmer Rouge

On further probing
no one suggests
that John F. Kennedy and
Martin Luther King perished—
both were assassinated

a few weeks later
i ask a Holocaust survivor
what words would properly describe
the actions by which
six million died

they were exterminated
he says
without hesitation

this word immediately reminds me
of my first months
in an apartment in Brooklyn
and the discovery of cockroaches
in my kitchen cupboards

honey
my next door neighbour
had told me then
look in the yellow pages
under exterminator

recently
i heard Mike Wallace of 60 Minutes
refer to all those who were lost
in Auschwitz

the word lost
makes me think
of my fear
of getting lost in foreign cities
on my travels abroad
when even maps
are of limited value
in those countries
which use different alphabets

the word also
calls up images
of thick forests
where hapless travelers
get lost
and i am reminded of
the story of Hansel and Gretel which used
    to make me appreciate
the safety of our crammed house
when i was a child

what with the twice a day roll-call
and the meticulous record keeping
of the German and Austrian concentration
    camp commanders
the chance of being lost in Auschwitz
or any other concentration camp
were very slim
my friend Dalia
explains to me
whose mother was gassed on the first day
of their arrival in Birkenau.

Ursula Duba is a non-Jewish German writer who was born in Germany shortly before the outbreak of World War II. She grew up during World War II during the impenetrable silence of the postwar years in Germany and has been living in the United States for the past 32 years. Her latest book is *Tales From a Child of the Enemy*. This story-poem is published here with the writer's permission.

Topic 3

The Mind of the Bystander: Indifference and Apathy

> *What hurts the victim most is not the cruelty of*
> *the oppressor but the silence of the bystander.*
>
> — Elie Wiesel

To watch as neighbors lost their rights, their homes, their freedoms, their lives; to stand behind closed doors and drawn curtains and ignore what was happening to friends in the streets beyond; to witness the torture of friends and neighbors and never raise a voice in opposition; to say, "I never knew"; this was the world of the bystander.

Raul Hilberg, an esteemed scholar of the Holocaust, in describing the bystander, wrote, "They were not 'involved,' not willing to hurt the victims and not wishing to be hurt by the perpetrators." Holocaust survivor Primo Levi explained that most Germans didn't know because they didn't want to know:

> In Hitler's Germany, a particular code was widespread: those who knew did not talk; those who did not know did not ask questions; those who did ask questions received no answers. In this way the typical German citizen won and defended his ignorance which seemed to him sufficient justification of his adherence to Nazism.

The truth, however, was that most of the population *did* know; how could they not know? Millions of people don't just disappear. How difficult, if not impossible, it would have been for the Nazis to murder millions if other millions had stood up and made their voices heard. Unfortunately, the general population did nothing; the victims had few allies, and the Nazis gained power and control.

How very different the outcome would have been if those who knew did talk, and those who did not know asked questions, and those who asked questions demanded answers.

Film: *The Hangman*

Source: CRM
           2215 Faraday, Suite F
           Carlsbad, CA 92008
           (800) 421-0833

Recommended for: Middle school and high school

Summary

Animation is used to illustrate a poem of the same name by Maurice Ogden about a town in which the people are hanged one by one by a mysterious hangman while the town stands by and rationalizes each victimization. This is an excellent film for understanding the mind of the bystander and the value of individual responsibility. It is 12 minutes long. The poem is as follows:

Hangman

by Maurice Ogden

1.

Into our town the Hangman came.
Smelling of gold and blood and flame—
And he paced our bricks with a diffident air
And build his frame on the courthouse square.

The scaffold stood by the courthouse side.
Only as wide as the door was wide;
A frame as tall, or little more,
Than the capping sill of the courthouse door.

And we wondered, whenever we had the time,
Who the criminal, what the crime,
That Hangman judged with the yellow twist
Of knotted hemp in his busy fist.

And innocent though we were, with dread
We passed these eyes of buckshot lead;
Till one cried: "Hangman, who is he
For whom you raise the gallows-tree?"

Then a twinkle grew in the buckshot eye,
And he gave us a riddle instead of reply"
"He who serves me best," said he,
"Shall earn the rope on the gallows-tree."

And he stepped down, and laid his hand
On a man who came from another land—
And we breathed again, for another's grief
At the Hangman's hand was our relief.
And the gallows-frame on the courthouse lawn
By tomorrow's sun would be struck and gone.
So we gave him way, and no one spoke,
Out of respect for his hangman's cloak.

2.

The next day's sun looked mildly down
On roof and street in our quiet town
And, stark and black in the morning air,
The gallows-tree on the courthouse square.

And the Hangman stood at his usual stand
With the yellow hemp in his busy hand;
With his buckshot eye and his jaw like a pike
And his air so knowing and businesslike.

And we cried: "Hangman, have you not done,
Yesterday with the alien one?"
Then we fell silent, and stood amazed:
"Oh, not for him was the gallows raised . . ."

He laughed a laugh as he looked at us:
". . .Did you think I'd gone to all this fuss
to hang one man? That's a thing I do
To stretch the rope when the rope is new."

Then one cried, "Murderer!" One cried, "Shame!"
And into our midst the Hangman came
To that man's place. "Do you hold," said he,
"With him that was meant for the gallows-tree?"

And he laid his hand on that one's arm.
And we shrank back in quick alarm,
And we gave him way, and no one spoke
Out of fear of his hangman's cloak.

That night we saw with dread surprise
The Hangman's scaffold had grown in size.
Fed by the blood beneath the chute
The gallows-tree had taken root;

Now as wide, or a little more,
Than the steps that led to the courthouse door,
As tall as the writing, or nearly as tall,
Halfway up on the courthouse wall.

3.

The third he took—we had all heard tell—
Was a usurer and infidel. And"
"What," said the Hangman, "have you to do
with the gallows-bound, and he a Jew?"

And we cried out: "Is this one he
Who has served you well and faithfully?"
The Hangman smiled: "It's a clever scheme
To try the strength of the gallows-beam."

The fourth man's dark, accusing song
Had scratched out comfort hard and long:
And "What concern," he gave us back
"Have you for the doomed—the doomed and black?"

The fifth. The sixth. And we cried again:
"Hangman, Hangman, is this the man?"
"It's a trick," he said, "that we hangmen know
for easing the trap when the trap springs slow."

And so we ceased, and asked no more,
As the Hangman tallied his bloody score;
And sun by sun, and night by night,
The gallows grew to monstrous height.

The wings of the scaffold opened wide
Till they covered the square from side to side;
And the monster cross-beam, looking down,
Cast its shadow across the town.

4.

The through the town the Hangman came
And called in the empty streets my name—
And I looked at the gallows soaring tall
And thought: "There is no one left at all

For hanging, and so he calles to me
To help pull down the gallows-tree."
And I went out with right good hope
To the Hangman's tree and the Hangman's rope.

He smiled at me as I came down
To the courthouse square through the silent town
And supple and stretched in his busy hand
Was the yellow twist of the hempen strand.

And he whistled his tune as he tried the trap
And it sprang down with a ready snap—
And then with a smile of awful command
He laid his hand upon my hand.

"You tricked me, Hangman!" I shouted then,
"That your scaffold was built for other men . . .
And I no henchman of yours," I cried,
"You lied to me, Hangman, foully lied!"

The a twinkle grew in the buckshot eye:
"Lied to you? Tricked you?" he said, "Not I,
For I answered straight and I told you true:
The scaffold was raised for none but you.

"For who has served me more faithfully
Than you with your coward's hope? Said he,
"And where are the others that might have stood
Side by your side in the common good?"
"Dead," I whispered; and amiably
"Murdered," the Hangman corrected me;
"First the alien, then the Jew . . .
I did no more than you let me do."

Beneath the beam that blocked the sky,
None had stood so alone as I—
And the Hangman strapped me, and no voice there
Cried "Stay" for me in the empty square.

Symposium: Critical Thinking and Discussion

The Hangman is an excellent vehicle for a discussion of a moral dilemma:

- After viewing the film *The Hangman,* read the poem aloud with classmates (choral reading).

- List the facts and issues presented, summarizing events, the people involved, and possible alternative actions the main character could have taken.

- Individually decide which alternative the main character should follow and describe (in writing) at least three reasons for your decision.

- Find other students who have selected the same alternative as you and focus on the most important reasons for taking this position.

- With your entire class, discuss the various alternatives selected and the reasons for it.

- Revaluate your position. Think about the facts, issues, and reasons discussed and then individually record what you think the main character should do and the most important reasons for taking this position. Compare your views now with your views before. Are there any changes? Explain.

Answer the following questions:

1. Discuss the meaning of the following line: "'He who serves me best,' said he, 'Shall earn the rope on the gallows' tree.'"

2. In what ways might the people have responded to the Hangman's question, "What concern have you for the doomed?"

3. From where did the Hangman get his power?

4. Describe your feelings after viewing and reading this poem. How did it affect you?

5. How would you connect the message or theme of this poem to your own life?

Reflections in Writing

1. Write a poem for today's world in which bystanders give power to perpetrators, such as bullies and gang leaders.

2. Write a lesson for life you learned from *The Hangman.* Find creative ways to disseminate this message, illustrate it, and display it in the classroom. Example of a slogan: "Stand up for what's right, even if you're standing alone."

3. Write and deliver a 1-minute speech to inspire and galvanize the community to stand up to the Hangman.

4. What is the main theme of *The Hangman?* Reread the poem and look for the various images and symbolism used to deliver its message. Write a paper that explores the use of these images and symbolism.

5. Compare the film and print versions. Which was the most impressive, effective, or thought-provoking? Write a commentary that explores this question.

Researching the History

1. Research ways in which people, individually and collectively, in Eastern Europe remained bystanders during the Holocaust years. What effect did the Nuremberg Laws have in promoting bystanders? Write an editorial that gives your impression of such bystanders and use support from the research you did.

2. How did ordinary men and women living in Germany in the early 1930s react to the Nazi policies and philosophy? How did the Church react?

3. Research other times in the history of this country in which Americans were bystanders to a social or political issue. Select one such event. On an index card, list the event, the date, the public response, and the effect(s) of this response. Put your index card together with those created by others in the class to create a timeline or a bulletin board to illustrate the effects of being a bystander.

Film: *The Voyage of the St. Louis*

Source: United States Holocaust Memorial Museum Shop
100 Raoul Wallenberg Place SW
Washington, DC 20024-2150
(800) 259-9998

Note: The questions and activities listed can be adapted to other films that also tell the story of the *St. Louis,* including: *The Double Crossing: The Voyage of the St. Louis* (29 minutes) and *The Doomed Voyage of the St. Louis* (50 minutes). Both can be ordered through Social Studies School Service, 10200 Jefferson Boulevard., P.O. Box 802, Culver City, CA 90232-0802, (800) 421-4246.

Recommended for: Middle school, high school, and college

Summary

This film tells the story of the more than 900 German-Jewish refugees who boarded the luxury liner *St. Louis* in May 1939 and sailed from Hamburg to Havana seeking refuge from the Nazi terror. Upon arrival in Havana, the Cuban government prevented most from disembarking. As the ship then traveled the coast of Miami Beach, attempts were made to petition the U.S. government to allow it entry, but to no avail. After nearly 40 days on the ocean, the passengers were returned to Europe and granted refuge in France, Belgium, Holland, and Britain. Unfortunately, three of these countries ultimately came under Nazi domination, so consequently hundreds of the original passengers of the *St. Louis* were murdered in the Holocaust, although over 600 did survive. The film is 52 minutes long.

Symposium: Critical Thinking and Discussion

1. Why did so much of the German-Jewish population wait until the late 1930s to try to escape Nazi persecution?

2. President Bru of Cuba claimed that the Jewish passengers of the *St. Louis* were being denied asylum because they had not complied with Cuban law. What other reasons would explain the failure of the Cuban government to allow the passengers to disembark?

3. Who, do you believe, is ultimately responsible for the fate of the passengers of the *St. Louis:* the Cuban government, the U.S. government, Jewish organizations in the United States, the officials of the Hamburg-Amerika Line, or other nations of the world? Explain.

4. What lessons did the Nazis draw from the world's response to the *St. Louis?*

5. What do you believe to be the most important lessons that can be drawn from the story of the *St. Louis* and its passengers?

Reflections in Writing

1. When the Cuban government denied passengers asylum, several American newspapers blamed the passengers for what ultimately happened. For example, the *Seattle Times* wrote: "Cuba had not invited them; had not even been asked if they would be received by residents; and harsh as it may seem, Cuba's President Bru perhaps had no alternative but to deny them admission."

   The *South Carolina State* wrote: "How could the refugees have been so careless about ascertaining whether and where they would be allowed to land? They had, it seems, only provisional permits from Cuba to land as travelers en route to the United States, where they hoped to gain admission later. What grounds were there for such hope? And just what does the word 'later' imply to Cuba?"

2. Write a persuasive paper that expresses your opposition to one of the above viewpoints.

3. Create a moral or ethical question raised by the story of the *St. Louis*. For example: "The U.S. had already provided asylum for many refugees. Is there a limit to how much the U.S. could do?" Discuss the question in groups or with the entire class.

4. Create a concept book on being a bystander for students younger than you that tells the story of the *St. Louis*. Include photos and illustrations.

5. Read several newspaper accounts of the *St. Louis*. Compile the information and, with others, create a newspaper in tribute to the passengers. Your paper may include articles that tell the *who, what, where, why,* and *how*; photos and captions; biographical sketches of some of the passengers of the *St. Louis*; an advice column related to the situation; an editorial cartoon; a letter to the editor.

Researching the History

1. Research current U.S. immigration policy. In what ways is it similar and in what ways is it different from the policy in the 1930s and 1940s?

2. In what ways are the experiences of refugees such as the Haitian, Cuban, Indochinese, or Central American similar to or different from those of the passengers of the *St. Louis*? Research the position of the United States concerning the *St. Louis*. Who was involved in the decision to make the *St. Louis* to return to Europe? What viewpoints were expressed? What were the political ramifications?

3. Obtain the names of some of the passengers on the fateful journey of the *St. Louis*. Select one and trace the events of this person's life from the time he or she returned to Europe. Look at the USHMM website link for this information.

4. Research the Evian Conference of 1938 and the Bermuda Conference of 1943. What generalizations can you make based on the results of these conferences?

Historical Novel: *Friedrich*

Author: Hans Richter (1987)

Recommended for: Middle school

Summary

Friedrich's best friend thought Friedrich was lucky. His family had a good home and his father had a good job, while many in Germany in the early 1930s were unemployed. As the Nazi Party gained power, Friedrich's world began to fall apart because he was Jewish. He was expelled from school, his mother was killed, his father was arrested, and Friedrich was left alone to survive. While exploring a friendship between two young boys and their families, Hans Richter's novel traces the ways in which the Nazi Party and the Hitler Youth transformed a generation and created a world of bystanders.

Symposium: Critical Thinking and Discussion

1. In the first part of the novel, Herr Resch, the landlord is described. How is his behavior symbolic of that of most of the citizens of Eastern Europe during the Holocaust?

2. Although this book is considered an historical novel, why is it an important book for studying the Holocaust?

3. What was the lure of the Jungvolk? Why did Friedrich want to join? How did it serve to transform a generation of boys and girls?

4. Of all the characters detailed in this book, whom do you most respect and whom do you least respect? Defend your answer with specific instances from the novel.

5. Read over the rules and laws listed in the chronology at the back of the book. How did the rules and laws affect the lives of the Jewish population? How did the rules and laws affect the lives of the non-Jewish population? Which rule or law seemed to mark the "beginning of the end" for the Jewish people?

6. Are we responsible for our friends and neighbors? If so, to what degree? If not, explain.

Reflections in Writing

1. Where does prejudice and hate originate? Write an essay from the perspective of *hate* or *prejudice*. Tell about your life, what gives you your power, how you influence people, and how you can be destroyed.

2. The novel *Friedrich* is told from the perspective of Friedrich's friend. Select one scene and rewrite it from Friedrich's perspective instead.

3. Read the judge's comments on page 53, "The Hearing," in which he speaks to Herr Resch about his membership in the NSDAP (Nazi Party). Then read the statement below by Martin Niemoller, a church leader who spoke out against the Nazis. Imagine that you had to rule on Herr Resch's petition. Write an opinion paper to explain your position.

> First they came for the communists and I did not speak out—because I was not a communist. Then they came for the socialists and I did not speak out because I was not a socialist. Then they came for the trade unionists and I did not speak out because I was not a trade unionist. Then they came for the Jews and I did not speak out because I was not a Jew. Then they came for me and there was no one left to speak out for me.
>
> Pastor Martin Niemoller

4. How does one go from becoming best friends with an individual to hating and persecuting people you don't even know who share a common religion with this friend? Create a list of reasons to explain this. Create a list that will guide others as they conduct life in today's multicultural world.

5. Primo Levi, a famous Holocaust survivor, once asked, "Did the German people know what was happening to the Jews?" Write a response to this question based on specific support from the novel *Friedrich*.

Researching the History

1. Why is propaganda such a powerful force? Research this phenomenon. Find several editorial cartoons that appeared in newspapers before and during the Holocaust years of 1933–1945 that promoted anti-Semitic feelings. Select one, describe it, and explain how it may have influenced perceptions.

2. Look at the chronology in the back of the book. Research one of the laws, decrees, or regulations listed. Write a paper to explain how this affected the lives of Friedrich and other Jews of Europe.

3. In the chapter "The Teacher," Herr Neudorf, Friedrich's teacher, gives an abbreviated history of discrimination in the world. Today, in all parts of the world, there are examples of hate and discrimination. Select one, research it, and write a newspaper article detailing the event.

4. Research the accomplishments of the Jewish people over the centuries. Create a poster that illustrates one or more of these accomplishments.

5. Research the topic *pogroms.* Describe pogroms of the past and present.

Memoir: *In the Shadow of the Swastika*

Author: Hermann Wygoda (1998)

Recommended for: Middle school, high school, and college

Summary

In his memoir, *In the Shadow of the Swastika,* Hermann Wygoda recounts his life as a Jew assuming a non-Jewish identity during the Nazi regime and thus was witness to many who were bystanders and watched as the ghetto walls were built. He was known first as a ghetto smuggler, bringing goods to the Jewish people imprisoned within the walls of the Warsaw Ghetto. Later he worked in the Resistance as Commandante Enrico and rose from commanding a platoon to leading a division of 2,500 partisans that ultimately liberated the city of Savona. Fluent in German and other languages, Wygoda understood what was happening to the Jewish people and with extraordinary spirit, courage, and strength fought against the Nazis in every arena. His actions were synonymous with the word *hero.* The following selection recounts Wygoda's recollections of the Warsaw Ghetto as it was being established and watched bystanders do nothing to assist Jews as they were being rounded up for the enclosed ghetto.

This book is also recommended for use in Topic 5, *Spiritual and Physical Resistance.*

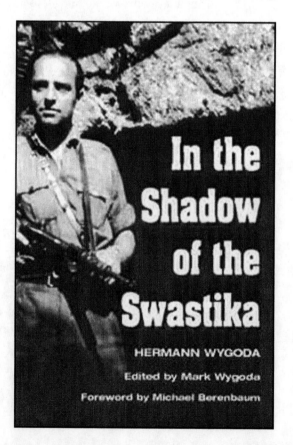

Excerpt from *In the Shadow of the Swastika*, by Hermann Wygoda, pp. 24–26. Reprinted with permission.

The shock of the quick Nazi victory over France is hard to describe. Our thoughts turned back to September 1939, when Poland had been invaded. Historically there had been a long, close, and friendly relationship between France and Poland, although that friendship had been marred somewhat during the period of flirtation between the Smigly-Rydz regime and Germany. It was hard to find an educated Pole who did not speak French, which was considered almost a second national tongue. Sentimentality set aside, one cold fact remained: the hope of regaining independence any time soon had been eliminated.

The increased feeling of insecurity, combined with the necessity of procuring the minimum amount of food required to sustain life, caused many people to dispose of whatever valuables they had managed to hide from the Nazis. This led to the development of a brisk black market. Businessmen and artisans also had been able to hide some of their merchandise and materials, from which they produced finished products in the relative safety of their cellars. Two of my close friends fit in this category: one owned a furrier business, and the other a jewelry business, before the outbreak of the war.

There were plenty of jobs around (except for Jews), but most were related to the Nazi war effort, and I was not ready to help the enemy unless forced to do so. Instead I joined with my two friends in the smuggling business. Each time I traveled into the countryside, I sold their goods to the farmers and purchased food to bring back to my friends in Warsaw. My willingness and ability to take risks were thus put to a profitable use.

Traveling almost every week gave me the opportunity to see things of which most people, particularly Jews, were not aware. I was especially intrigued by the defense preparations going on in the vicinity of Warsaw during the summer of 1940. Some places were camouflaged, while others were painted with a special color, such as the dark blue that covered the railroad station windows. No one (except of course the Nazis) knew what enemy the concrete bunkers were supposed to deter.

In midsummer of 1940 those mysterious walls in Warsaw began to go up at a faster pace. What in the spring had appeared to be a crossword puzzle with scattered pieces now began to look like a medieval fortress. But no medieval fortress had ever covered so much territory. In some places the walls ran down the centers of streets right between the streetcar tracks. In other places whole rows of apartment buildings had their gates blocked up with bricks.

One day, in the early fall of 1940, an edict appeared signed by Hans Frank, who was the Nazi governor general of the General gouvernement. It stated" "Effective immediately, the Jews who are now scattered throughout the city and the surrounding area are ordered, under penalty of death, to make arrangements to move to the sector especially provided for them. Those Jews found after the fifteenth of October outside the Jewish sector will be shot on sight." Even for the efficient Nazis, however, the time allotted for the resettlement of such a large number of people turned out to be too short. It was thus necessary to postpone the deadline until November 15.

A few days after that proclamation, an angry article appeared in a German newspaper printed in Warsaw, the *Warschauer Zeitung*, complaining that the Jews and plutocrats were spreading rumors—intended to besmirch the name of the Germans—that the Jews were being pressed into a so-called ghetto. Nothing, claimed the German paper, could be further from the truth. That sector arrangement had nothing to do with a ghetto; it was intended as a place where Jews could live in peace and security and further their cultural heritage, a place where the Germans could protect the Jews from their Polish neighbors. After that famous article, rumors circulated that anyone mentioning the term *ghetto* would be summarily executed.

The resettlement took place on an exchange basis. Any Gentile living in the now official Jewish sector had to move out to make room for incoming Jews. I too decided to exchange my apartment with a family from inside the ghetto, although I did not intend to live there. Living in a ghetto was tantamount to living in a jail or worse, particularly under the Nazis. It made me furious just to think about it.

The first and only night I spent in the ghetto, November 15, 1940, was the night after I had moved my furniture. My new residence was located close to a major checkpoint at the corner of Pawia and Okopowa Streets. The next morning I walked outside and noticed a large crowd assembled near a group of German police who were blocking the exit. The haste with which the Nazis acted in sealing the ghetto had caught many Gentiles inside, and these people were now concentrated at the exit waiting for passage out. I too approached that point and waited with a made-up excuse. In the meantime I discovered that the reason for the delay was that the German police did not know what to do. They kept everyone there until they received the order to let only the Gentiles through. I told them that I was a Gentile and that I had not quite been able to leave the day before. I was let out without problem, and for the time being I stayed with my friends in Praga.

The ghetto was not an indisputable fact. From that time on, the ghetto was closed, but the Nazis were unable to seal it hermetically for a technical reason: to reach a major railroad station, they had to run the streetcars through the ghetto. To solve that problem, the Nazis ordered the streetcar operators to drive through the ghetto at a high rate of speed without stopping. It was impossible to obey that order, however, because the Nazi bigwigs—who lived mostly in the newer sections of the capital, with its wide promenades—failed to take into consideration the narrow width of the ghetto streets and the tight curves at their intersections, where slowing down to almost a complete stop was imperative. I used the streetcar to enter and leave the ghetto at least once a week, smuggling out merchandise and returning with food for several friends who by now needed help badly. One in particular was the wife of a good friend who never returned home from the war. They had a little girl my son's age.

The Polish police, of course, knew about the streetcar traffic problems within the ghetto. After the collapse of Poland, they had come out of hiding and had reported to the Nazis for service. In their wildest dreams the Nazis could not have hoped for more loyal elements than the Polish police. They turned out to be far better at collaboration than were the police in any other conquered territory. At first the Nazis ordered a Polish police to be placed on each of the streetcars, but they soon discovered that one man was not enough to keep things under control. Next they tried placing an officer on each of the four platforms. But this still did not succeed in stopping the traffic to and from the ghetto.

Faced with such a colossal problem, they decided to eliminate the streetcar traffic from the ghetto altogether. To accomplish this they reduced the size of the ghetto by taking out one street and then used that street for streetcar traffic after blocking up the cross streets with masonry. Thus, the streetcar problem was finally solved, and the one-half million or more Jews inside the ghetto were faced with a ten-foot-high brick wall capped with broken glass. To maintain contact with the rest of the city, the inhabitants made holes in the wall here and there. The Polish police were aware of this, however, and had to be bribed so that these holes could be used to supply the people inside. Such holes were mainly reserved for professional smugglers only. I had to pay dearly for help to get in, but I got in—not once a week anymore, but every two weeks—no matter what the price.

Symposium: Critical Thinking and Discussion

1. What is a *ghetto*? How does your definition of the term *ghetto* differ from the types of ghettos established during the Holocaust?

2. Locate Warsaw, Poland, on a European map. What reason did the Germans give for establishing the Warsaw Ghetto? What was the real reason behind its creation?

3. Why does Wygoda compare the ghetto with a "medieval fortress?" In what ways are they alike and in what ways are they different?

4. How did the establishment of the ghetto affect the Jewish people, and how did it affect the non-Jewish people of the area?

5. Discuss the title of the book and the images it evokes.

Reflections in Writing

1. Wygoda explains how he rode in the streetcar that ran through the ghetto along with the other passengers who were not Jewish. Discuss the different ways in which the Nazis promoted apathetic "bystander" behavior among the Polish population in Warsaw.

2. What is your definition of a hero? Read the remaining chapters of *In the Shadow of the Swastika*. What qualities does Wygoda share with your definition of a hero? Write a paper that expresses your interpretation of a hero and, using support from the book, explain why Wygoda is considered a hero.

3. Herman Wygoda's daughter Sylvia Wygoda lives in Atlanta, Georgia, and has dedicated her life to teaching the lessons of the Holocaust to students like you. Write a letter to Ms. Wygoda to express your reaction to *In the Shadow of the Swastika*. (You may write to her in care of the publisher, the University of Illinois Press.) Ms. Wygoda speaks frequently to school groups and can be contacted at the Georgia Commission on the Holocaust.

Researching the History

1. Research how the Jewish people kept their culture alive as they struggled to survive in the ghetto. Write a journal entry that reflects your findings for historians to read in the future. What impressed you most about survival in the Warsaw Ghetto?

2. Research the Warsaw Ghetto. Discuss some of the major problems that the Jewish population faced living in this confined area. What happened to the original inhabitants of the area before the Jewish people were forced into the area established as a ghetto? How were their lives changed?

3. Read the remaining chapters from *In the Shadow of the Swastika*. On a map, trace Wygoda's route from the beginning of the Holocaust until its end and discuss all his heroic accomplishments at each geographical location.

Lessons for Today

Moral or Ethical Dilemma

1. Think about a time in your life when you might have been considered a bystander. For example, perhaps you witnessed discrimination toward others, or you have knowledge of a classmate who has made threats to other students. In view of what you have learned about bystanders, if you were to witness a similar event, what would you do differently? Explain.

2. Create a moral dilemma of your own based on personal experiences or from a local news report, such as those mentioned above. Write the dilemma and use it as a basis for discussion in your class or small group.

Making Connections

1. *The White Rose* was an underground organization of German non-Jewish teens who wanted to warn the German citizens about the evils of the Nazi regime. What do we have in place today to safeguard the rights of the individual?

2. On the subject of bystanders, historian Edmund Burke wrote, "The only thing necessary for the triumph of evil is for good men to do nothing." A poem written by a Holocaust survivor expressed a similar philosophy and suggested that the biggest fear we have to face is the fear of "the indifferent who permit the killers and betrayers to walk safely."

3. Consider the times in the history of our country that have proven these quotes true. Along with others, create a campaign that focuses attention on the problem of being a bystander and encourages others to take action, to right a wrong.

4. Discuss how an individual could possibly begin as a bystander, and then either become a collaborator or even possibly a rescuer. Give examples from your reading and research.

Topic 4

Life in the Ghetto: Images of Hope and Despair

Alongside the horrible suffering, terror and death,
there was a pulsating life in the ghettos—a life
filled with meaning, with dignity and even with
hope. This was the essence of resistance.

— Vladka Meed

During the 1930s, life for the Jewish people in Germany became increasingly difficult. Laws were passed that not only put restrictions on their lives but also took away their rights of citizenship. By 1939, when Germany invaded Poland, persecution of the Jews had continually escalated, and Eastern European Jews became the target for violent crimes and murder. At this time, too, the Nazis began a program of relocating Jews, taking them to major cities and imprisoning them in ghettos, barricaded run-down sections of cities in Eastern European countries.

Hundreds of thousands of Jews were forced into ghettos, under the harshest of circumstances. Starvation and diseases such as typhus were rampant, and life was precarious at best. The cold of the winters, combined with hunger and disease, took the lives of thousands and thousands—young and old alike, and those living in the ghetto were often reduced to begging, smuggling, and fighting for every morsel of food. Travel in and out of the ghetto was prohibited unless a person had a work permit that allowed him or her to leave the ghetto during the day. Many, however, climbed the ghetto walls or went underground through the sewers in order to get to the other side to find food and, in some cases, obtain weapons.

Two of the largest ghettos were in Lodz and Warsaw, Poland. Hundreds of thousands of Jews were packed into small areas. In Lodz 150,000 to 200,000 Jewish people were crammed into 20 blocks, and in the Warsaw Ghetto, at its peak, 400,000 people lived in an area of approximately 3.5 square miles.

By the end of the war, almost all of the inhabitants of these ghettos were dead, either from conditions in the ghettos or after being transported to the concentration camps.

While the Nazis controlled the ghetto, they established a Jewish Council, or *Judenrat,* which was composed of 27 male leaders of the community. The *Judenrat* was responsible for ensuring that Nazi dictates were followed. The *Judenrat* distributed food, ran hospitals, and was often given the unbearable task of selecting men, women, and children for deportation to the East—the concentration camps. An ongoing debate questions the role of the *Judenrat:* Did it make life better for its people, or were its members guilty of complicity?

The memoirs and films included in this chapter's topic focuses on the realities of life in the ghettos. They offer a look at the efforts of a people to keep alive their Jewish identity, their culture and traditions, and to retain their humanity. They also make us aware of the "choiceless choices" that were made on a daily basis. Ultimately, it is a story of the struggle to survive under the most horrific and unimaginable conditions.

Film: *Korczak*

Source: U.S. Holocaust Memorial Museum Shop
100 Raoul Wallenberg Place SW
Washington, DC 20024-2150
(800) 259-9998

Note: Additional information on the life of Janusz Korczak can be found at http://fcit.coedu.usf.edu/holocaust/people/Korczak. Once on the site, follow links to people—specifically, "resisters."

Recommended for: High school and college

Summary

Janusz Korczak was a famous Jewish pediatrician who established and directed the Jewish orphanage in Warsaw. When deportations to the Treblinka death camp began in the summer of 1942, Korczak refused to try to save his own life and chose to stay with his children. With dignity and grace, holding a child in each arm, Korczak led his children from the ghetto to the train station to the cattle cars. In August, 1942, Korczak and his children were taken to Treblinka, where all perished. This 2-hour film traces the life of Korczak and "his children" in the orphanage in the Warsaw ghetto. In black and white with English subtitles, the film is extremely moving in its portrayal of the plight of the children and the heroism of the adults who struggled to keep alive hope and humanity.

Symposium

1. After watching this film, how would you describe Janusz Korczak? Often in film we watch the emergence of the "tragic hero." Would you consider Korczak to be such a person? Why or why not?

2. What factors might have influenced Korczak's decision to allow the children to show up for deportation rather than try to hide them?

3. Of all the deeds Korczak and his staff accomplished, why was the last walk with the children remembered most? What does this walk symbolize?

4. Korczak and the children perished in the Treblinka death camp. Today Treblinka is surrounded by forests, and the only reminder of what was are the 17,000 rocks put there to represent the cities and villages from which those murdered in Treblinka came. There is only one rock with a personal name: Janusz Korczak. Why?

Stones at Treblinka

5. How did the film change or augment your understanding of life in the ghetto? Explain.

Reflections in Writing

1. Create a study guide for others your age who are watching this film as part of their study of the Holocaust. Include questions that will guide them in understanding the film and help them to focus on the scenes that you believe are most important.

2. Select one scene from the film that will stay with you. Describe the scene and the impact it has had.

3. In August 1942, 192 children and 10 adults were deported from the Warsaw Ghetto to Treblinka. With Korczak at the front of the line, 192 children and 10 adults marched through the street. Those who witnessed the final march are haunted by the memory. Create a poem, or essay, that relates the story of Korczak and "his children."

4. Create a photobiography of Janusz Korczak using photos and captions.

5. Courage took many forms in those dark times. What kind of courage did Korczak show that was different from the Resistance Fighters, yet still courageous?

Researching the History

1. Read "The Last March: August 6, 1942" (below) from *The King of Children: The Life and Death of Janusz Korczak* by Betty Jean Lifton (1997). What did you learn from the text that you weren't aware of from the film alone?

Dr. Betty Lifton is a local known child psychologist and author who spent many years researching the life of Korczak for her book. We gratefully acknowledge and thank her for the permission to reprint. Excerpt from "The King of Children" by Betty Lifton reprinted with permission.

The Last March:

August 6, 1942

What matters is that all of this did happen.

— Ghetto Diary

Korczak was up early, as usual, on August 6. As he leaned over the windowsill to water the parched soil of "the poor Jewish orphanage plants," he noticed that he was again being watched by the German guard posted by the wall that bisected Sienna Street. He wondered if the guard was annoyed or moved by the domestic scene, or if he was thinking that Korczak's bald head made a splendid target. The soldier had a rifle, so why did he just stand there, legs wide apart, watching calmly? He might not have orders to shoot, but that hadn't deterred any SS so far from emptying his ammunition into someone on a whim.

Korczak began speculating about the young soldier in what was to be the last entry of his diary. "Perhaps he was a village teacher in civilian life, or a notary, a street sweeper in Leipzig, a waiter in Cologne. What would he do if I nodded to him? Waved my hand in a friendly gesture? Perhaps he doesn't even know that things are—as they are? He may have arrived only yesterday, from far away . . ."

In another part of the compound, Misha Wroblewski and three of the older boys were getting ready to leave for the jobs Korczak had been able to arrange for them at the German railway depot on the other side of the wall. Every morning they were marched out under guard and counted, and marched back again every night. It was hard work, but it gave them a chance to barter what few possessions they had for food.

They left the orphanage quietly without communicating with anyone. It seemed like just another day they had to get through. Promptly at seven Korczak joined Stefa, the teachers, and the children for breakfast at the wooden tables, which had been pushed together once the bedding was removed from the center of the room. Perhaps they had some potato peels or an old crust of bread, perhaps there was some carefully measured ersatz coffee in each little mug. Korczak was just getting up to clear the table when two blasts of a whistle and that dread call, "Alle Juden raus!" ("All Jews out!"), rang through the house.

Part of the German strategy was not to announce anything in advance, but to take each area by surprise: the plan that morning was to evacuate most of the children's institutions in the Small Ghetto. The lower end of Sliska Street had already been blockaded by the SS, squads of Ukrainian militiamen, and the Jewish police.

Korczak rose quickly, as did Stefa, to still the children's fears. Now, as always, they worked intuitively together, knowing what each had to do. She signaled the teachers to help the children gather their things. He walked into the courtyard to ask one of the Jewish policemen for time to allow the children to pack up, after which they would line up outside in an orderly fashion. He was given fifteen minutes.

Korczak would have had no thought of trying to hide any children now. During the past weeks, he had seen people who had been discovered hiding in cupboards, behind false walls, under beds, flung from their windows or forced at gunpoint down to the street. There was nothing to do but lead the children and teachers straight into the unknown, and, if he was lucky, out of it. Who was to say that, if anyone had a chance of surviving out there in the East, it might not be them?

As he encouraged the children to line up quietly in rows of four, Korczak must have hoped that no matter how terrible the situation in which they found themselves, he would be able to use his charm and powers of persuasion to wheedle some bread and potatoes and perhaps even some medicine for his young charges. He would, above all, be there to keep their spirits up—to be their guide through whatever lay ahead. He had to try to reassure the children as they lined up fearfully, clutching their little flasks of water, their favorite books, their diaries and toys. But what could he tell them, he whose credo it was that one should never spring surprises on a child—that "a long and dangerous journey requires preparation." What could he say without taking away their hope, and his own? Some have speculated that he told them they were going to their summer camp, Little Rose, but it seems probable that Korczak would not have lied to his children. Perhaps he suggested that the place where they were going might have pine and birch trees like the ones in their camp; and, surely, if there were trees, there would be birds and rabbits and squirrels.

But even a man of Korczak's vivid fantasy could not have imagined what lay in wait for him and the children. No one had yet escaped from Treblinka to reveal the truth: they were not going East, but sixty miles northeast of Warsaw to immediate extermination in gas chambers. Treblinka was not even an overnight stay.

The Germans had taken a roll call: one hundred and ninety-two children and ten adults. Korczak was at the head of this little army, the tattered remnants of the generations of moral soldiers he had raised in his children's republic. He held five-year-old Romcia in one arm, and perhaps Szymonek Jakubowicz, to whom he had dedicated the story of Planet Ro, by the other.

Stefa followed a little way back with the nine- to twelve-year-olds. There were Giena, with sad, dark eyes like her mother's; Eva Mandelblatt, whose brother had been in the orphanage before her. Halinka Pinchonson, who chose to go with Korczak rather than stay behind with her mother. There were Jakub, who wrote the poem about Moses; Leon with his polished box; Mietek with his dead brother's prayer book; and Abus, who had stayed too long on the toilet.

There were Zygmus, Sami, Hanka, and Aronek, who had signed the petition to play in the church garden; Hella, who was always restless; big Hanna, who had asthma; and little Hanna with her pale, tubercular smile; Mendelek, who had the bad dream; and the agitated boy who had not wanted to leave his dying mother. There were Abrasha, who had played Amal, with his violin; Jerzyk, the fakir; Chaimek, the doctor; Adek, the lord mayor; and the rest of the cast of The Post Office, all following their own Pan Doctor on their way to meet the Messiah King. One of the older boys carried the green flag of King Matt, the blue Star of David set against a field of white on one side. The older children took turns carrying the flag during the course of their two-mile walk, perhaps remembering how King Matt had held his head high that day he was forced to march through the streets of his city to what he thought was to be his execution.

Among the teachers were many who had grown up in the orphanage: Roza Sztokman, Romcia's mother, with her blond hair parted in the middle and plaited into two thick braids like her daughter's; Roza's brother Henryk, who typed the diary, blond like her, a good athlete, popular with the girls. (He could have escaped to Russia before the fall of Warsaw, but he had stayed behind to be with their father, the old tailor.) There were Balbina Grzyb, whose husband Feliks (away at work that day) had been voted king of the orphanage as a boy; Henryk Asterblum, the accountant for thirty years; Dora Solnicka, the treasurer; Sabina Lejzerowicz, the popular sewing teacher who was also a gymnast; Roza Lipiec-Jakubowska, who grew up in the orphanage; and Natalia Poz, who worked in the office for twenty years, limping as a result of polio contracted as a child just before she came under Korczak's care.

The sidewalks were packed with people from neighboring houses, who were required to stand in front of their homes when an Aktion was taking place. As the children followed Korczak away from the orphanage, one of the teachers started singing a marching song, and everyone joined in: "Though the storm howls around us, let us keep our heads high." They walked past the Children's Hospital, a few blocks down on Sliska Street, where Korczak had spent seven years as a young doctor, past Panska, and Twarda, where he had gone at night to see his poor Jewish patients. The streets here were empty, but many people watched from behind closed curtains. When Jozef Balcerak, who had moved into the ghetto the year before to be with his parents, caught sight of the little procession from his window, he gasped, "My God, they've got Korczak!" The orphans marched half a mile to the All Saints Church on Grzybowska Square (where they had once asked to play in the garden), joining up with thousands of others, many of them children from institutions that had also been evacuated that morning. They continued on together through the Small Ghetto to the Chlodna Street bridge that crossed over to the Large Ghetto. Witnesses say that the youngest children stumbled on the uneven cobblestones and were shoved up the steps of the bridge; many fell or were pushed down to the other side. Below the bridge some Poles were shouting: *"Goodbye, good riddance, Jews!"*

Korczak led his children down Karmelicka Street, past Nowolipki, home of the Little Review, and past the sausage shop where he used to take his reporters on Thursday nights. Michael Zylberberg and his wife Henrietta, living in the basement of a house on the corner of Nowolipki and Smocza, happened to look out as the orphans passed by. He was relieved to see that the police were not beating and shoving them as they did with other groups.

The little procession walked past Dzielna Street, past the Pawiak prison, and up Zamenhofa toward the northernmost wall of the ghetto. The younger ones were wilting by now in the intense heat; they dragged their feet; they moaned that they wanted to rest, that they were thirsty, that they were hot, that they had to go to the bathroom. But the Jewish police, who were escorting them, kept the group moving forward. Joanna Swadosh, a nurse, saw the orphans as they were approaching their destination. She was helping her mother set up a small infirmary in the evacuated hospital next to the Umschlagplatz. It was no use asking why the Germans, so intent on killing, were bothering to open such a unit. There was no apparent logic in anything they did. She no longer dwelled on such questions, but went numbly about her routine. Not until later would she understand that the infirmary was just a cover to allay any suspicion about resettlement.

She was unpacking a crate when someone glanced through a window and called, "Dr. Korczak is coming!" It could mean only one thing, she thought—they had Korczak. If Korczak had to go, so would they all. The Jewish police were walking on both sides, cordoning them off from the rest of the street. She saw that Korczak was carrying one child, and had another by the hand. He seemed to be talking to them quietly, occasionally turning his head to encourage the children behind. Word that Korczak's orphanage had been taken spread quickly through the ghetto. When Giena's brother, Samuel, heard the news, he rushed out of the furniture factory, two friends following in fast pursuit to prevent him from trying to join Giena. He ran first to the Judenrat office to ask Abraham Gepner if it was really true. Gepner, who had always seemed so powerful, sat slumped in his chair as he acknowledged it was.

"Can you help me get Giena out of the Umschlagplatz?" Samuel pleaded. *"It's impossible,"* Gepner said, almost inaudibly. *"Yesterday they took my daughter's best friend—remember, I called her my adopted daughter. I couldn't save her."*

As Samuel turned to leave, Gepner roused himself. *"Even if I had a way of getting Giena out of there, she might refuse to go. She may be better off with Korczak and Stefa and the other children."* Samuel dashed out of the Judenrat office and headed for the Umschlagplatz, his friends still trailing after him. But as he neared the loading area, he found that Mita Street, Niska, and part of Zamenhofa were blocked off. He tried to slip through the crowd of people also desperate to save their loved ones, but his friends held on to him and managed to drag him back to the factory.

All that night Samuel lay on his bed staring into the darkness, unable to think of anything but Giena. What was it like for her on the Umschlagplatz? What was she thinking? Was she scared? Was she crying for him? He would take part in the Ghetto Uprising the following year, and survive Maidanek and Auschwitz, but his inability to save his sister would torment him all his life.

In spite of the pandemonium in the ghetto, one could still telephone out to the Aryan side.

Harry Kaliszer, who had arranged the bribe for Korczak's release from Pawiak two years earlier, phoned Igor Newerly with the terrible news that he had seen everyone being led away. Newerly immediately phoned Maryna Falska, who rushed over to his apartment to join him, his wife, and their nine-year-old son in their vigil. She paced back and forth for quite a while, and then sat in silence. When the telephone finally rang, Newerly leapt for it.

"They're at the Umschlagplatz," Harry told him. *"It looks like this is it." "Call us if there's any hope,"* Newerly said. *"We won't hear from him again,"* Maryna said hoarsely. Her prediction was correct.

At the gate where the ghetto ended, fresh squadrons of SS and Ukrainians were waiting with their whips, guns, and dogs. The children were pushed and shoved through the gate, across the tram tracks on the Aryan side, and through another gate, this one opening into the large dirt field by the railway siding which was the Umschlagplatz. Thousands of people—crying, screaming, praying—were already waiting there in the broiling sun. Families huddled together, their meager belongings tied up in pillowcases or sacks; mothers clung to their children; old people sat in a daze. There was no water, no food, no place to relieve oneself, no protection from the German whips and curses.

Nahum Remba, an official of the Judenrat, had set up a first-aid station in the Umschlagplatz through which he was able to rescue a few of those caught in the dragnets. Word that Korczak and his children were on their way had just reached him when they arrived. He seated them at the far end of the square against a low wall; beyond was the courtyard of the evacuated hospital, now filled with yet more Jews waiting to be loaded onto the trains.

Korczak's children weren't the only ones that Remba had to worry about that day: four thousand youngsters had been gathered with their caretakers from other institutions. But Korczak's children—well, they were Korczak's. The trains carried from six to ten thousand people daily, but Remba hoped that if he could hold Korczak's entourage there until noon, he might possibly save them until the following day. in a mad world such as this, each day counted—each hour.

Remba took Korczak aside and urged him to go with him to the Judenrat to ask them to intervene. But Korczak wouldn't consider it; if he left the children even for a moment in this terrifying place, they might panic. He couldn't risk that. And there was always the danger that they might be taken away in his absence.

"The loading of the railway cars began then," Remba wrote in his memoirs. *"I stood next to a column of ghetto policemen who were transferring the victims to the train, and watched the proceedings with a pounding heart, hoping that my plan of delay would succeed."* The Germans and Ukrainians kicked and shoved people into the chlorinated cars, and still there was room left. A tall, thin young man with a violin case pleaded in perfect German with an SS officer to let him join his mother, who had been crammed into one of the cars. The officer laughed derisively and said: *"It depends on how well you play."* The young man took out the violin and played a Mendelssohn Requiem. The music floated over the crazed plaza. But the German, tired of his game, signaled the violinist to get into the car with his mother and sealed the door behind him.

Then, to Remba's dismay, Schmerling—the sadistic chief of the ghetto police in charge of the Umschlagplatz—ordered that the orphanages be loaded. Korczak signaled his children to rise.

There are some who say that at that moment a German officer made his way through the crowd and handed Korczak a piece of paper. An influential member of CENTOS had petitioned the Gestapo on his behalf that morning, and the story goes that Korczak was offered permission to return home—but not the children. Korczak is said to have shaken his head and waved the German away.

Remba records in his memoir that Korczak headed the first section of children and Stefa the second. Unlike the usual chaotic mass of people shrieking hysterically as they were prodded along with whips, the orphans walked in rows of four with quiet dignity. *"I shall never forget this scene as long as I live,"* Remba wrote. *"This was no march to the train cars, but rather a mute protest against this murderous regime . . . a procession the like of which no human eye has ever witnessed."*

As Korczak led his children calmly toward the cattle cars, the Jewish police cordoning off a path for them saluted instinctively. Remba burst into tears when the Germans asked who that man was. A wail went up from those still left on the square. Korczak walked, head held high, holding a child by each hand, his eyes staring straight ahead with his characteristic gaze, as if seeing something far away.

2. As an advocate for children, Korczak imagined a Declaration of Children's Rights long before it was created by the U.N. General Assembly in 1959. The declaration he envisioned was never completed. Research Korczak and his thoughts concerning the rights of children. Along with others, create a list of children's rights based on what you learned. Send your list to a local paper to help bring attention to the rights of children.

3. *The King of Children: The Life and Death of Janusz Korczak* by Betty Jean Lifton is the most recent, definitive book on Korczak. Read this book and select a chapter that best captures the man and his spirit. Discuss this choice with others in your class.

4. Read about H.J. Res. 165—a joint resolution introduced to the House of Representatives in February 1939 and written to authorize the admission of a limited number of German refugee children. What was the fate of this resolution? What are the implications both in terms of its impact on the children and on world perception?

Film: *Kovno Ghetto: A Buried History*

Source: Social Studies School Services
10200 Jefferson Boulevard
Culver City, CA 90232-0802
(800) 421-4246

Recommended for: High school, and college

Summary

The Jewish ghettos in Europe were set up in haste, as soon as the Nazis invaded and took control of a community. Although most ghettos were closed, life went on. Families adjusted to new realities as survival became a daily challenge. Governance of the ghetto was administered through the *Judenrat* (Jewish Council), Jewish officials charged with controlling the life within the ghetto.

Before the war, 40,000 Jews had lived in Kovno, the provisional capital of Lithuania. In the Kovno Ghetto, desperate Jews vowed to resist in the only way they could, by documenting what was being done to them. After the war, copies of official German orders, minutes of Jewish Council meetings, personal diaries, and photographs were found buried beneath the ground of the ghetto.

This 100-minute film weaves together the memories of survivors of the Kovno Ghetto along with the artifacts recovered to create a detailed portrayal of the daily life and resistance efforts of those imprisoned in the Kovno Ghetto. An important value of this film is that it depicts the ways in which people of spirit and strength fought to survive, a legacy to us all.

Symposium: Critical Thinking and Discussion

1. Why did the Lithuanians at first welcome the Soviets? How did their initial feelings turn to general distrust?

2. What do you believe to be the most difficult circumstances that the people in the Kovno Ghetto were forced to experience?

3. In June 25, 1941, the Germans entered Kovno, Lithuania. Why did the Jewish people at that time think, even for a moment, that this was a good sign?

4. How does the point of view from which the story of the Kovno Ghetto is told affect the viewer?

5. Dr. Elkes, a physician, was highly respected for his leadership of the Jewish Council. What decisions did Dr. Elkes have to make? What choices did he have?

6. The Jewish Council set up many committees, such as housing and work. Select one and describe the purposes of the committee and its accomplishments.

7. Why was it so difficult for people to escape from the ghetto? What were the ramifications to the population in the ghetto if someone attempted to escape?

8. The few survivors of the Kovno Ghetto have made enormous contributions in life. Discuss the final thoughts they expressed on this film. What responsibility do they ascribe to the German people for the terror they experienced?

Reflections in Writing

1. The Jewish Committee established a plan to record the events in the ghetto. Research some of the journal entries and photographs that were found, and describe their impact upon your understanding of life in the ghetto.

2. With classmates, create an illustrated timeline of significant events in the Kovno Ghetto. On index cards, give additional information about each event.

3. Select a single "snapshot" from this film that had a significant impact upon you. Describe this snapshot and write your reaction to it.

4. Discuss the concept of *free choice*. Write an opinion paper that explores the question, "Did free choice exist in the ghetto?"

5. "There is a desert inside me—my soul is scorched." These were words found in the diary of Dr. Elkes, the leader of the Jewish Council in the Kovno Ghetto. Write a piece to complete this diary entry.

Researching the History

1. Locate Lithuania and the city of Kovno, presently known as Kaunus, on a map. Research this area to learn how the politics during World War II affected the country.

2. Research the efforts of Sugihara, the Japanese consul in Lithuania. What did he and his family do in order to rescue Jewish men, women, and children? What makes his efforts especially heroic?

3. In 1943 the Kovno Ghetto was officially declared a concentration camp. Research the escape planned from this camp and its limited success.

4. Some small children in the Kovno Ghetto miraculously escaped death. Research and recount one child's survival.

Memoir and Film: *The Pianist*

Author: Wladyslaw Szpilman (1999)

Recommended for: High school and college

Summary

On September 23, 1939, Wladyslaw Szpilman played *Chopin's Nocturnal in C-sharp minor* live on the radio as shells exploded all around him. It was the last live music broadcast from Warsaw. That day, Germany invaded Poland and a German bomb hit the station, which went off the air.

The Pianist is the memoir of composer and concert pianist Wladyslaw Szpilman, who lost his entire family to the Holocaust. Szpilman survived in hiding and, in the end, was saved by a German officer who heard him play the same Chopin piece on a piano found among the rubble of the Warsaw Ghetto.

The film, which is 2 hours long, is based on the memoir. The questions and activities in this chapter can be used with both.

Symposium: Critical Thinking and Discussion

1. Explain the dichotomy that initially existed in the ghetto. How did it mirror the world outside the ghetto?

2. *The Pianist* is a testament to the essential human desire to live. What passage (scene) do you believe most clearly reflects this?

3. Based on the diary (or from remarks in the film), to what do you attribute the motives of Captain Wilm Hosenfeld for saving Szpilman's life? Szpilman wrote," Just as there were 'good' Germans and bad, there were 'good' Poles and bad." Give examples to support this.

4. How does a person survive? Some say it is because of the goodness of others, others will tell you it's luck. In Szpilman's case, what do you believe was most instrumental in keeping him alive? Explain.

5. At the Umschlagplatz, the dentist said, "It's a disgrace to us all! . . . We're letting them take us to our death like sheep to the slaughter! If we attacked the Germans, half a million of us, we could break out of the ghetto, or at least die honorably, not as a stain on the face of history!" (p. 101) Why didn't more people fight back at that time? Now that you know the history, do you agree that not fighting back would be a stain on the face of history? Explain.

6. The dentist referred to above said he was "ninety percent sure they plan to wipe us all out!" The author's father replied, "Look. . . . We're not heroes! We're perfectly ordinary people, which is why we prefer to risk hoping for that ten percent chance of living." Do you think that those who fought back were heroes? Explain. What lessons does this debate pose for today?

Reflections in Writing

1. In the scene at the Umschlagplatz, as the ghetto was being liquidated and Jews were being "resettled," various viewpoints concerning their situation were expressed. Summarize this exchange of ideas.

2. Wladyslaw Szpilman wrote his story in Warsaw directly after the war. In the epilogue to the book, Wolf Biermann, one of Germany's best-known poets, songwriters and essayists, wrote about the melancholy detachment with which the book was written. This same emotional detachment is reflected in the film. Write a piece that might explain this phenomenon.

3. Why would the majority of people who were living and working together with their Jewish neighbors allow themselves to follow the dictates of Nazi policy and often help the Nazi cause? Select one such person mentioned in the book (or film) and write a piece from a first-person point of view to express his or her change of heart.

4. After more than 50 years, the first person account that Szpilman wrote about in the 1940s has gained immense popularity. Write a book review or film review that includes reasons why the book or film has such a widespread audience.

5. In poetic form, create a portrait of life in the Warsaw Ghetto based on what you have read or viewed. Make sure your writing expresses your feelings and observations.

Researching the History

1. The Jewish police played an important role in the ghetto. Research this role and create a chart that reflects the positives and negatives of the Jewish police. What would motivate a person to join the Jewish police?

2. In what ways did the book or film alter your perceptions of life in the Warsaw Ghetto? Select one of the most important impressions you have from the book or film and research this to see how it captured the realities of life in the ghetto.

3. The Szpilman family would like to have Wilm Hosenfeld, the Nazi officer who saved Wladyslaw's life, recognized as a "righteous gentile," a non-Jew who risked his or her life to save the life of a Jewish person during the Holocaust. Research the debate between the family and the reaction of those connected with Yad Vashem, the Holocaust authority established by the State of Israel.

4. At the end of the book, Wladyslaw Szpilman reflects on his survival and the need to go on with his life. He wrote, "Tomorrow I must begin a new life. How could I do it, with nothing but death behind me? What vital energy could I draw from death?" Interview survivors of the Holocaust and discuss the choices they had to make both during and after the Holocaust. What vital energy did they draw from to help them go on? Compile your findings.

Memoir: *Images of the Holocaust: A Literature Anthology*

Editors: Jean Brown, Elaine Stephens, & Janet Rubin (1997)

Recommended for: High school and college

Summary

This is an excellent, comprehensive anthology of short, well-written memoirs authored by Holocaust survivors, witnesses, and their descendants. Some are works written by well-known writers such as Elie Wiesel, Primo Levi, and Simon Wiesenthal. The collection is organized thematically and chronologically, covering all aspects of the Holocaust, from the beginning of prewar anti-Semitism to families reuniting after the Holocaust.

From this book, read the memoir of David Sierakowiak entitled "Lodz Ghetto." It chronicles the daily life of a Polish teen (p. 117, *Images from the Holocaust*) beginning with the German invasion of Poland in 1939, when he was 15 years old. Sierakowiak graduated from the Lodz Ghetto Gymnasium (the equivalent of high school), was active in ghetto politics, and was a member of the ghetto underground. He died in the Lodz Ghetto of tuberculosis at the age of 19.

Symposium: Critical Thinking and Discussion

1. Describe the chaos and panic that seized the Jews of Lodz when they were forced into the Lodz ghetto based on Sierakowiak's diary.

2. What is the power in reading a diary such as this one rather than learning of the events from 3rd person narration?

3. Describe the loss of human rights for the Jews of Lodz on September 15, 1939.

4. What kinds of decisions does the Jewish Council (*Judenrat*) have to make that could be classified as "choiceless choices"?

Reflections in Writing

Read the following speech below made by Chaim Rumkowski, the leader of the Judenrat in the Lodz ghetto of which David Sierakowiak writes in the diary you read.

Rumkowski's Address at the Time of the Deportation of the Children from the Lodz Ghetto, September 4, 1942

. . . The ghetto has been struck a hard blow. They demand what is most dear to it—children and old people. I was not privileged to have a child of my own and therefore devoted my best years to children. I lived and breathed together with children. I never imagined that my own hands would be forced to make this sacrifice on the altar. In my old age I am forced to stretch out my hands and to beg: "Brothers and sisters, give them to me!—Fathers and mothers, give me your children. . . ." (Bitter weeping shakes the assembled public). . . . Yesterday, in the course of the day, I was given the order to send away more than 20,000 Jews from the ghetto, and if I did not—"we will do it ourselves." The question arose: "Should we have accepted this and carried it out ourselves or left it to others?" But as we were guided not by the thought: "how many will be lost?" but "how many can be saved?" we arrived at the conclusion—those closest to me at work, that is, and myself—that however difficult it was going to be, we must take upon ourselves the carrying out of this decree. I must carry out this difficult and bloody operation, I must cut off limbs in order to save the body! I must take away children, and if I do not, others too will be taken, God forbid . . . (terrible wailing).

I cannot give you comfort today. Nor did I come to calm you today, but to reveal all your pain and all your sorrow. I have come like a robber, to take from you what is dearest to your heart. I tried everything I knew to get the bitter sentence cancelled. When it could not be cancelled, I tried to lessen the sentence. Only yesterday I ordered the registration of nine-year-old children. I wanted to save at least one year—children from nine to ten. But they would not yield. I succeeded in one thing—to save the children over ten. Let that be our consolation in our great sorrow.

There are many people in this ghetto who suffer tuberculosis, whose days or perhaps weeks are numbered. I do not know, perhaps this is a satanic plan, and perhaps not, but I cannot stop myself from proposing it: "Give me these sick people, and perhaps it will be possible to save the healthy in their place." I know how precious each one of the sick is in his home, and particularly among Jews. But at a time of such decrees one must weigh up and measure who should be saved, who can be saved, and who may be saved.

Common sense requires us to know that those must be saved who can be saved and who have a chance of being saved and not those whom there is no chance to save in any case. . . .

"Rumkowski's Address at the Time of the Deportation of the Children from the Lodz Ghetto, September 4, 1942," *Documents on the Holocaust: Selected Sources on the Destruction of the Jews of Germany and Austria, Poland, and the Soviet Union.* Yitzhak Arad, Yisroel Gutman, Abraham Margaliot, eds. Jerusalem: KTAV Publishing House, 1981. Used with permission of Yad Vashem Archives.

1. Describe the impact this speech had on you.

2. Prepare and present a monologue based on your reaction to Rumkowsi's speech. Do you agree or disagree with the stand he took?

3. In one paragraph, create a visual picture of the Lodz Ghetto.

4. Select one of the diary entries written by Sierakowiak and create a journal entry in which you react to it.

Researching the History

1. With others in your group, select one of the ghettos that was established during the Holocaust to isolate and imprison Jews. Create a photo essay of life in this ghetto. Combine these with other photo essays generated by classmates and compile a booklet on life in the ghettos.

2. Read about the *Judenrat*. What was its function? How were its members selected? What choices did it have to make? What moral dilemma did it face?

3. Read about the *Judenrat* in ghettos such as Vilna and Kovno. What did their religious leaders advise when the *Judenrat* was ordered to select people for "relocation" to the concentration camps? What did the leaders of the *Judenrat* ultimately decide?

Lessons for Today

Moral or Ethical Dilemma

Reread Rumkowski's speech on page 73. Based on your knowledge of the ghettos and the way in which the Nazis selected leaders from the population of Jews to enforce their rules, what other choices did Rumkowski have?

Making Connections

In the ghettos, the leaders were forced to make many kinds of decisions. They were also responsible for selecting those to be sent to concentration camps. Many of their decisions would be classified as "choiceless choices." As a class, brainstorm the choiceless choices we face. Brainstorm these as a class and then, in groups, select one choice. Determine how you would ultimately make a decision.

Topic 5

Fighting Back:
Spiritual and Physical Resistance

*Brothers, it is better to die like free fighters
than to live by the murderer's grace.
Resist until your last breath!.*

— Mordecai Anielewicz, Jewish Resistance
Leader in the Warsaw Ghetto

There was resistance. From the forests where fugitives of the Nazi regime joined forces with the partisans, to the armed resistance of a handful of teens in the Warsaw Ghetto, individuals and groups did what they could to defy the Nazis. *There was resistance.* From the mother who shielded her baby from the Nazi bullets with her own body, to the prisoners in the concentration camps who gave away their last morsels of bread to those dying of starvation, life was sanctified.

Although resistance is often defined as organized armed opposition, it is important to recognize the contributions of those who resisted spiritually as well. Whether the battle was fought with guns or words, these daring men, women, and children made their voices heard.

Resistance fighters sabotaged the German ammunition plants. Resistance fighters did battle in the mountains, in the forests, in the death camps, and behind the ghetto walls. Resistance fighters fought oppression and moral degradation. Resistance fighters dreamed of the past and spoke of the promise of tomorrow. Resistance fighters did what they could, used what they had, to save a life, lift a soul, or stop the Nazis, if only for a moment in time.

Resistance took the form of the 15,000 children of Theresienstadt concentration camp who wrote prose and poetry and produced plays. Resistance was in the hearts of the thousands of teens like Anne Frank whose words and lives inspired a generation of people throughout the world to live up to the ideals of human decency. Resistance was in the spirit of the hundreds of men and women like Vladka Meed who fought the Nazis with little more than their courage, determination, and indomitable spirits.

With little to sustain them, abandoned by the world, starving, and diseased—they found a way. *There was resistance.*

Film: *Daring to Resist*

Source: Women Make Movies, Inc.
          462 Broadway, Suite 500
          New York, NY 10013
          (212) 925-0606

Recommended for: Middle school, high school, and college

Summary

Daring to Resist paints a portrait of three teenage girls who fought back in very unique ways during the Holocaust. Faye Schulman was a photographer and partisan fighter in the forests of Poland; Barbara Rodbell was a ballerina in Amsterdam who obtained food and transportation for Jews who were hiding, and Hungarian Shulamit Lack acquired false documents and safe houses for Jews trying to escape Nazi domination. The film is 57 minutes long.

Symposium: Critical Thinking and Discussion

1. How do the three stories in *Daring to Resist* counter the myth that the victims of the Holocaust did not fight back?

2. Discuss the contributions of each young woman. What would you consider the greatest risk each took? What would you consider to be the greatest legacy of each?

3. What did each young woman do during the early years of the war as each became aware of the Nazi plan to make Europe free of all Jews?

4. Historically, young men and women have been involved in revolutionary movements. What circumstances make it possible for teenagers to often become more involved in resistance activities than their parents?

5. What qualities do these young women share that were instrumental in their involvement in forms of resistance? What generalizations can you make? What factors compel some to engage in active resistance while the majority did not? What things were they able to do that would have been more difficult for men?

Reflections in Writing

1. As you watch the film, record impressions concerning these young women who dared to resist.

2. With a partner, create a definition of *resistance,* and write about the challenges faced by women who resisted during the Holocaust.

3. Create a web or cluster based on one of the young women highlighted in the film. Use this web or cluster to write an outline that describes her life. Include such main topics as: early life and background; character traits and special skills; schooling; people or events that influenced her life; resistance work with which she was involved.

4. Take on the persona of one of the young women in the film. Prepare and deliver a 1-minute monologue that this person might present to students your age to describe what she did and why and to encourage others to stand up for what they believe.

5. Read the Jewish partisan song (the beginning is included below), which was sung by partisans during the Holocaust. It was originally written in Yiddish by Hersh Glick, a resistance fighter who was killed at the age of 22. Its very message is to resist evil, to have the courage to face adversity and the determination to embrace life. Create an additional stanza for the song that would be appropriate for today's world.

Song of the Partisans

Never say that you have come to your journey's end,
When the days turn black, and clouds
Upon our world descend,
Believe the dark will lift, and freedom yet appear.
Our marching feet will tell the world
That we are here.

Researching the History

1. In recent years the role of women in the Holocaust has been explored. Research their role by viewing such sites as: www.holocaust-trc.org or www.interlog.com. The latter is created by Judy Cohen, a Holocaust survivor. Write a summary of your impressions in general about the role of women at this time.

2. Research the life of another woman of the Holocaust. Write a character sketch of this person and include a picture. Combine your piece with those of others in the class to create a book dedicated to the *Women of the Holocaust*. Research books and articles written by Dr. Rochelle Saidel, a scholar on women in the Holocaust.

3. Read selections from women's memoirs about World War II and the Holocaust to deepen your understanding of the particular contributions women made and the challenges they faced. Use the website www.interlog.com for a complete listing.

4. Are there any questions you'd like to know about the making of this film or any aspects of the subject matter? Contact the filmmakers, Barbara Attie and Martha Lubell, at daringtoresist@aol.com.

5. Although many examples of Jewish resistance can be found in the ghettos, in the forests, and in the concentration camps, there was also resistance in the non-Jewish population. *The White Rose* was an organization created by a group of non-Jewish teenagers living in Germany. Research *The White Rose*. Who were its leaders? What happened to them? What caused these German teens to resist when so many others were bystanders or perpetrators?

Film: *Uprising*

Source: Warner Home Video
4000 Warner Boulevard
Burbank, CA 91522
(Available at most video rental stores)

Recommended for: High school, and college

Summary

A remarkable story of relentless heroism, *Uprising* re-creates the saga of the Warsaw Ghetto Uprising, as Jewish men and women fought back against their oppressors. The Warsaw Ghetto Uprising, in April–May 1943, was the largest campaign of armed Jewish resistance to Nazi tyranny during World War II. This fact-based film, about 3 hours long, is presented in semi-documentary style. It is both poignant and powerful as it stirs the emotions and touches the heart.

Symposium: Critical Thinking and Discussion

1. Discuss the question that was posed in the beginning of this film: "Can a moral man maintain his moral code in an immoral world?" Discuss this quote extensively and give examples of today's events to support your position.

2. What dilemma faced the Jews who were part of the Jewish Council or part of the Jewish police? What were their choices and the consequences of these choices?

3. How does a person keep his or her humanity amid such degradation and inhuman conditions?

4. What aspects of society (e.g., newspaper, schools) were present in the Warsaw Ghetto, and why was each so important?

5. Discuss the concept of collective responsibility. How did this keep many from fighting back? What do you think of collective responsibility in today's news events?

6. The film ended with images of Jewish life and Jewish customs. Explain the significance of this ending.

Reflections in Writing

1. Study the picture "The Warsaw Ghetto Uprising—Heroism and Resistance" by Israel Bernbaum (from his 1985 book *My Brother's Keeper*). Although the book is out of print, the pictures are available on SVE Video and CD through Society for Visual Education, 6677 North Northwest Highway, Chicago, Illinois 60631, (800) 829-1900. Based on what you have learned about the uprising from the film, write a piece that explains various images in the picture.

2. Read the letter (from Yad Vashem Archives) written by 19-year-old Mordecai Anielewicz, the leader of the Warsaw Ghetto Uprising, shortly before he and others fighters were killed on May 8, 1943. After reading the letter, dated April 23, answer the questions that follow.

   - On the brink of destruction, how could Anielewicz believe that what took place (the uprising) exceeded all expectations?
   - What does he refer to when he mentions "partisan methods of fighting"?
   - How did the "last wish of my life" affect the way in which others perceive Jewish resistance?
   - At the end of his letter, Anielewicz asked, "Where will rescue come from?" How would you respond to this?

The Warsaw Ghetto Uprising assumed a significance beyond the revolt itself. As news of the heroic Warsaw Ghetto fighters spread through the underground network, Jews in other ghettos were inspired to resist deportation to their deaths. The Warsaw ghetto uprising would become a defining moment in Jewish history, ZOB leader Mordechai Anielewicz seemed to recognize when he wrote his last letter two weeks before his death on May 8, 1943:

> *It is now clear to me that what took place exceeded all expectations. In our opposition to the Germans we did more than our strength allowed—but now our forces are waning. We are on the brink of extinction. We forced the Germans to retreat twice—but they returned stronger than before.*
>
> *One of our groups held out for forty minutes; and another fought for about six hours. The mine which was laid in the area of the brush factory exploded as planned. Then we attacked the Germans and they suffered heavy casualties. Our losses were generally low. That is an accomplishment too. Z. fell, next to his machine-gun.*
>
> *I feel that great things are happening and that this action which we have dared to take is of enormous value.*
>
> *We have no choice but to go over to partisan methods of fighting as of today. Today, six fighting-groups are going out. They have two tasks—to recoinniter the area and to capture weapons. Remember, 'short-range weapons' are of no use to us. We employ them very rarely. We need many rifles, hand-grenades, machine-guns, and explosives.*
>
> *I cannot describe the conditions in which the Jews of the ghetto are now 'living.' Only a few exceptional individuals will be able to survive such suffering. The others will sooner or later die. Their fate is certain, even though thousands are trying to hide in cracks and rat holes. It is impossible to light a candle, for lack of air. Greetings to you who are outside. Perhaps a miracle will occur and we shall see each other again one of these days. It is extremely doubtful.*
>
> *The last wish of my life has been fulfilled. Jewish self-defense has become a fact. Jewish resistance and revenge have become actualities. I am happy to have been one of the first Jewish fighters in the ghetto.*
>
> *Where will rescue come from?*

Documents on the Holocaust: Selected Sources on the Destruction of the Jews of Germany and Austria, Poland, and the Soviet Union. Yitzhak Arad, Yisroel Gutman, Abraham Margaliot, eds. Jerusalem: KTAV Publishing House, 1981. Used with permission of Yad Vashem Archives.

3. What headline would you use if you were a newspaper editor in the United States reporting the uprising in the Warsaw Ghetto? Create an article to accompany this headline and include a photograph and caption.

4. In the April 23, 1943, edition of *The New York Times,* an article appeared with the headline "Warsaw Ghetto Fights Deportation." The article stated, "After Warsaw, the Cracow ghetto is to be liquidated . . . deportations have already started. . . . Polish circles here believe 1,300,000 Polish Jews already have perished under the German occupation." After reading this article, write a paper to explain why there wasn't any type of outcry from the United States as a country or from individuals across the globe.

Researching the History

1. Mordecai Anielewicz, the leader of the Warsaw Ghetto revolt, died in the command bunker at 18 Mila Street. Read the book *Mila 18* by Leon Uris (1962) and identify the facts upon which this book was based.

2. Research articles from national and international newspapers (such as *The Times* of London and *The New York Times*) that reported news of the Warsaw Ghetto Uprising. Write a news article that synthesizes the information you've gathered. How did each article cover the story. With validity and facts or not?

3. Research the history of the "Song of the Partisans." The song, written by partisan Hersh Glick, was sung to the tune of a Russian folk song and became the anthem of the Jewish underground fighters What else can you learn about this historically significant piece?

4. The fight in Warsaw was not an isolated event, and evidence of Jewish armed resistance in many ghettos has been documented. Create a map that highlights Jewish resistance in the ghettos and attach research that summarizes the resistance movement in each one. The following ghettos are recognized as having the largest armed resistance organizations in addition to the Warsaw Ghetto:

   • Bialystok, August 16, 1943
   • Czestochowa, June 25, 1943
   • Bedzin and Sosnowiec, August 1, 1943
   • Tarnow, September 2, 1943
   • Krakow, December 22, 1942
   • Minsk, December 1941

5. Armed resistance was also evident in the death camps: Treblinka, August 1943; Sobibor, October 1943; Auschwitz, October 1944. Although millions died before these heroic events took place, there were many factors that affected an earlier decision not to fight. Research the factors that prevented earlier retaliation and explain what ultimately led to the acts of armed resistance in one of the death camps.

Memoir: *Anne Frank: The Diary of a Young Girl*

Author: Anne Frank (1995) edited by Otto Frank and Mirjam Pressler

Recommended for: Middle school, high school, and college

Summary

Anne was given a diary for her 13th birthday, June 12, 1942. Less than one month later, she and her family were forced into hiding when the Nazis, in their goal to annihilate all the Jews of Europe, called her sister Margot for deportation. Life in hiding was difficult, but Anne's spirit and courage allowed her to soar beyond the physical restraints. After two years in hiding, Anne and her family were discovered and deported to concentration camps. Eventually, she and her sister were transferred to Bergen-Belsen, where Anne died only weeks before the British liberated the camp. She was 15 years old.

The pages of Anne's diary reveal not only the events of World War II and the Holocaust as witnessed by one of its victims, they are also a deeply revealing commentary on human nature.

Symposium: Critical Thinking and Discussion

1. In the introduction to the book, Eleanor Roosevelt said that Anne's diary shows the "nobility of the spirit." Cite examples from Anne's diary that exemplify this.

2. What do you and your friends have in common with Anne?

3. What aspects of life in hiding would you find most difficult? Explain.

4. Discuss the concept of lost childhood as it applies to Anne and other children and teens of the Holocaust.

5. Anne Frank's wish to "go on living even after [her] death" has come true. How will you remember Anne? What lessons for life will you remember as a result of Anne's words?

Reflections in Writing

1. Select one paragraph from Anne's diary that especially affected you. Write a journal entry that explores its meaning and impact on you.

2. Write a descriptive character piece that captures the personality of one of the people living in the secret annex. Focus on the ways in which this person exhibited physical resistance.

3. Close your eyes and imagine that you are looking through Anne's window in the secret annex. Describe what you see, hear, and feel.

4. After reading Anne's diary, reread the introduction by Eleanor Roosevelt. Write your own introduction to the diary and include your own assessment of Anne and the power of her words.

5. Otto Frank, Anne's father and the only person from the secret annex to survive, wrote, "We cannot change what happened anymore. The only thing we can do is to learn from the past and to realize what discrimination and persecution of innocent people means. I believe that it's everyone's responsibility to fight prejudice." Write a paper to respond to Mr. Frank's challenge and include what you personally can do to fight prejudice.

Researching the History

1. *Anne Frank: Diary of a Young Girl* has achieved enormous popularity and has been translated into 55 different languages throughout the world. Research the publication history of the diary, and consider why Anne Frank has become the voice for the 1.5 million Jewish children killed in the Holocaust.

2. Research the life of Miep Gies, the person most responsible for helping Anne and her family while they were in hiding, and the woman who found and saved Anne's diary. What about her background and personality created an individual who would risk her life to save another? Write a brief paper to explore this question.

3. The life of Anne Frank has been captured on film and stage. The most recent film was aired as a "made for TV movie" in 2001. View this film (available from local video rental stores), which goes far beyond the pages of the diary and brings Anne Frank to life in an even more poignant way. Write a review that explores the way in which both the film and the diary affected you.

   Other audiovisual materials based on Anne Frank and her life are also available:

   • *Bill Moyers: Anne Frank Remembered*—deals with the life and legacy of Anne Frank on what would have been her 60th birthday. Available from WNYC-TV, One Centre St., New York, NY 10007, (212) 669-7800.

   • *The Diary of Anne Frank.* Twentienth-Century Fox's 1959 drama is available from CBS Fox Video, Industrial Park Drive, Farmington Hills, MI 48024, or Social Studies Service, 10200 Jefferson Boulevard., P.O. Box 802, Culver City, CA 90232-0802, (800) 421-4246.

   • *Anne Frank: A Legacy for Our Time* (1984) discusses Anne Frank's life, human rights, prejudice, morality, and the values that sustained Anne during her years in hiding. Available through SVE, 6677 N. Northwest Highway, Chicago, IL 60631-1304, (800) 829-1900.

4. Take a tour of Anne Frank's secret annex. With others, create a model of this hiding place. Visit www.annefrank.com for information about the annex.

5. Many Web sites contain information on Anne Frank. Visit several of them and see what you can add to your knowledge and understanding of Anne and her family that go beyond the diary.

   United States Holocaust Museum
   www.ushmm.org

   Anne Frank: Her life and times
   www.annefrank.com

   The Anne Frank House in Amsterdam
   www.annefrank.nl

Memoir, Poetry, Drawings:
I Never Saw Another Butterfly

Editor: Hana Volavkova (1993)

Recommended for: Middle school, high school, and college

Summary

I Never Saw Another Butterfly is a compilation of poems and drawings created by the children in the Terezin (Theresienstadt) concentration camp between 1942 and 1944. The children of all ages used art and poetry to convey their feelings about life—their hopes, dreams, fears, and reality. These images are all that remain of the children of Terezin. It is their legacy to us. Of the 15,000 children who went through the gates of Terezin, only 100 survived.

Symposium: Critical Thinking and Discussion

1. Read the title poem, "The Butterfly." What does the butterfly symbolize? Why can't butterflies live in the ghetto? Based on this poem, describe the poet—his hopes, dreams, fears.

2. Select any poem or picture included in the book. From this selection alone, what inferences can you make about the poet or artist? What gives you this impression? What feelings does the poem or picture evoke? Why?

3. Select one poem or picture that evokeded an emotion in you. Lead a class discussion of this work to see what additional insights can be gained.

4. What subjects do the majority of the poems and pictures reflect?

5. Why is the collection of poems and pictures such an important one? Why do they symbolize what is called "spiritual resistance"?

Reflections in Writing

1. Read the first-person memoir (below) reprinted with permission by Arno Erban, Holocaust survivor, who was a young man when he arrived at Terezin. Born in Prague, he was sent to Terezin during the Holocaust and put in charge of Home Number 9. Later, Erban was sent to Auschwitz and several labor camps. After the war, he returned home but left Czechoslovakia when it fell under communist control. He moved to Venezuela and finally the United States. Today he lives in Miami Beach, where he visits schools and speaks to students to explain what happened during the Holocaust.

   After reading the testimony, explain this statement: "Terezin was just one part of the Big Lie perpetrated by the Nazis."

Terezin

Testimony by Arno Erban, Holocaust Survivor

Let's talk about Terezin—where it is and what it was. Until the beginning of World War II it was a small and quite insignificant town located in the northern part of the Czech Republic. It became world-renowned, however, by playing a tragic role during the Nazi occupation of Czechoslovakia. It was built in the year 1782 by the Austrian emperor Joseph II as a fortress with all the things which characterize a fortress, that is, a city with a number of barracks for the soldiers around a place for the civil population and surrounded by high walls. It was named Terezin or in German, Theresienstadt after the emperor's mother Maria Theresa and the reason was to block the Prussian invasions to that part of Europe. It was never used as a fortress because the Prussian army just bypassed it. After that, it remained a place for soldiers and a part of it, the so called "Little Fortress," was converted to one of the most terrible prisons in Europe. For example—the students, who killed the Austrian archduke Ferdinand in Sarajevo in the year 1914, the event that started the First World War, were imprisoned and finally killed in Terezin. Jews were a special group of prisoners in the Little Fortress. The Gestapo sent the Jews there for violating some of the anti-Jewish regulations. The Little Fortress was an extermination camp for them because the guards were there either to kill them in their cells, at work or in roll call.

During World War II, the Nazis expelled about 140,000 Jews, mostly from the Czech part of Czechoslovakia, but also from central and western Europe, to the ghetto in Terezin. The idea of building a ghetto within the walls of Terezin was made effective in November 1941. At that time Czechoslovakia was already in the hands of Germany, and there were no Czech soldiers in Terezin anymore. The first transports of Jews started soon after Germany's decision to convert Terezin to a ghetto. In the first few months the Jews were installed in the barracks. Men and boys were together and the women, girls and little children were in different barracks There was no possibility of any kind of communication between the barracks. Later the Germans evacuated the civil population to make space for new transports of Jews. After that, they sealed the ghetto completely.

Following the first transport of Jews from Prague on 24 November 1941, the Council of Elders was formed. This council ran the internal affairs of the ghetto and was directly responsible to the SS Commander, who gave them the orders and established the rules. The Jewish Council had the terrible task of compiling the lists of those to be deported to the "EAST." Nobody really knew the meaning of "EAST." The only thing we knew was that it was something really bad. The Jewish government was also responsible for all the activities in the ghetto, like maintaining order, distribution of food, assignment of quarters, sanitation and last, but not least, the care of the children. Shortly before the end of the war all members of the Council were sent to Auschwitz and murdered.

Of all the big lies conceived by the Nazi propaganda, to say that the Terezin ghetto was a paradise, that ranks as one of the greatest. The Nazi bosses were saying textually: "While the German soldiers are dying in the battlefields, the Jews in Terezin are sitting in the coffeehouses eating cakes." The math could not have been more different. From November 1941 until May 1945 this place was "the anteroom of hell." About 150,000 people were deported to Terezin, 35,000 died there from starvation and almost 90,000 were shipped out to the death camps. Through Terezin passed 74,000 Czech Jews, 43,000 from Germany, 15,000 from Austria, 5,000 from Holland and some 500 from Denmark. In the last period of the war the camp received 1,500 Slovaks and 1,000 Hungarian Jews. Of the 15,000 children under the age of 15 who passed through Terezin fewer than 100 survived.

In a place with a garrison of about 3,500 soldiers and about the same number of civil inhabitants, the Germans established a ghetto with 50,000 people. Prisoners lived in large barracks and houses in the town including cellars and backyards. Men and women lived separately in large buildings. Children under 15 years of age were separated from their parents and lived in so called "homes." There were about 10 to 20 children squeezed in one room, most of the time sleeping on the floor.

Prisoners at Terezin had to observe a number of various prohibitions. They could not have cigarettes, medications, money, matches or lighters and they couldn't communicate with the outside world. Punishments for violation of the regulations, imposed by the SS commander, were very severe. For instance, early in the year 1942 the Nazis hanged 16 men, who had secretly sent letters from the camp. The objective of these executions was the intimidation of the other prisoners. After that, the other offenders were sent to the Little Fortress where they were killed.

Yet with all the hunger, cruelty and death, the inhabitants of the Ghetto preserved their essential humanity. The artists continued to paint, the singers to sing and poets to write while expecting to die or to be deported. The deportation to Auschwitz was an everyday possibility and we never knew when it would be our turn.

The International Red Cross was invited by the Nazis to inspect Terezin. After a long preparation for that event, directed by a special propaganda group, on June 23, 1944 the commission arrived. Before their arrival, just to reduce the overcrowding, some 7,500 prisoners were sent to Auschwitz. Buildings were repainted, 1200 rose bushes from Holland were planted, playgrounds for the children were constructed and even a cafe house was adorned with tablecloths. Goebbels, the propaganda boss of Nazi Germany, ordered a film called "The Führer gives the Jews a Town" to be made. In that film you can see happy and healthy people, enjoying the sunshine. Good looking men and women are shown at work in factories and workshops or vegetable gardens, children were playing soccer and acting in the children's opera Brundibar. Apparently the Red Cross delegation was fooled. After the war a Swiss newspaper explained that they didn't believe the show, that they were afraid to say so. Who knows what was the truth?

In September 1943 there was a transport to Auschwitz; 4,000 people survived the first "selection" after their arrival. They were families and they were put into a new, so called, Family Camp, something completely new. Families lived together in one camp, surrounded by barbed wire, of course. The camp had its own kitchen, latrine and washing facilities. In December, the same year, two other transports from Terezin arrived to join the people in the family camp. It gave an impression of another ghetto and the people inside started to be optimists, hoping that the end of the war might save them. There were about 12,000 people, men, women and children. In March 1944 all people who came last September were loaded into trucks, taken to the gas chamber and killed. The rest of the people stayed in the camp. More people came in May. On June 29, six days after the Red Cross commission had been persuaded by the Germans in Terezin that the Jews in the camps were treated so well, liquidation of the last German showplace, the Family Camp in Auschwitz-Birkenau, was completed. The Germans didn't need it any more. The International Red Cross was satisfied. Very few strong men and women were saved. Over 500 children were gassed. Ninety-eight boys over 16 years old were transferred to the men's camp. About 30 of them survived the war.

Now, let's talk about the children in Terezin. The Jewish Council was really interested in doing everything possible to get some advantages for them. There was a special department for child care and also a separate kitchen with a little better food. They couldn't do much for the babies and little children who stayed with their mothers. The children from 10 until 15 years had their own "homes." The girls occupied a big building in the main plaza next to the SS commando. The boys occupied the former school building, which was divided into 6 homes. I was called to become a teacher or leader of one of the homes because of my former experience with children as teacher and counselor in different vacation camps.

Our home was Home No. 9 and was well known in the ghetto. Forty-two boys, 13 and 14 years old in a room with 3 story beds and a big table in the center, became a substitute for a real home for all of them during 1942 to the end of 1944. There were several hundreds of them, because they were coming and leaving with the transports. They were separated from their families and became a group of friends who lived together and loved each other. Home No. 9 became the place of their new family. Most of them had to work in the fields and gardens, in maintenance or in different workshops. The education permitted by the Germans was only for manual skills. But against the orders, education was a major issue in our life. There were many educators in Terezin who helped us to teach the children. Many famous writers and poets visited our home and so did famous musicians and philosophers. Home No. 9 was known for its good organization. It had its own boys' self-government. They published their own magazine and also there was a daily competition where the boys competed in different disciplines of their life and were awarded points for their behavior, for fixing their beds, for playing chess or other games, for their studies, for poetry, for drawings etc. The points were calculated daily and the results were posted on a blackboard.

We practiced the ideas of the Boy Scouts movement. It was a little strange, because the ideas of this organization are connected with nature and that was exactly what we didn't see in Terezin but on the other hand the other things, like every day one good deed, or one day without talking (and that was important to learn in a prison) and so on, were quite acceptable in our situation. One day I met two of my boys in the plaza who were carrying a stretcher with a dead body. To my question as to what they were doing, they told me that they were helping two old men who were carrying the stretcher and that this was their good deed for the day. After that I was not too sure of my educational methods. Normally the funeral vehicles were used to carry bread.

Just to be able to understand the bizarre situation of some of the children, I wish to describe a certain episode. One of my boys, as I have called them my whole life, was sent to Terezin after his 13th birthday. He was not of the Jewish religion and never knew a thing about Jews. But his father and mother were Jewish and after his father died, when he was still a baby, his mother married a very nice non-Jewish man. The man adopted the boy, gave him his name and later, when they had 2 more children, they all lived as one happy family. When he was sent to the ghetto, he was completely confused.

On one of my birthdays the boys gave me a great present. They gave me a book, made by them with painted emblems of 3 different scout groups, the Beavers, the Archers and the Wolves. It was signed by all who were in our home at this time. I was lucky to recover the book after the war and it has become my greatest treasure. After the first pages with the emblems it contains the best Czech and world poetry.

The boys suffered from many different diseases like encephalitis, scarlet fever, typhus, impetigo and other infections. There were very good doctors in Terezin, but very little medicine. Due to insufficient food rations their weakened bodies became easy prey to various diseases.

The children in Terezin were quite creative. They wrote poems and they produced a lot of good drawings and paintings. Some of them survived the war and are shown around the world. The Terezin motto to survive and to demonstrate that the Germans could beat us but they cannot subdue us was "I live as long as I create and I am able to absorb culture." That was our cultural resistance. As a member of the Czech resistance movement I began practicing some paramilitary exercises with the boys for an armed revolution in the ghetto. Unfortunately the transports to Auschwitz made our plans impossible.

Now I want to recall something that was really very special for the children and the grownups in Terezin, the children's opera, Brundibar. The music and the songs are beautiful and the words tell an allegorical tale. Two impoverished children, little Joey and little Mary, try to earn money as street entertainers to buy milk for their ailing mother. The bad organ player, Brundibar, angered by the competition, steals the money they earned. With the help of 3 guardian spirits, the dog, the cat and the bird, all the children defeated the bad guy. As the last song says: Brundibar is defeated, we finally got him, the bad people lost and the good people won. The boy, who played Brundibar was from our home and so were most of the other actors. The Germans didn't object, they knew that we were all going to Auschwitz to be murdered. The Red Cross either didn't understand or did not want to understand that the bad Brundibar was meant to be Hitler. Not one of the boys survived. The opera was performed 54 times in the building where our home was and once for the Red Cross Commission

From hundreds of boys, who passed through our home No. 9, in Terezin, there were only 14 alive after the war. In 1992 we met in Prague. It was a very emotional meeting. We were very happy to see each other and we were very sad for those who could not make it.

2. Of all the things he has done in his life, Erban says that the time spent with the children in Home Number 9 was the most important. From the hundreds of boys who passed through Home Number 9 in Terezin, there were only about 14 alive after the war. Several years ago, Arno Erban met with his "children" in Prague, Czechoslovakia. He writes, "It was a very emotional meeting. We were very happy to see each other and we were very sad for those who could not make it." The "boys"—now all over the age of 60—gave him a diploma. Read the words of the diploma below and answer the questions that follow.

"Diploma" presented to Arno Erban by his "boys"

Not everyone in this world can be as proud of having his own "list" as Mr. Schindler. But you—you have your own "list." It is not as long as the other one, but it is a "list" that was produced by great risks and enormous physical and sentimental sufferings. The desperation for the losses of our families and best friends, and the suffering of our impotence to do anything to remediate the situation. With your patience, your optimism, and your efforts to educate us—us, the children who were on their way to become young boys—you did not let us become an uncontrollable group of savages. Instead of that, you led us to believe and conserve a strong and solid moral base with the possibility and opportunity to grow and eventually someday join the human race again. With all this, you have formed your unfortunately not too long "list" from the remains of the boys from No. 9. We will never stop thanking you for everything you have done for us.

- What were the physical and sentimental sufferings that the "boys" endured?
- What do you believe are the most important things Mr. Erban did for his "boys"? Explain.
- What qualities did Arno Erban exhibit that reflected spiritual resistance?
- What did the "boys" seem to value most? What does this tell you about the kind of people they are?

3. Select one of the pictures from this book. Describe the picture in writing so that others can see it without looking at the picture itself. You may also wish to study and describe pictures that adults drew while imprisoned in Terezin. You can find many of these pictures in Lawrence L. Langer's (1995) book *Art from the Ashes: A Holocaust Anthology.*

4. Create a PowerPoint presentation using the pictures and verses in *I Never Saw Another Butterfly* as a tribute to the children of Terezin. Write a narration to accompany it.

5. Create your own picture or poem promising the children of Terezin that they will be remembered.

Researching the History

1. The Terezin (Theresienstadt) concentration camp lies approximately 37 miles from Prague, Czechoslovakia. It was established as a "model camp" for the Nazis to proudly show to foreigners who investigated the concentration camps. Research this camp. Compare and contrast it to other concentration camps in Eastern Europe.

2. View the video *The Journey of the Butterfly* (see Appendix C) in which the poetry of the children of Terezin is put to music and sung by a boy's choir from the United States when they visited Czechoslovakia. Throughout the video the viewer is also introduced to survivors of Terezin who share their experiences.

3. Read excerpts from Vladka Meed's 1997 book *Both Sides of the Wall* about resistance in the ghettos. Compare acts of resistance described in this book with those of the children of Terezin.

4. Obtain the name and postal address or e-mail address of a survivor of Terezin through one of the Holocaust Resource Centers in the United States (see Appendix E). Obtain the name and address of a survivor of Terezin and write or e-mail this individual to express how the stories of the children of Terezin has impacted you. Arno is available at AErban@aol.com.

5. Learn more about the children of Terezin by visiting various Web sites (see Appendix D). Combine your findings with those of others in your class to create an afterword to the book *I Never Saw Another Butterfly.*

Memoir: *On Both Sides of the Wall*

Author: Vladka Meed (1999)

Recommended for: High school and college

Summary

On Both Sides of the Wall is a moving, inspirational first-person memoir of life in the Warsaw Ghetto. Through the eyes of Feigele Peltel (Vladka Meed), readers are transported to the Warsaw Ghetto to vicariously experience life there from July 1942 to August 1944 and witness the way in which the Jews of the Warsaw Ghetto existed under the most horrific conditions. Left to fend for herself as a young teenage girl, Vladka found the strength to become a leader of the Warsaw Ghetto Uprising. Through the pages of this book, we follow Vladka's dangerous missions and heroic exploits as an underground courier on "both sides of the Wall," as she risked her life to protect the ghetto's remaining Jewish community.

Symposium: Critical Thinking and Discussion

1. In his foreword to the book, Elie Wiesel says that the ghetto was "occupied by half a million souls, yet for the most part [the ghetto] did not become a jungle." How was this possible? Describe how a sense of community developed under the harshest of circumstances.

2. Discuss the importance of the Jewish police in the Warsaw Ghetto. For what did the Nazi police rely on them? Why were they "feared but also objects of envy"?

3. How did Feigele (Vladka) learn to survive once she was left entirely on her own after her family was deported?

4. Describe the eyewitness account of Elie Linder, an escapee from the death camp Treblinka. How did her words determine the actions that Feigele (Vladka) and her friends were now resolved to take in their resistance efforts?

5. What was the specific assignment given to Feigele (Vladka) that would one day make her the most revered female resistance fighter in the history of the Holocaust? Describe her actions and what motivated her to undertake such a dangerous mission.

6. In chapter 14, "Blackmailers," what happened to shatter Vladka's illusion that the non-Jews on the Aryan side cared about the Jews inside the ghetto? What did the Polish blackmailers do that was morally reprehensible? How would you react to the belief that in their own way they killed the Jews?

7. Discuss the vignettes at the end of the book that describe the lives of several leaders in the uprising and their attempts to hide among the non-Jewish people on the other side of the wall.

Reflections in Writing

Read the following chapter from Vladka Meed's memoir entitled "Volunteers."

"Volunteers" reprinted with permission of Vladka Meed, Holocaust survivor, author, and a leader of the Warsaw Ghetto uprising.

Vladka Meed

Vladka Meed was the "Aryan" name that Feigel Peltel-Miedzyrzecki took when she left the Warsaw ghetto. Born in Poland in 1922, she was an active member of the Polish underground throughout the Nazi occupation, although she was only seventeen when the Nazis first arrived. Her Aryan appearance and ability to speak fluent Polish helped her to be an effective member of the underground. She served as a courier, helping Jews to escape and smuggling guns into the ghetto. She is the author of On Both Sides of the Wall: Memoirs from the Warsaw Ghetto, which was originally published in Yiddish in 1948 and from which the following excerpt is taken.

The following excerpt from Meed's memoirs presents an ironic view of volunteering.

"Volunteers"

Ten days since the deporations had begun—could it have been so short a time? We had been through so much . . .

Thousands upon thousands of Jews had already been deported and there was no reliable knowledge of their whereabouts. Some still thought the deportees had been assigned to some kind of work. One rumor was that they had been dispatched to the city of Smolensk, close to the Russo-German front, to dig trenches. But by now an ever-growing number of Jews tended to believe the horrible new rumors that all the German promises were false and that the so-called "resettlement" actually meant only one thing—death! We fought against accepting that grisly thought. Our loved ones were among the deportees. No, they must be alive; they surely must be alive . . . somewhere . . . Throughout each day, while the raids continued, individuals and small groups of Jews, parents and children, trudged through the comparatively deserted streets, weighed down by bundles, baskets, and battered valises, their last pitiful belongings, towards the *Umschlagplatz*. Some walked slowly with heads bowed; others hurried along, as if pressed for time. No one detained them or barred their way; they were the "volunteers." The ghetto watched their mute, resigned march without surprise. In hiding places and workshops, hearts ached with silent admiration for the strength that had enabled these people to take at least this decisive step. My sister and I could summon no such courage.

Gloom pervaded the ghetto. There was no security whatsoever. Exhausted by privation, emaciated or bloated by hunger, crushed by the incessant fear of being trapped, many simply gave up the struggle. The Germans' diabolical tactics reaped their harvest. Hunger drove famished Jews to the bread line, where each receive his three kilograms of bread—before being pushed into the waiting railroad cars. Three kilos of bread loomed very large in the eyes of a starving man. The temptation, even for once to still that gnawing hunger eclipsed all other considerations, including the dread of the unknown, the destination of the railroad cars. In his tragic helplessness, the victim let himself be lulled by the Germans' soothing promises of an end to his daily struggle for survival. Perhaps it was true, after all, that there would be jobs waiting for them.

Yakub Katz, a barber from Kalisz, an intelligent man whom I knew from my work in the underground, had been driven in 1940, together with his wife and two daughters, from his home to Warsaw, where his family languished in the refugee compound at Leszno 14 for some time. Katz had worked hard, enduring hunger and cold, barely making ends meet, hoping that he and his family would weather the storm. I met him during the early days of the German roundups. Unnerved and starved, he informed me that his wife was ready to surrender to the

Germans. "And you?" I asked, astonished. After all, Katz was familiar with the underground press. He knew better than to have any faith in the German promises. What had come over him?

"One can't go on starving forever," he answered gloomily. "We have no strength left to go on. We'll perish here anyway." His sallow, emaciated face and sad, sunken eyes underscored his words. The very next day I learned that he had left the ghetto.

The widow Chaveleh, whose husband had died in the war, came often to our home. She lived at Mila 48, gladly accepting a bowl of soup and a piece of bread in payment for her services as a seamstress. The evening after my mother and brother had been taken away, Chaveleh came to my mother's apartment while I happened to be there. A small, wizened old woman carrying a basket, she halted timidly at the threshold, inquiring after my mother. She had come to beg a few zloty—for the last time, she said, adding, "You see, I am about to go to the *Umschlagplatz* to get three kilograms of bread, and perhaps I'll find odd sewing jobs in some other town.

When she learned of our misfortune, her deadened eyes suddenly showed a strange gleam, she seemed jubilant. She had better hurry along, she said, if she wanted to catch up with my mother. It was easier to travel with friends.

Hunger was not the only reason for voluntary surrender. There were Jews who could have remained safely in the ghetto, who had bona fide employment cards, as well as jobs at German factories. They were not crushed by the trying conditions around them. On the contrary, they still harbored a strong will to live, to resist, yet they proceeded voluntarily to the waiting railroad cars. They did this for only one reason: they did not want to be separated from their families.

Abramek Bortensteing had been well aware of the fate that awaited the deportees. He worked at Roerich's factory at Nowolipki 74. He could have obtained an employment card and remained in Warsaw. But during the roundup on Mila Street, when his wife and year-old daughter were threatened with eviction, he had abandoned his job—the only secure place then—and had gone into hiding with his family. Together with a group of other Jews, they had hidden in a loft. The atmosphere in the attic was stifling and the baby whined. The others in the group, fearing that the baby's cries would give them away, forced Abramek and his family to leave the hideout. Meanwhile, out in the street, the Germans continued to "select" the inhabitants of the ghetto: idle Jews to the left, employed to the right. Abramek did not present his employment card, but silently followed his family, rather than forsake them even in the face of death.

Yurek Blones, a classmate of mine, who was to be a participant in the ultimate uprising, was also taken to the *Umschlagplatz* along with his younger brother Lusiek. While some were being loaded into the railroad cars, other young men were singled out and sent back to work. Twenty-two years old and an able auto mechanic, Yurek would have been saved. But his little brother would not have been permitted to remain. Just then Yurek was spotted by a German fellow worker, who motioned him to step aside. "Your services could still be utilized in the factory," he said.

"But what about my little brother?" Yurek countered.

"He has to be deported," was the reply.

"In that case, I'm staying with him; he wouldn't be able to take care of himself."

Yurek and his brother were shoved into a freight car destined for Treblinka. Somehow Yurek cut a hole in the wall of the car and the two brothers jumped off the speeding train.

Miraculously, they survived and reached Warsaw. I met them shortly after they had smuggled themselves back into the ghetto. Eventually the two brothers joined the ranks of the resistance organization and distinguished themselves in the Warsaw ghetto uprising.

My sister and I made a similar choice. Learning that the public kitchen on Nowolipki Street, where she was working, was scheduled for a raid, I rushed there to warn her of the imminent danger and pleaded with her to go into hiding with me. We were the only two survivors of our family, I said; we should at least stick together. Either both of us would escape or else we would go down the last road together. She listened attentively, then replied in a trembling voice: "I'm sorry, but I cannot leave my post."

To put my mind at ease, she tried to assure me that the Germans were not likely to bother a working crew. No amount of pleading on my part could dissuade her. That very day, the entire staff of the kitchen was loaded into one of the wagons for deportation. My sister went with them.

1. Based on this piece, create a higher-level thinking question that will guide discussion and writing related to this piece. For example: After reading the excerpt, write a paper to describe the dilemmas the various volunteers faced.

2. "If it is our fate to die anyway, then let us die with dignity! Let us resist and make the enemy pay dearly for our lives." Write what would have been your own call to action to inspire others to resist the Nazis even when they know they are doomed to die.

3. After reading this memoir of the Warsaw Ghetto and the uprising, write a brief paragraph that might be found in history textbooks to contradict the presumption that Jews did not fight back.

4. Write a composition that contrasts life on both sides of the wall.

5. Many Holocaust survivors have explained that what kept them alive was hope. Take the persona of *hope* and explain the part you played in the Warsaw Ghetto Uprising. As an alternative, what quality would you most attribute to the men and women involved in the uprising? Take the persona of that quality and explain your part in the uprising. Example "I am hope . . ." "I am perserverance . . ." "I am determination . . ."

6. Five months after the war, Vladka and Ben Meed returned to Warsaw and the area that once was the Warsaw Ghetto. Of this experience, Vladka wrote, "Nothing. Nothing was left of my past, of my life in the ghetto, not even my father's grave." What would you say to her in response? Write a journal entry in either prose or poetry that addresses the profound loss that Holocaust survivors experience.

Researching the History

1. Read about the Warsaw Ghetto. Write 10 facts you learned about life in the ghetto that helped you to better understand the people and events described in *On Both Sides of the Wall*.

2. Research several other well known ghettos in Eastern Europe. Compare them to the Warsaw Ghetto.

3. What was the Z.O.B.? How was it started? Describe its leaders. What were the main objectives of the organization? Did they accomplish them?

4. Read *Mila 18* by Leon Uris (1962) and/or view the movie by the same name. Both are based on the Jewish Fighting Organization under the command of Mordecai Anielewicz. Write a review of either the book or the film. With your classmates, discuss the will to resist, to fight deportation, and to die with dignity.

5. Research the lives of various leaders of the Warsaw Ghetto Uprising. Select one and write a brief biography that includes what you consider to be the person's major contributions then and now.

Lessons for Today

Moral or Ethical Dilemma

As Vladka Meed (author of the memoir *On Both Sides of the Wall*) watched the ghetto in flames from the Aryan side, she wondered, "Why was there no response from the rest of the city? Where was the help our neighbors had promised? And the rest of the world was silent—why was it so silent?" Hold a class discussion on her words, not only in reference to this uprising but in relation to other world events since the Holocaust.

Making Connections

1. In 1985, Ben and Vladka Meed started the first teacher training program in the United States on "Teaching the Holocaust and Resistance." There were 29 teachers in the first group, and today there are more than 850 teachers (including co-author Miriam Klein Kassenoff) who have been trained by Ben and Vladka to teach the lessons of the Holocaust in the public schools. As a student of the Holocaust, what would you suggest that Holocaust education classes include? With others in your class, create an outline for a Holocaust curriculum for your grade level that will teach the importance of resistance, not only during the Holocaust but also in the world today.

2. In her diary, Anne Frank wrote, "It's utterly impossible for me to build my life on a foundation of suffering and death. I see the world being slowly transformed into a wilderness. I hear the approaching thunder that, one day, will destroy us too. I feel the suffering of millions. And yet, when I look up at the sky, I somehow feel that everything will change for the better, that this cruelty too shall end, that peace and tranquility will return once more. In the meantime, I must hold on to my ideals. Perhaps the day will come when I'll be able to realize them!" Think about the world in which you live today. What are your ideals? How do you hope to realize them? Create a plan of action.

3. Begin a diary of your own. A diary is one way to learn more about yourself, who you are, and to develop your own voice. Select a special blank notebook for your diary. You may wish to write in it daily, after special events, or when you have something on which you wish to reflect.

4. The title poem, "The Butterfly," along with other poems in *I Never Saw Another Butterfly*, were put to music. Think of a world event to which you would like to pay tribute. Create a poem and put it to music, using an existing melody or writing your own.

Chapter 6

Courage and Compassion: Stories of Rescue

Whoever destroys a single life destroys the
entire world. He who saves one life,
saves the world entire.

— *Talmud*

During the Holocaust, human beings were responsible for committing the worst hate crimes imaginable. Yet there were other human beings who stood up to the evil, and their noble deeds shined through the darkness. Although their numbers were few, it is these rescuers who will be remembered for risking their own safety to save another. It is their stories that are beacons to us, reminding us of the courage and compassion that shapes our actions.

Although the deeds of rescuers such as Raoul Wallenberg and Oskar Schindler have become legendary, the majority of rescuers were the common men and women who did what they did simply because it was the right thing to do. In addition to the individual rescuers of the Holocaust, there were pockets of combined resistance in cities, towns, and villages across Europe as well as in countries such as Denmark and Bulgaria. Had more people refused complicity in carrying out the dictates of the Nazis, the Holocaust could have been prevented or greatly reduced in scope.

A study of the choices made by these people of courage and compassion during a time of chaos gives rise to an analysis of those qualities that allow individuals to stand up for what they believe in and take action to fight injustice. As we explore these qualities, we hope that the next generation will recognize the power that each person has in determining and shaping the future.

Film: *Diplomats for the Damned*

Source: Social Studies School Services
10200 Jefferson Boulevard
P.O. Box 802
Culver City, CA 90232-0802
(800) 421-4246

Recommended for: Middle school, high school, and college

Summary

During the Holocaust, several diplomats sacrificed their careers to save the lives of thousands of Jewish people and others who were trying to escape from Nazi persecution. This film profiles four such individuals of courage: Aristedes de Sousa Mendes, the Portuguese consul in Bordeaux; Harry Bingham, the American vice-consul in Marseilles; Carl Lutz, a Swiss diplomat in Hungary; and George Duckwitz, a German attaché to Denmark. The film is 43 minutes long.

Symposium: Critical Thinking and Discussion

1. The film gives an interesting overview of the events leading to the Holocaust. One such event was the Evian Conference. What was the outcome of this conference? How did this further Hitler's objective to make Europe free of Jews? Describe Kristallnacht. Why is it often considered "the beginning of the end"?

2. How did Aristedes de Sonsa Mendes get involved in helping Jews to escape from France? Why was Lisbon, Portugal, a safe destination?

3. What did these diplomats have in common? What motivated them to help the victims of the Holocaust? What qualities did they share? What chances did they take? In what ways did they jeopardize their careers?

4. Throughout the country of Denmark, four million Danes aided their Jewish countrymen and hid them from Adolf Eichmann's roundup. Describe the ways in which the Jews of Denmark were saved. Compare the way in which the Jews were treated in Denmark with that of their treatment in other countries. To what do you attribute the intense protection of Jews by their Danish neighbors?

5. Discuss the fate of each of the diplomats described in the film.

Reflections in Writing

1. Select one of the diplomats highlighted in the film. Create a memory box that includes the person's photo and artifacts that represent his life and deeds. Put a brief biography of the person in the box. Share with other students in a presentation.

2. Hold a tree-planting ceremony on your school grounds to honor rescuers during the Holocaust: the common man or woman and the diplomats. For each tree planted, write a poem inspired by the efforts of the individual being recognized.

3. Hiram Bingham worked with Varian Fry, an American journalist, to help Jewish artists and writers such as Marc Chagall and Thomas Mann escape from France and immigrate to the United States. Hiram Bingham was later reassigned to Argentina, and Fry returned to the United States and wrote his memoir. Based on your knowledge of their accomplishments, write a short memoir that Fry might have written about this chapter in his life.

4. These diplomats prove that help was possible during the Nazi regime. Elie Wiesel asks the haunting question, "Why didn't others do the same?" How would you answer this?

Researching the History

1. Other diplomats, such as Japan's Chiune Sugihara who served as consul in Lithuania, and China's Feng-Shan Ho, who was consul general in Vienna, deserve special recognition. Research the heroic efforts of one such individual not highlighted in the film. Write a short biography of the person's life.

2. Select one of the diplomats featured in the film. Research this individual's life to learn what happened to him after the war. Do you think, given the opportunity, he would make the same choice to help? Explain.

3. Each diplomat featured represented a different country. Select one of the diplomats and research the political, social, and economic climate in his native country during the Holocaust years. How did it affect the country's policy toward Jewish immigration?

4. Select one concept or event from this film that especially captured your interest. Do additional research on the topic or event and create an original way to present it to others in the class. Research the history of Jewish Rescue by such organizations as the HIAS (Hebrew Immigration Aid Society).

Film: *Rescuers: Stories of Courage—Two Couples*

Source: USHMM Bookstore

Recommended for: Middle school, high school, and college

Summary

Amid the horror of the Holocaust, there were people who risked everything, including their lives and the lives of their families, to save another. *Rescuers: Stories of Courage—Two Couples*, produced by Barbra Streisand and Cis Corman, tells the true-life compelling stories of two ordinary families living in Nazi Europe during extraordinary times. Both stories exemplify the goodness and courage of individuals who would not simply stand by and let evil happen. The first story is of a newlywed couple in Holland who hides Jewish refugees in their home. The second story is about a small town in Belgium, where young Jewish boys are hidden at a Catholic school for the children of prisoners of war. The film is 105 minutes long.

Symposium: Critical Thinking and Discussion

1. Discuss the concepts of moral courage and goodness. What shapes people's actions and enables them to risk everything to help others?

2. How did people in leadership positions appear to follow Nazi policy and yet resist?

3. What part did faith have in the choices made by the individual rescuers?

4. Many rescuers are described as nonconformists. How does this apply to the rescuers in this film?

Reflections in Writing

1. In each story, rescuers and other characters in the film went through changes in their perceptions and attitudes. Select one of the characters and describe the ways in which he or she changed and what you think inspired this change.

2. What challenges did the hidden children face? For example, many had to change their names and hide their roots and their heritage. Write a narrative or poem from the hidden child's point of view that addresses these challenges.

3. Imagine a world of universal human decency. What would this world be like? What expectations would be made of each member of society?

4. How do these stories illustrate "the power of one"? Write a memoir in which you relate a time when you or someone you know helped to make this world a better place.

5. A poem written after the Holocaust talks about the fact that the writer didn't do anything to help, but that next time he'd be ready. Write a journal entry that describes a time in your life in which you were a bystander. If the circumstances were to be repeated, discuss how you would react next time.

Researching the History

1. This film is based on the book *Rescuers: Portraits of Moral Courage in the Holocaust* by Gay Block and Malka Drucker (1992). Research the story of one of the individuals highlighted in the book. Prepare an oral presentation that describes the way in which this person's story inspired you.

2. Research the role of the Church during the Holocaust. What acts of resistance and rescue can you find? What more might have been done?

3. Rescuers have often been described as nonconformists. Select an individual you admire in any field, such as politics, entertainment, sports, or literature, who might be considered a nonconformist. Create a poster that highlights this individual's contributions.

4. Many hidden children such as the ones portrayed in the film lost everything during the Holocaust, including their families, their roots, and their heritage. Research your heritage and create a family tree to have for postentry.

5. In both films, stereotypes of Jewish people were mentioned. Research the phenomenon of stereotypes. What are stereotypes? Where do they originate? How can they be eliminated?

Film: *The Courage to Care: Rescuers of Jews During the Holocaust*

Source: Anti-Defamation League of B'nai B'rith
International Center for Holocaust Studies, Dept. LM 2
823 United Nations Plaza
New York, NY 10017

Recommended for: High school and college

Summary

Nominated for an Academy Award by the Motion Picture Academy of Arts and Sciences in the category of Best Documentary Short, *The Courage to Care: Rescuers of Jews During the Holocaust* is the story of several individuals who risked their lives during the Holocaust to aid Jews. It is a story of people who opened their homes and hearts to the plight of others while the rest of the world closed theirs.

The film focuses on the deeds of several men and women, including the following:

1. Irene Opdyke, a Polish Catholic who hid 12 Jews in the cellar of the villa of a German military officer where she was a prisoner-housekeeper.

2. Marion P. Van Binsbergen of the Netherlands, who helped to find homes and hiding places for Jewish children and adults after the deportations started in 1942.

3. Magda Trocme, a French Protestant living in LeChambon-sur-Lignon, whose husband led the population in sheltering thousands of Jews.

This film is 28 minutes long. A resource guide is available from ADL.

Symposium: Critical Thinking and Discussion

Select one of the rescuers highlighted in the film and answer the questions that follow. Be ready to discuss and support your responses with the rest of the class.

1. What did this person do in order to rescue Jews from the Holocaust?

2. What risks did this person face in his or her rescue efforts?

3. How did the person exhibit the courage to care?

4. Debate the choices this rescuer faced. What options were available?

5. What qualities would you attribute to this person that allowed him or her to take action and have the courage to care?

Reflections in Writing

1. Elie Wiesel said, "It is possible for a human being alone, often alone, to say no to death." Synthesize the information you gained from the film *The Courage to Care* and write a paper to explain how some people during the Holocaust were lucky enough to be able to say no to death.

2. Create a visual artifact to symbolize the rescue efforts of one of the rescuers depicted in the film. On an index card, summarize what the artifact represents. Display both.

3. What are some moral and ethical issues brought up in this film? Select one and write a paper to explain your thoughts on this issue and how it impacts you.

4. In the film, Marion Pritchard said, "We all have memories of times we should have done something and didn't." Write about a time you wish you had made a different choice and discuss what you would do differently the next time.

Researching the History

1. Irene Opdyke's story is highlighted in the film. Her first-person narrative, "Nobody Has a Right to Kill and Murder Because of Religion or Race," appears in the book *Images of the Holocaust: A Literature Anthology* (Brown, Stephens, & Rubin, 1997) and gives additional insight into Opdyke's life and philosophy. Read the piece by Opdyke and answer the following questions:

   • How does Opdyke explain why she could not stand by while the Nazis captured Jewish people? What family values helped her in later life to make the decision to do the right thing?

   • What events led Opdyke to hide the Jews? What "miracle" seemed to lead her in that direction?

   • Opdyke explained that she "became the eyes and ears for the Jewish people." In what ways was this true?

2. *The Avenue of the Righteous* in Yad Vashem, Israel, is a memorial to the rescuers of the Holocaust. Research this memorial to discover more about these rescuers.

3. Select one of the people highlighted in the film and do additional research on the person's life. What can you find in the person's background that might have led him or her to risk his or her life for another?

4. Contact one of the resource centers (see Appendix E) and invite a survivor of the Holocaust to speak about his or her life and about the rescuers he or she has met or knows.

Memoir: *Into the Arms of Strangers: Stories of the Kindertransport*

Authors: Mark Harris & Deborah Oppenheimer (2000)

Recommended for: Middle, high school, and college

Summary

At a time when other nations were unwilling to alter their immigration quotas, Britain alone agreed to provide sanctuary for children fleeing Nazi Europe. While the rest of the world waited and watched, more than 1.5 million Jewish children perished in the Holocaust. *Into the Arms of Strangers* recognizes Britain's extraordinary rescue mission and highlights the lives of several of the 10,000 children whose lives were saved due to the heroic efforts of the British government.

The memoir, and the film by the same name, is also an excellent resource to use for topic 8, "The Power of Perseverance: Children Surviving the Holocaust."

Symposium: Critical Thinking and Discussion

1. In the introduction to the book, Lord Richard Attenborough spoke of his parents, who provided a home for two young girls: "My parents' attitude to life was always that there is such a thing as society, and that it involves obligations of concern, tolerance, and compassion for those less fortunate than we are." Discuss this concept of *society*. What would you add to this or change?

2. Based on the individual testimonies in this book, who do you think made the greater sacrifice, the parents of the children or the foster parents? Support your answer with specific facts related in the testimonies.

3. What problems and adjustments might the children have had to overcome in their new country and their new homes?

4. From the stories you read, what do you believe was the most remarkable outcome of the British Kindertransport?

5. It was said that the "Kindertransport was great . . . if flawed." How would you react to that statement? Give support.

Reflections in Writing

1. Create an exhibit on the story of the Kindertransport. Each student group can focus on a different individual's story.

2. Write a radio advertisement that might have been aired in Britain to attract attention to the plight of the Jewish children and to help find them homes.

3. Select one of the photographs from the book and make interpretations from the picture. Discuss your interpretations with those of others who analyzed the same picture.

4. Lord Attenborough wrote in the introduction that if he hadn't had the background he had, if he had not known Irene and Helga (the two Jewish children his parents took care of for 8 years), he doubts that he would have had the passion and determination to "demonstrate those feelings through my work." How will a study of the Holocaust affect your life?

Researching the History

1. Research America's reaction to saving the Jewish children of Europe. Cite specific instances.

2. Research the Kindertransport more fully. Who helped to establish it? What obstacles were faced?

3. Watch the film *The Power of Good* (see chapter 8) which movingly depicts the efforts of one British man, Nicholas Winton, to provide sanctuary for 669 children and protect them from the Nazi destruction of European Jewry. Discuss the similarities in this story with those in the book *Into the Arms of Strangers*. What scene in this film had the most profound effect? Why did it affect you as it did?

Memoir: *Rescue: The Stories of How Gentiles Saved the Jews During the Holocaust*

Author: Milton Meltzer (1991)

Recommended for: Middle and high school

Summary

Dozens of righteous gentiles defied the Nazi plan to murder the Jews and risked their lives to save the lives of others. You will meet a peasant girl, a housemaid, a countess, a bricklayer, a policeman, a pastor, a priest, a consul, an industrialist, a washerwoman, a clerk, and a librarian. Their stories remind us of the good that people are capable of and show us that one need not be passive or silent in the face of evil.

Symposium: Critical Thinking and Discussion

Select one of the rescuers highlighted in the book and complete the questions that follow. Be ready to discuss and support your responses with the rest of the class.

1. What did this person do in order to rescue Jews from the Holocaust?

2. What risks did this person face in his or her rescue efforts?

3. Discuss the choices this rescuer faced. What options were available?

4. What qualities would you attribute to this person that allowed him or her to take action despite the risks?

5. Why do you think this person risked his or her life to help others?

Reflections in Writing

1. Think about the following quote from the Talmud (the collection of writings constituting Jewish civil and religious law): "He who saves one life, saves the world entire." Explain the truth and wisdom in this quote.

2. After reading about the different rescuers in this book, synthesize the information you gained and complete the following in outline form, adding details for support:
   - Reasons non-Jews risked their lives to save Jews
   - Reasons non-Jews did not risk their lives to save Jews
   - Reasons that governments (countries, cities, villages) got involved in rescuing the Jews
   - Reasons that governments refused to get involved

3. What characteristics do rescuers seem to have in common? Review the stories of the rescuers of the Holocaust you have read about and create a profile of a rescuer.

4. Select one of the rescuers from the book. Create a certificate for this person that includes the reason that this individual is being honored. Display your certificate with those created by others in the class.

5. In the final chapter of the book, Milton Meltzer explained that most of the men and women whose stories are in the book were honored at Yad Vashem as righteous Gentiles, non-Jews who risked their lives to save others. He wrote, "They are, all of them, human spirits whose lives witness the truth that there is an alternative to the passive acceptance of evil. Where they lived, goodness happened. And where we live, goodness can happen." Explain what you believe Meltzer meant by his final line. How can we ensure that goodness can happen where we live?

6. What if the acts of rescue you read about were more the rule than the exception during World War II? How might history have been changed?

Researching the History

1. Do additional research into the life of Raoul Wallenberg, one of the individuals highlighted in the book in the chapter "A Legend Among Jews." Based on your research, what do you believe happened to Wallenberg after the war? Support your answer.

2. Select your favorite story of rescue from the book. Do additional research on this individual and retell his or her rescue efforts through the creation of a mural, or dramatic.

3. If you were to teach another class about the lessons of rescue, what would you do? With a group of students, research the topic more fully, design a lesson, and teach it to another class in your school.

4. When the topic of rescue is discussed in terms of the Holocaust, why is the country of Denmark almost always the first mentioned? Do additional research into the rescue efforts of the Danish people. Also, learn about the attitude of the Danish people toward the Jews of Denmark during World War II. How did their attitudes and actions differ from most of Europe's?

5. The White Rose was an organization created by non-Jewish teens in Germany. Though not mentioned in Meltzer's book, it would nevertheless have been a perfect addition. Research this organization. Who were its leaders? What happened to them? Write a chapter for *Rescue*

based on the efforts of the members of *The White Rose.* Be sure to include the final words and meaning behind the words of Professor Kurt Huber, a philosophy professor who guided the members of *The White Rose:* "You shall act as if on you and on your deeds depended the fate of all Germany and you alone must answer for it."

Memoir: *Dry Tears: The Story of a Lost Childhood*

Author: Nechama Tec (1984)

Recommended for: High school and college

Summary

Dry Tears is the memoir of a young girl who at the age of 11 lived with various Polish-Christian families during the Holocaust, passing as a gentile (a non-Jew). Nechama Tec, winner of the National Jewish Book Award for her *Resilience and Courage: Women, Men and the Holocaust* (2003), is one of the most eminent scholars and authors of the Holocaust. In *Dry Tears,* her landmark tale describing how she was shifted from one Polish family to another, Tec often feels so alone and unloved that one wonders at her strength and courage to resist and survive in the midst of terrorizing times.

Dry Tears is an important book for readers today as our society grapples with how to survive traumas in a world of terrorism and fear. Recounting one young girl's resilience and spirit, *Dry Tears* inspires the reader to be strong in the face of evil. *Dry Tears* does not paint a rosy picture that all rescuers were by nature good. Instead, it tells the truth that must be told: Some rescuers were indeed righteous in their attempts to save Jews, but a few others did shelter Jews for money and sometimes were very cruel. These truths must be admitted if students are to have meaningful dialogues about the moral and ethical implications of choices made during the Holocaust and what responsibilities we as humans have for our fellow human beings.

Symposium: Critical Thinking and Discussion

1. Describe the early life of Nechama before she went into hiding. How do you think her life would have been different if there had been no Holocaust? How did she change? What qualities, attitudes, and motivations do you attribute to her experiences in hiding?

2. What is the significance of the title *Dry Tears: The Story of a Lost Childhood?*

3. During the Holocaust, what types of sacrifices did a family have to make in order to save others? Were all people capable of being rescuers? What precautions had to be taken when a Jewish child went into hiding with a non-Jewish family?

4. Nechama relates, "Inside a church, I felt like neither a Christian nor a Jew, but only a human being." Discuss this concept.

5. As Nechama explains, some families kept Jews in hiding as a business proposition. How does this differ from stories you have read of righteous gentiles? What are the moral and ethical implications of saving people as a business rather than for altruistic reasons?

Reflections in Writing

1. Posing as a non-Jew, Nechama would often hear the comments of her "friends" about Jewish people. Write a journal entry that discusses the hypocrisy, prejudice, and stereotypes described in the following excerpt from *Dry Tears,* by Nechama Tec.

   > Pointing in their direction, my friend said indifferently, "Jews." Afraid to show my pain, I shrugged and said nothing, but that night I cried tears of helplessness as I described the scene to my parents. "It will soon be over," my father consoled me. I could not feel sure that he believed what he said. Although my friends were not interested in Jews as living and suffering beings, Jews were a part of their everyday speech, constantly referred to as symbols of greediness, dishonesty, and guile. And yet I played with these Polish children, and valued some of them as my friends. It was hard for me to understand and accept that those I thought of as kind, considerate, and helpful were often the most vehement in their remarks about Jews.
   >
   > In a sense, they were unconsciously telling me that I was their friend only for as long as they thought I was one of them. I could not doubt that their friendship would turn into denunciation if they knew who I really was.
   >
   > Janka was a friend to whom I felt especially close. Two years older than I, she was a big, plain-looking girl who felt protective toward me and treated me with special kindness. We enjoyed each other's company, and sometimes we would leave the rest of the children to chat and gossip alone.

2. Select a scene from the book that you found especially powerful. Rewrite it as a play and present it with others in your group.

3. In 1945 many parts of Poland had been liberated. When the Russians arrived, Nechama, emerging from a bomb shelter, remembered, "We came out into a free world. All was silent." Read her description of this memory on page 211 and write a paper that addresses those things that impressed her most.

4. Nechama faced many conflicts and dilemmas. Select one and describe it. Write about the choices Nechama had and the choice she made. Discuss her choice with others in the class.

5. Many first-person memoirs have been written by children who were hiding during the Holocaust, yet since its first publication in 1982, *Dry Tears* has remained in a category by itself, considered to be the most informative first-person memoir of a teenager in hiding as a Gentile. What specific qualities makes Nechama's story so effective? Write a review of this book that addresses the criteria that make it so well received.

Researching the History

1. Read another memoir written by a child who was hidden during the Holocaust. What similarities can you find in their experiences and the way these experiences shaped their lives?

2. Nechama Tec's book ends with her arrival back in Lublin. She said she ended the story where she did because "at that time I could go no further." However, Nechama Tec *has* gone much further—further than she had ever dreamed. Research Nechama Tec by going on the Web to www.google.com. Learn what she has done since the end of World War II and the Holocaust. Write an epilogue for her book, including everything she has accomplished to the present.

3. Research the topic of rescuers during the Holocaust. Although many of the rescuers Nechama Tec came into contact with did what they did because they believed it to be the right thing to do, others were rescuers for profit. Consider this latter group. Would you consider them courageous since they still risked their lives, or would you look at them differently since they did what they did for personal gain? Explain.

Lessons for Today

Moral or Ethical Dilemma

1. Think of a time you were faced with a situation in which you had to put yourself in some type of danger, whether physical or emotional, to help another. Write a summary of the dilemma and the options you had. Have others in the class discuss the dilemma and discuss what alternatives they can discern and what actions they might have taken.

2. Read the story below, "The Merit of a Young Priest" (from *Hasidic Tales of the Holocaust* by Yaffa Eliach, 1982). Discuss with classmates the moral dilemma faced by the priest in the story. What options did he have? What decision did he make? What do you think are the merits of his choice?

From *Hasidic Tales of the Holocaust* by Yaffa Eliach. Reprinted with permission of the author.

The Merit of a Young Priest

It was June 1942; the murder of Jews in the Cracow Ghetto was at its height. About 5,000 victims were deported to the Belzec death camp. Hundres were being murdered in the ghetto itself, shot on its streets on the way to deportation. Among them were Dr. Arthur Rosenzweig, head of the Judenrat, the famous Yiddish poet Mordechai Gebirtig, and the distinguished old artist, Abraham Neumann.

The Hiller family realized that their days in the Cracow ghetto were numbered; they too would soon be swept away in one of the frequent Aktions. Yet there was still a glimmer of hope. They were young and skilled laborers; if they were deported to a labor camp, perhaps they would still have a chance of survival. But the fate of their little son Shachne was a different matter. Small children had become a rare sight in the ghetto; starvation, disease, and the ever-increasing selections took their constant toll. Helen and Moses Hiller began feverishly to plan the rescue of their little Shachne. After considering various possibilities they decided to contact family friends on the Aryan side in the small town of Dombrowa, childless Gentile people named Yachowitch.

Helen Hiller, with the help of the Jewish underground, made her way to Dombrowa. She went to Mr. and Mrs. Joseph Yachowitch and begged them to take care of her little son. Although they could do so only at great risk to their own lives, the Christian friends agreed to take the child.

Despite the ever-increasing dangers of the ghetto, the young parents could not bring themselves to part from their only child. Only after the large Aktion of October 28, 1942, when 6,000 additional Jews were shipped to Belzec and the patients at the Jewish hospital, the residents of the old-age home, and 300 children at the orphanage were murdered on the spot, did the Hiller family decide to act.

On November 15, 1942, Helen Hiller smuggled her little boy out of the ghetto. Along with her son, she gave her Christian friends two large envelopes. One envelope contained all the Hillers' previous valuables; the other, letters and a will. One of the letters was addressed to Mr. and Mrs. Yachowitch, entrusting them with little Shachne, and asking them to bring up the child as a Jew and to return him to his people in case of his parents' death. The Hillers thanked the Yachowitch family for their humanitarian act and promised to reward them for their goodness. The letter also included the names and address of relatives in Montreal and Washington, D.C.

The second letter was addressed to Shachne himself, telling him how much his parents loved him, that it was this love that had prompted them to leave him alone with strangers, good and noble people. They told him of his Jewishness and how they hoped that he would grow up to be a man proud of his Jewish heritage.

The third letter contained a will written by Helen's mother, Mrs. Reizel Wurtzel. It was addressed to her sister-in-law Jenny Berger in Washington. She wrote to her of the horrible conditions in the ghetto, the deportations, the death of family members, and of the impending doom. "Our grandson, by the name of Shachne Hiller, born on the 18th day of Av, August 22, 1940, was given to good people. I beg you, if none of us will return, take the child to you; bring him up righteously. Reward the good people for their efforts and may God grant life to the parents of the child. Regards and kisses, your sister, Reizel Wurtzel."

As Helen was handing the letters to Mrs. Yachowitch, she once more stated her instructions: "If I or my husband do not return when this madness is over, please mail this letter to America to our relatives. They will surely respond and take the child. Regardless of the fates of my husband or myself, I want my son to grow up as a Jew." The two women embraced and Mrs. Yachowitch promised that she would do her best. The young mother hurriedly kissed her little child and left, fearing that her emotions would betray her and she would not be able to leave her little son behind in this strange house, but, instead, would take him back with her to the ghetto.

It was a beautiful autumn day. The Vistula's waters reflected the foliage of a Polish autumn. The Wavel, the ancient castle of the Polish kings, looked as majestic as ever. Mothers strolled with their children and she, the young Jewish mother, was trying to hold back her tears. She slowed her hasty, nervous steps so as not to betray herself and changed her hurried pace to a leisurely stroll, as if she too were out to enjoy the sights of ancient Cracow. To thwart all suspicion, Helen displayed a huge cross hanging around her neck and stepped in for a moment to the Holy Virgin Church in the Old Square.

Smuggling little Shachne out from the ghetto to the Aryan side was indeed timely. In March 1943, the Cracow ghetto was liquidated. People in the work camp adjacent to the ghetto were transferred to nearby Plaszow and to the more distant Auschwitz. Anyone found hiding was shot on the spot. Cracow, the first Jewish settlement on Polish soil, dating back to the thirteenth century, was Judenrein!

Mr. and Mrs. Joseph Yachowitch constantly inquired about the boy's young parents. Eventually they learned that the Hillers had shared the fate of most of Cracow's Jews. Both of them were consumed by the flames of the Holocaust.

The Yachowitches, too, faced many perilous days. They moved to a new home in a different town. From time to time, they had to hide in barns and haystacks. When little Shachne suffered from one of his crying spells, calling for his mother and father, they feared that unfriendly, suspicious neighbors would betray them to the Gestapo. But time is the greatest healer. Little Shachne stopped crying. Mrs. Yachowitch became very attached to the child and loved him like her own. She took great pride in her "son" and loved him dearly. His big, bright, wise eyes were always alert and inquiring. She and little Shachne never missed a Sunday service and he soon knew by heart all the church hymns. A devout Catholic herself, Mrs. Yachowitch decided to baptize the child and, indeed, make him into a full-fledged Catholic.

She went to see a young, newly ordained parish priest who had a reputation for being wise and trustworthy. Mrs. Yachowitch revealed to him her secret about the true identity of the little boy who was entrusted to her and her husband, Joseph, and told him of her wish to have him baptized so that he might become a true Christian and a devout Catholic like herself. The young priest listened intently to the woman's story. When she finished her tale, he asked, "And what was the parents' wish when they entrusted their only child to you and your husband?" Mrs. Yachowitch told the priest about the letters and the mother's last request that the child be told of his Jewish origins and returned to his people in the event of the parents' death.

The young priest explained to Mrs. Yachowitch that it would be unfair to baptize the child while there was still hope that the relatives of the child might take him. He did not perform the ceremony. This was in 1946.

Some time later, Mr. Yachowitch mailed the letters to the United States and Canada. Both Jenny Berger, from Washington, D. C., and Mr. and Mrs. H. Aron from Montreal responded, stating their readiness to bring the child to the U.S.A. and Canada immediately. But then a legal battle began on both sides of the Atlantic that was to last for four years! Polish law forbade Polish orphan children to leave the country. The immigration laws of the United States and Canada were strict, and no visa was issued to little Shachne. Finally, in 1949, the Canadian Jewish Congress obtained permission from the Canadian Government to bring 1,210 orphans to the country. It was arranged for Shachne to be included in this group, the only one in the group to come directly from Poland. Meantime a court action was instituted in Cracow, and Shachne was awarded, by a judge in Poland, to the representatives of the Canadian American relatives.

In June 1949, Shachne Hiller boarded the Polish liner *MS Batory*. The parting from Mrs. Yachowitch was a painful one. Both cried, but Mrs. Yachowitch comforted little Shachne that it was the will of his real mother that one day he should be returned to his own people.

On July 3, 1949, the *Batory* arrived at Pier 88 at the foot of West 48th Street in New York City. Aboard was little Shachne, first-class passenger of cabin No. 228. He was met by his relatives, Mrs. Berger and Mrs. Aron. For the next year, Shachne lived in Montreal. On December 19, 1950, after two years of lobbying by Jenny Berger, President Harry S. Truman signed a bill into law making Shachne Hiller a ward of the Berger family. When Shachne arrived at the Bergs' home on Friday, February 9, 1951, there was a front-page story in the Washington Post.

It was more than eight years since Shachne's maternal grandmother Reizel Wurtzel, in the ghetto of Cracow, had written the letter to her sister-in-law (his great aunt) Jenny Berger, asking her to take her little grandson to her home and heart. Her will and testament were finally carried out.

Years passed. Young Shachne was educated in American universities and grew up to be a successful man, vice-president of a company, as well as an observant Jew. The bond between him and Mrs. Yachowitch was a lasting one. They corresponded, and both Shachne and his great aunt Jenny Berger continually sent her parcels and money, and tried as much as possible to comfort her in her old age. He preferred not to discuss the Holocaust with his wife, twin sons, family, or friends. Yet all of them knew about the wonderful Mr. and Mrs. Joseph Yachowitch who saved the life of a Jewish child and made sure to return him to his people.

In October 1978, Shachne, now Stanley, received a letter from Mrs. Yachowitch. In it she revealed to him, for the first time, her inclination to baptize him and raise him as a Catholic. She also went on to describe, at length, her meeting with the young parish priest on that fateful day. Indeed, that young parish priest was none other than the man who became Cardinal Karol Wojtyla of Cracow, and, on October 16, 1978, was elected by the College of Cardinals as Pope—Pope John Paul II!

When the Grand Rabbi of Bluzhov, Rabbi Israel Spira, heard the above story, he said, "God has mysterious, wonderful ways unknown to men. Perhaps it was the merit of saving a single Jewish soul that brought about his election as Pope. It is a story that must be told."

Based upon several of my conversations with Shachne Hiller (Stanley Berger), his family, and his mother-in-law, Mrs. Anne Wolozin. September 1977–October 1, 1981. (Yaffa Eliach)

Making Connections

1. The United States Holocaust Memorial Museum designated *Memories of Courage* as the theme for the 2002 Days of Remembrance, our nation's annual commemoration of the victims of the Holocaust. What memories of courage have you witnessed or learned about in your lifetime? For example, several years ago, in Billings, Montana, the entire town put menorahs in their windows at Hanukkah to show solidarity with their Jewish neighbors and to send a message to the neo-Nazis in their area who had been trying to divide the community. Create a tribute to a person or community who has displayed courage and compassion in the face of overwhelming odds.

2. With others in your class, create a traveling exhibit to recognize these individuals, their choices, and their actions.

3. Create an advertisement campaign to remind students your age that you do have the power and choice to make a difference and fight prejudice and oppression.

4. Hold a panel discussion on the topic "The Courage to Care." Why do some stand up and others stand by? Research more information on Pope John Paul II and his relationship to Jews of the Holocaust.

5. Raoul Wallenberg, the Swedish diplomat responsible for saving the lives of at least 20,000 Hungarian Jews, disappeared after the war. Some evidence suggests that he was arrested by the Soviet secret police and held in captivity until his death. Unfortunately, in today's world, people are being unjustly incarcerated. Write to Amnesty International USA to find out what you can do to help.

Topic 7

The Final Solution:
The Camps

*The things I saw beg description and I made the
visit deliberately, in order to be in a position to
give firsthand evidence of these things, if ever in
the future there develops a tendency to charge
these allegations merely to "progaganda."*

— General Dwight D. Eisenhower
Supreme Allied Commander

In January 1942, high-ranking Nazi leaders met in the Berlin suburb of Wannsee. Their objective was to discuss the "Final Solution to the Jewish Question." Fifteen men, many with doctorates from German universities, met to discuss and craft a systematic plan, with rules and regulations, created to exterminate the entire Jewish population of Europe. "The language of the Wannsee Conference sanctioned the industrialization of death" (*The Holocaust Chronicle,* 2000). The Jews of Europe were to be evacuated and sent to ghettos, and from there transported East to death camps. By the middle of 1942, six camps served as death camps in which victims were gassed: Auschwitz-Birkenau, Belzec, Chelmno, Majdanek, Sobibor, and Treblinka. Auschwitz and Majdanek were slave-labor and penal camps as well.

However, even before the Wannsee Conference, the Jews of Europe had been forced into concentration camps and labor camps. Mass murders of Jews by the Einsatzgruppen (SS squads) and at the Chelmno death camp had already occurred. In 1933, the first concentration camp was established at Dachau. Concentration camps served three major purposes:

At first, they were penal colonies; later, large camps were established to supply labor for special projects; and finally, the camps were used for "liquidation," or murder. . . . There were more than 9,000 camps scattered throughout German-occupied Europe. They included transit camps, prisoner-of-war camps, private industrial camps, work-education camps, foreign labor camps, police detention camps, even camps for children whose parents had been sent to slave-labor camps. More than 300 camps were for women only. (Berenbaum, 1993, p. 119)

Conditions in these camps were inhumane at best, and the treatment of prisoners went beyond the scope of human comprehension. Millions of people, mostly Jews, were murdered in the concentration camps, dying from starvation, disease, medical experimentation, shooting, or gassing.

As American GIs liberated hundred of concentrations camps in Germany and Austria, from Ohrdruf to Buchenwald to Dachau to Ebensee, they became witness to the most inhumane of circumstances. As they entered various villages along the way, one question kept surfacing: "How could you?" GIs had witnessed untold death and destruction throughout World War II, but nothing prepared them for the enslavement, torture, and murder of innocent men, women, and children. At liberation, as Allied troops spread out through Eastern Europe and Germany, they saw firsthand the horror of the camps.

The statistics are staggering. The only way to even begin to understand the enormity of the loss is through the voices of the victims: the men, women, and children who were in the camps, who lost their childhoods, their innocence, and their worlds. This chapter's topic takes us back in time to a period of death and suffering, hope and survival. It contains films and memoirs that each have profound effects on the viewer or reader, that each reach into our hearts and souls, compelling us to remember always.

Film: *Genocide, 1941–1945*
(*World at War* Series)

Source: Social Studies School Service
10200 Jefferson Boulevard
P.O. Box 802
Culver City, CA 90232-0802
(800) 421-4246

Recommended for: High school and college

Summary

Part of the definitive film series on World War II, this documentary tells the story of the destruction of European Jewry through archival footage and the testimonies of victims, perpetrators, and bystanders who represent a variety of European countries. Often graphic in content, the film captures the times in footage that is unsettling but ultimately memorable. This film is destined to impact viewers and make them vow "Never again." It is 52 minutes long.

Symposium: Critical Thinking and Discussion

1. In January 1939, Hitler threatened that if world Jewry forced Germany into war it would be the end of the Jews. Do you believe that this statement was rhetoric, or do you believe that Hitler, in 1939, had plans to annihilate the Jews of Europe?

2. What event precipitated World War II? With this in mind, how could Hitler rationalize his belief that if there were a war it would be caused by world Jewry?

3. How would you characterize Heinrich Himmler? What part did he play in the events of the Holocaust?

4. What made it possible to implement the "Final Solution"? What considerations had to be in place?

5. At what point do you believe that the Nazis' victims realized they would be killed? Why didn't they know sooner?

6. Trace the progressive violence of Nazi actions.

7. Study Table 7-1, "Estimated Jewish Losses in the Holocaust." Based on this, what inferences can you make? What conclusions and/or generalizations can you form?

Table 7-1. Estimated Jewish Losses in the Holocaust

For a variety of reasons, Holocaust-related figures may never be definitively known. It is important to keep in mind that the available Holocaust statistics do include a wide margin of error for many reasons, which include the following: Not all victims of the Holocaust were registered; countless records that did exist were destroyed by the Nazis or lost in military actions; different scholars have used different base dates for computing their figures, and this situation results in statistical differences due to the changing national borders of the Holocaust period.

Country	Initial Jewish Population	Killed	Percentage of Prewar Population
Austria	185,000	50,000	27.0 %
Belgium	65,700	28,900	44.0%
Bohemia & Moravia	118,310	78,150	66.1%
Bulgaria	50,000	0	0 .0%
Denmark	7,800	60	0.7%
Estonia	4,500	2,000	44.4%
Finland	2,000	7	0.3%
France	350,000	77,320	22.1%
Germany	566,000	141,500	25.0%
Greece	77,380	67,000	86.6%
Hungary	825,000	569,000	69.0%
Italy	44,500	7,680	17.3%
Latvia	91,500	71,500	78.1%
Lithuania	168,000	143,000	85.1%
Luxembourg	3,500	1,950	55.7%
Netherlands	140,000	100,000	71.4%
Norway	1,700	762	44.8%
Poland	3,300,000	3,000,000	90.9%
Romania	609,000	287,000	47.1%
Slovakia	88,950	71,000	79.8%
Soviet Union	3,020,000	1,100,000	36.4%
Yugoslavia	78,000	63,300	81.2%
Total	**9,796,840**	**5,860,129**	**59.8%**

Sources: Bauer, Yehuda, & Rozett, Robert. (1990). *Encyclopedia of the Holocaust* (p. 1799).
Grolier Encyclopedia. (1996). *The Holocaust* (vol. 3, p. 370).

Reflections in Writing

1. As many survivors testify, the will to survive is amazingly powerful. Discuss this phenomenon with survivors and write an essay to reflect your findings.

2. Many camps were surrounded by electrical wires. Yet the vast majority of prisoners resisted any suicide attempts. As one survivor remembered, "To die was easy." Complete this statement and compare your ending of the statement with that of others in your class.

3. Nazi anti-Jewish propaganda was extremely aggressive. Pause on one of the propaganda posters in the film. Describe its content, purpose, and how it was interpreted by the general non-Jewish population.

4. With all the evidence and testimony concerning the Holocaust, how do you explain those who deny the Holocaust happened? Write an editorial or create an editorial cartoon that allows the public to understand the real motivation of these deniers.

5. As American GIs liberated the camps, they constantly asked villagers, "How could you?" Their question was usually answered with "We didn't know." At camp after camp, the GIs forced the local citizens to dig mass graves. Many GIs took pictures of the atrocities they witnessed. Find several photos taken by GIs at liberation. After looking at these photos, write a paper that addresses the answer the majority of citizens of Europe gave: "We didn't know."

6. *Genocide* graphically shows the repercussions of heeding or ignoring the idea behind, "Am I my brother's keeper?" Select any historical or contemporary situation that applies to this theme. Create a picture book for young students to help them understand the importance of watching out for one another.

Researching the History

1. Differentiate and explain the terms *labor camps, concentration camps,* and *death camps.*

2. Heinrich Himmler was Reichsfuehrer of the SS. Once the Nazi party gained power, it allowed him to realize his dream of awakening the Germanic race within Germany to re-create the older "Aryan" Germany. Research this older "Aryan" Germany. How did it compare to the one the Nazis tried to create? What characteristics led to the end interpretation which prompted the ideas of genocide and the Holocaust?

3. Nazi ideology was a form of neo-Darwinism. Research Darwin's theory of the "survival of the fittest." How did it apply to Nazi philosophy and action? How did the Nazis interpret it?

4. Using a Web site such as www.historyplace.com, locate information on other genocides of the 20th century. Select one and prepare an oral presentation. For example:

> Bosnia-Herzegovina
> Rwanda
> Pol Pot in Cambodia
> Nazi Holocaust
> Rape of Nanking
> Stalin's Forced Famine
> Armenians in Turkey

5. Read the article "Freeing the Survivors" in *U.S. News & World Report*, April 3, 1995. It was written on the 50th anniversary of the beginning of the liberation of the concentration camps in Germany and Austria by American troops. What questions does this article answer for you? Search for the article on one of the websites in Appendix D, Webography.

Film: *Schindler's List*

Source: United States Holocaust Memorial Museum Shop
100 Raoul Wallenberg Place SW
Washington, DC 20024-2150
(800) 259-9998

Recommended for: High school and college

Summary

Schindler's List presents the true story of Oskar Schindler, a German businessman who comes to Poland as an opportunist and leaves as a rescuer responsible for saving more than 1,000 lives. Using his power and business skills, Schindler takes over a run-down factory in Krakow and selects workers from the Jewish community to work there. As the Nazis attempt to send the workers to labor camps and to Auschwitz, Schindler uses his influence to keep them in his factory. Finally, in 1944, as all the Jews of Krakow are being deported to be murdered, Schindler uses the fortune he has amassed to bargain with the Nazi leader, Amon Goeth, for the lives of his workers. The film is 3 hours long.

Symposium: Critical Thinking and Discussion

1. How does Schindler change from the beginning of the film to the end?

2. What is the symbolism of the girl in the red coat? Why did Steven Spielberg use black and white through most of the film but choose to picture this little girl in red?

3. Would Schindler fit your definition of a hero? Explain.

4. Discuss the concepts of conscience, gratitude, and altruism as they connect to this story.

5. Why is *Schindler's List* an important film? How has it affected attitudes about the Holocaust? What do you think is the most important message a person should come away with after watching *Schindler's List?*

Reflections in Writing

1. At what point, in your opinion, did Schindler become more of a humanitarian than an opportunistic businessman? Describe this scene.

2. Create a character sketch of Schindler that captures the essence of this complex man.

3. Write a paper that deals with the issue of individual responsibility and the concepts of right and wrong in terms of the events that unfolded in this film.

4. Create a conversation between Oskar Schindler and a friend in which Schindler explains his reasons for spending his life's savings to save the lives of Jewish men, women, and children. Present this conversation to your class.

5. At the end of the film, members of the families of "Schindler's Jews" paid their respects to the memory of Oskar Schindler. Replay this scene in your mind and create a poem that captures your feelings and describes the impact one person can make.

Researching the History

1. Read Thomas Keneally's *Schindler's List* (1992). What similarities and differences exist in the story and in the way in which Schindler was portrayed?

2. With others in your group, research the Nazi invasion and occupation of Poland during the Holocaust. Present your findings.

3. What was the Jewish response to the Nazi occupation and Nazi dictates? What was the response of the Polish people in general?

4. Research Steven Spielberg's interest and intentions in capturing the story of Oskar Schindler.

5. *Schindler's List* shows different types of camps: labor, concentration, and death camps. Do additional research to learn the differences between these camps designed by the Nazis.

Read the following first-person account by Arno Erban of his experiences in Auschwitz. Discuss the importance of first person Holocaust survivor testimony when studying the Holocaust.

AUSCHWITZ

Testimony by
Arno Erban, Holocaust Survivor

Peering thorough a crack in the side of the car, I noticed an unusual movement outside the train. The SS who had accompanied us until now were replaced by others. The trainmen left the train. We were at the end of our journey. The lines of cars began to move again and some 20 minutes later stopped. Through the crack I saw a desert-like terrain. Concrete pylons stretched in even rows to the horizon, with barbed wire strung between them from top to bottom. Signs warned us that the wires were electrically charged with high-tension current. Hundreds of searchlights were strung on the top of the concrete pillars. With intensive clarity I saw hundreds of barracks, inside the enormous squares, covered with green tarpaper and arranged to form a long rectangular network of streets as far as my eyes could see. Figures, dressed in the striped burlap of prisoners, moved inside the camp. The barbed wire enclosure was interrupted every 30 or 40 yards by elevated watch towers, with SS guards who stood leaning against a machine gun mounted on a tripod. Heavy footsteps crunched on the sand.

The seals on the car doors were broken. The doors slid slowly open and we could hear somebody giving us orders. We jumped to the ground, the parents helping their children, because the level of the cars was about 5 feet from the ground. The guards had us lined up along the tracks. They divided us according to sex, leaving all children under 14 with their mothers. The guards told us, that we would be taken off for a bath and to be disinfected. Afterwards we would all be reunited with our families.

We arrived in front of a young SS officer, impeccable in his uniform a gold rosette gracing his lapel. Later I learned that he was the head of the SS group, and that his name was Dr. Mengele. In addition he was the chief physician and also the head of the Auschwitz concentration camp. In the moment, that followed, we experienced what was called in Auschwitz selection. Dr. Mengele was in charge of forming two groups. The left-hand group included the aged, the crippled, the feeble and the women with children under 14. Those too sick to walk, the aged and insane were loaded into "Red Cross" vans. They departed with the left-hand group. The right-hand group started to enter the concentration camp.

One object immediately caught our eyes. It was an immense square chimney, built of red bricks. It was like a two story building and looked like a strange factory chimney. We saw enormous tongues of flame coming from its square top. Somebody told us that, what we saw, was a crematorium. Later we saw the second and third one with the same flames. A faint wind brought the smoke to us. Our noses, then our throats, were filled with the nauseating odor of burning flesh and scorched hair. Later we found out that what was burning in the crematoriums were dead bodies of our families and friends, who came with us in the same train. After being selected to go to the left, they walked about 300 yards from the ramp, then they advanced along a path about 100 yards from where 10 or 12 steps led them down to an underground room, described in several languages as a "bath and disinfecting room." There were 3 rooms. The first one was about 200 yards long and it was brightly lit. In the middle of the room were rows of columns and along the walls were benches. Above the benches were numbered coat hangers. They got instructions to leave their clothes and shoes together to avoid confusion after the bath. The next room was equipped with showers. They were ordered - in spite of the fact that there were men, women and children - to take their clothes off. The young girls, especially, were uneasy, but they had to obey. An SS man entered and opened a door to the second room. There were no benches, but every 30 yards there were columns, not to support the ceiling, but square sheet-iron pipes, with numerous perforations. After everybody was inside, the SS left the room, the lights were switched off and instead of water a gas escaped through the perforations and within few seconds filled the room. Within 5 minutes everybody was dead. The bodies were not lying here and there, instead they were piled in a mass to the ceiling. The reason for that was that the gas inundated the lower levels first and then rose slowly toward the ceiling. This forced the victims to trample one another in a frantic effort to escape. Yet a few feet higher the gas reached them anyway. What a struggle for life there must have been. They could not think, they did not know that they were trampling over their children, wives and friends. Their action was only an instinct of self-preservation.

After it was over a crew of men, called Sonderkommando, who performed all the duties in the area of crematorium, entered the gas chamber to wash and remove the bodies to the third and final place of their existence. They loaded 20 to 25 corpses into an elevator. The elevator stopped in the incineration room. After stripping the victims of their clothes and shoes, the kommando extracted or broke off all the golden teeth and fillings and stripped the bodies of all the valuables, The corpses were then taken over by the "incineration-kommando." They always laid 3 bodies on a metallic pushcart. The heavy doors of the ovens opened automatically, and the pushcart moved into a furnace heated to incandescence. Each crematorium worked with 15 ovens and there were 4 crematoriums.

For years many thousands of people passed through the gas chambers and incineration ovens. The crematoriums were attended by a group of prisoners that got great privileges, compared with others in the camp. They had special dormitories, good food, and cigarettes and didn't wear prison uniforms. They did their work for about 4 months. After that new people were called for crematorium work. Their first duty was to incinerate the corpses of the previous group of crematorium workers, who had been shot by the SS. The Germans didn't want any witnesses to that, even if they were absolutely sure that they would win the war. They probably didn't want even the German people to find out about the bestiality of their leaders.

People whose destiny had directed them into the left-hand column were transformed by the gas chambers into corpses within an hour after their arrival. Less fortunate were those whom the adversity had singled out for the right-hand column. They were still candidates for death, but with the difference, that for 3 or 4 months or as long they could endure, they had to submit to all the horrors, the concentration camp had to offer until they dropped dead from utter exhaustion. They bled from a thousand wounds, their bellies were contorted with hunger, their eyes were haggard and they moaned like the demented. They dragged their bodies across the snow or mud until they couldn't go any farther. They were the living death, and in prisoners language called "musulmans." Trained dogs snapped at their wretched fleshless bodies and only death was their liberation.

Who then was more fortunate, those who went to the left or those, who went to the right? After our "right-hand" column left the ramp, we passed in-between the different camps until we arrived at a barracks on which "Bath and Disinfecting" was written over the entrance. We entered and were objects of the same routine as in the gas chambers with the remarkable difference that in the second room there was water and not gas coming from the pipes. Outside of the barracks were the barbers who first shaved our heads and then the rest of our bodies. Then they rubbed our heads with a solution of calcium chloride, a blinding disinfectant. We were told by one of the SS that we were not human beings any more, and we had no right to live and from that moment were to forget our names. We would be numbers only and not even that for a long time. Almost immediately a man tattooed a number on our arms.

After that we were taken to an empty barracks, which would be our immediate home. We learned that Auschwitz was not a concentration camp, but an extermination camp. In the barracks there were about 600 people. We were unable to stretch out completely, and we slept there both lengthwise and crosswise, with one man's feet on another's head, neck or chest. Stripped of all human dignity, we pushed and shoved and kicked each other in an effort to get a few more inches of space on which to sleep. We didn't have much time to sleep because they woke us at 3 in the morning. Guards armed with rubber clubs had us line up immediately outside. Then began the most inhumane of all my stay in the concentration camps—"the roll call."

The prisoners had to stand in rows of five. The SS in charge arranged us in order. The prisoner in charge of the barracks, usually a man imprisoned for murder, lined us by height, the taller ones in front and the shorter behind. He was in prison uniform, but a clean one and neatly pressed and he was very well fed. Then another SS guard, who was in charge of the section that day, arrived and shouting at us put the taller ones behind the little ones. We never knew the reason. The SS guard never accepted the word of the barracks chief that everything was in order. They counted us again and again, sometimes for several hours because they counted us from front to back and back to front or in any other possible direction. If the rows were not straight, or our hands were not raised correctly above our heads we stood there an hour more. In winter or in summer roll call began at 3 am and lasted until 7 am when the SS officers arrived. The barracks leader, an obsequious servant of the SS with his green insignia, which distinguished him from other prisoners, snapped to attention and made his report. Then the SS officers counted us again and put the numbers in their notebooks. If there were any dead in the barracks they had to be brought for inspection, naked and supported by 2 living prisoners. Sometime the kommando in charge of the dead didn't show up and the dead had to be physically present every day.

On several occasions roll call became a "selection," similar to the one on our arrival at Auschwitz. The SS officers headed by Dr Mengele came, accompanied by SS soldiers and dogs, surrounded us and those chosen for the gas chamber were pushed into vans with no possibility to escape or resistance. Some of the prisoners were used for medical experiments almost always with fatal results.

Those who were in charge of Auschwitz were murdering people all day, but at night they retired to their homes outside the camp to live a comfortable life with their families. They had no remorse for their "work" during the day.

That is how I remember Auschwitz. (Arno Erban, April, 2004)

Memoir: *Night*

Author: Elie Wiesel (1982)

Recommended for: High school and college

Summary

Night is Elie Wiesel's personal account of the Holocaust as seen through the eyes of a 15-year-old boy. The book describes Wiesel's first person testimony of the Holocaust and details the persecution of a people and the loss of his family. Wiesel's experiences in the death camps of Auschwitz and Buchenwald are detailed; his accounts of starvation and brutality are shattering—a vivid testimony to the consequences of evil. Throughout the book, Wiesel speaks of the struggle to survive, the fight to stay alive while retaining those qualities that make us human. Although Wiesel lost his innocence and many of his beliefs, he never lost his sense of compassion or his inherent sense of right.

Symposium: Critical Thinking and Discussion

1. Wiesel's village was invaded by the Nazis in 1944, years after the murder of Jews had begun. Why, after all this time, did the people have so little, if any, information about what had been happening to Jews all over Europe?

2. Wiesel was given two contrasting pieces of advice about how to survive. One was from a young Pole, a prisoner in charge of one of the prison blocks, and the other was from the head of one of the barrack blocks at Buchenwald who spoke to Wiesel as his father lay dying. Summarize these two philosophies of survival and discuss the wisdom of each.

3. At one point, upon arrival at Auschwitz, the prisoners considered revolting. What stopped them? Many people ask survivors why there was so little resistance in the death camps. Although there is documented evidence of some resistance in the various camps, tell why from your reading there were so few possibilities of resistance efforts.

4. At one point in the book, Wiesel said that he had ceased to feel human. What did he mean by this, and what kinds of things can cause people to lose their sense of dignity and humanity?

5. In what ways did Wiesel's experiences affect his beliefs today? Recount one specific experience.

Reflections in Writing

1. The following are possible themes for discussion: *Silence, A Journey from Darkness to Light, The Loss of Innocence, Fathers and Sons.* Choose one for discussion and extension of ideas.

2. Over the years, Wiesel, in a sense, has become the "soul of the Holocaust." After reading *Night*, explain why Wiesel was given this title.

3. After the war, Wiesel took a 10-year vow of silence before he attempted to put into words the horror and pain of the Holocaust. When he finally wrote *Night,* he had difficulty finding a publisher, for it was believed that few would want to read such heart-wrenching words. Research the publication history of *Night.* Today it is one of the most read and respected books on the Holocaust. Write an essay explaining why this is so.

4. Wiesel wrote of those things he will never forget. After reading *Night,* what images, ideas, and feelings do you think you will never forget?

5. Select a recurring word, phrase, or symbol from *Night.* For example, the word *night* is used frequently throughout the book. Analyze the word, phrase, or symbol and explain the images it evokes.

6. Recount one instance of kindness Elie experienced in the dark hours of *Night.* What impact did this have on the reader having been absorbed in reading this book *Night?*

Researching the History

1. In 1985, Elie Wiesel was the recipient of the Congressional Gold Medal, and in 1986 he was honored with one of the greatest of all awards, the Nobel Peace Prize. Research the life of Elie Wiesel in order to understand the reasons why he received such recognition.

2. Read another of Wiesel's work, such as *Against Silence: The Voice and Vision of Elie Wiesel* (Schocken Books, 1988) and *All Rivers Run to the Sea.* What impressions did you get of Wiesel from the book you read?

3. Wiesel was born in Sighet in Transylvania. Locate the region of Transylvania on a pre–World War II map of Europe. Discover what happened to this area during and after World War II. Share five facts you find most significant about pre-Holocaust years in the community of Sighet and others like it. Why didn't the Jews of Sighet leave when they first heard of the Nazi atrocities?

Memoir: *Hasidic Tales of the Holocaust—* Excerpt "Stars"

Author: Yaffa Eliach (1982)

Recommended for: High school, and college

Summary

"Stars," a selection from the book *Hasidic Tales of the Holocaust* by Yaffa Eliach, dramatically retells the experience of Michael Schwartz as he "beat the Nazis' system," saving his cousin from the gas chamber in Auschwitz.

A Holocaust survivor, Yaffa Eliach was born in Vilna, Poland, in 1935. She, her parents, and one brother survived the war by hiding in caves, in the woods, and among the partisans. Her mother and brother were killed by Poles after they returned home following the Holocaust. Her father was imprisoned by the Russians and sent to Siberia. Eliach was taken to Israel and later, in 1954, immigrated to the United States. She earned a doctorate in Russian intellectual history, is a professor at Brooklyn College, and founded the Center for Holocaust Studies. Her "Tower of Faces" is one of the most powerful and often visited exhibits at the United States Holocaust Memorial Museum in Washington, D.C. Eliach is also the author of the award-winning book *There Once Was a World: A Nine Hundred Year Chronicle of Eishyshock* (1999) and the editor of Hasidic Tales of the Holocaust, from which the selection below is taken.

"During the Holocaust," Yaffa Eliach explains, "when European Jews were systematically destroyed and cultural achievements were fragmented, Hasidism continued to create its magnificent tales in ghettoes, hiding places, and camps. In fact, the Hasidic tales helped the survivors to come to terms with the Holocaust and its aftermath." *Hasidic Tales* contains stories of the Holocaust that were gathered by the author from interviews and oral histories. Together these stories offer a window into the souls of those who lived the terror of the Holocaust.

The following selection dramatically retells the experience of Michael Schwartz as he "beat the Nazis' system" and saved his cousin from the gas chamber.

Stars

(From Hasidic Tales of the Holocaust, by Yaffa Eliach. Reprinted with permission.)

Michael Schwartz arrived in Auschwitz-Birkenau in August of 1944 with one of the last transports from the Lodz ghetto. Though a veteran of this first and last ghetto of Nazi Europe, Michael was in a state of shock when he was shoved out of the cattle car into the Auschwitz kingdom. The railway platform with its barking dogs, screaming S.S. men, kicking Ukrainians, and the sorrowful eyes of quick-moving prisoners in striped uniforms inspired terror, hopelessness, and a strange wish to get it over and done with as quickly as possible. Before he realized what was happening, he was separated from his family and was led away in the opposite direction with a group of young men. The men marched beneath a barrage of leather truncheons, near the edges of flaming pits where people were tossed alive. The air was filled with sulfur and the stench of burning flesh.

A few hours later, his hair shaven, his body stinging from disinfectants, wearing a striped, oversized uniform and a pair of skimpy, broken clogs, Michael along with hundreds of young men was led off to a barracks. There in the barracks, he found a cousin from whom he had been separated earlier at the platform. Only after looking at his cousin did Michael realize the transformation that he himself had undergone since his arrival on that accursed platform. That night in the barracks the cousins promised each other never to part again. It was the first decision Michael had made since his arrival in Auschwitz.

Michael quickly learned the realities of Auschwitz. Survival depended on one's ability to "organize" anything and everything, from an additional sip of coffee to a better sleeping place on the three-tiered wooden planks, and of course one had to present a healthy and useful appearance if one hoped to pass selections.

One day rumors spread in Michael's barracks that the impending selection was of particular importance, for those selected would be transferred out of Auschwitz to work at another camp. Michael was especially anxious to pass that selection. In the few months he had been in Auschwitz he had learned that Auschwitz would eventually devour everybody, even those who deciphered its survival code.

Dr. Joseph Mengele himself was supervising the selection. It was apparent to Michael that Mengele was using what was known among the Auschwitz old-timers as the "washboard" criterion. Each inmate was ordered to lift his hands high above his head as he approached Mengele. If his rib cage protruded and each vertebra was clearly visible, Mengele would smile and motion with his snow-white glove to the left.

The moment came. Michael and his cousin stood in front of Mengele, whose clean, shaven face glittered in the sun and whose eyes shown. The angel of death was in his moment of bliss. Michael's turn came and Mengele's finger pointed: "Right!" Then Michael heard Mengele's death sentence on his cousin: "Left!"

A moment later Michael stood before a table where three people sat dressed in white coats. One was holding a stamp pad, one a huge rubber stamp, and the third a pen and a white sheet of paper. Michael felt the cold rubber stamp press against his forehead and saw a pen mark a line on the white sheet of paper.

Michael moved on to a group of young men, all naked like himself, wearing only a huge ink star on their foreheads. Michael realized that this star was the passport that would take him out of the camp, and that his cousin in the other group just a few meters away would be taken to the chimneys.

In the commotion of the selection Michael decided to act. He walked briskly over to his cousin, spat on his cousin's forehead, pressed his own forehead against his cousin's, took his cousin by the hand, and led him to the group marked with stars. Only then did he dare look at his cousin. There in the middle of his forehead was the imprint of the lucky star, the passport that would lead them out of the Auschwitz hell.

From Birkenau, Michael and his cousin were transported to Neuengamme, Braunschweig, Watenstadt, Beendorf, Ravensbrück, and Ludwigslust, where they slaved in the Hermann Goering works in private German companies engaged in the war industry.

On a May day in 1945 a tank entered a camp near Ludwigslust. On it was painted a huge white star and inside the tank sat a black-faced soldier wearing a steel helmet. After six years in the Nazi slave kingdom, Michael and his cousin were once again free men.

Symposium: Critical Thinking and Discussion

1. Describe the scene when the transports arrived at Auschwitz. Discuss the way in which prisoners were dehumanized. Why would the Nazis go to such extremes to dehumanize the prisoners?

2. Michael didn't realize his transformation since his arrival at Auschwitz until he saw his cousin. Explain this statement.

3. Michael explained that he learned the realities of Auschwitz. Upon what did survival in part depend?

4. In the selection process in the death camp, what did "going to the right" ultimately represent? What did "going to the left" represent?

5. How did Michael save his cousin's life? Why is this story so important?

Reflections in Writing

1. Write an essay to explain how the concentration camps exemplify the lowest level of inhumanity that the Nazis had finally reached.

2. Create a eulogy (a speech in praise) for the millions of victims of the Holocaust. Read this eulogy to the class.

3. Locate photographs taken at concentration camps. Select one picture that affects you and write a paper that lets the reader "see" the picture.

4. Medical experiments were performed on concentration camp prisoners by doctors such as Josef Mengele, "the angel of death." How do you suppose that doctors, who take an oath to work for the good of their patients, were recruited to carry out these experiments?

5. Opportunities for keeping diaries in the concentration camps were fewer than in the ghettos, but some people did manage to write and preserve their memories. Research diaries that were kept in certain camps and look for indications of hope.

Researching the History

1. Research the six major killing center camps established. Notice where they are located. Why do you suppose they were built where they were rather than in Germany?

2. Research concentration camps and death camps. Compare and contrast conditions in each.

3. How did the first concentration camps differ from those built later? There were three phases in the development of the concentration camps: 1933–1936, 1936–1942, 1942–1945. Create a chart to explain the purposes behind the development of camps in each of these time periods.

4. Slave labor was vital to the Nazis, especially toward the end of the war. Research this phenomenon.

5. The word *camps* was used as a euphemism. Research what the Jews knew about the camps before they were transported to them. How did the Nazis keep their plans and actions such a secret?

Memoir: *The Cage*

Author: Ruth Sender (1986)

Recommended for: Middle school and high school

Summary

The Cage is a memoir of an extraordinary young girl named Riva Minsky (Ruth Sender). It is 1939, and Riva is living a relatively happy life with her family in Lodz, Poland, when the Nazis shatter her world by taking her mother during an early deportation of the Jewish community. Riva, a young teenage girl, becomes the sole caretaker of her brothers in the Lodz Ghetto and then ultimately is left alone to survive labor camps and the horror of Auschwitz. What keeps her spirit alive and ultimately allows her to share her harrowing experiences is expressed in this classic story of the Holocaust. This memoir is a must-read for its lasting message of hope.

Symposium: Critical Thinking and Discussion

1. Riva describes the new Jewish generation as "the new link in an old chain." What does she mean by that?

2. What is the "caravan of horror" to which Riva refers? Where do all the men go to on this "caravan of horror"?

3. While in the ghetto, Laibele wonders if the world outside "the cage" has forgotten about them. What do you think? How could a world forget about the atrocities of perpetrators?

4. Reread the poem on page 194. What is the underlying theme and message of this poem? How does this theme recur throughout the book?

5. When discussing the Holocaust, Riva's daughter Nancy told her mother, "But Mommy, it could not happen here. Our neighbors, our friends, they would help." Do you agree or disagree with Nancy's conclusion? Explain.

Reflections in Writing

1. Hope is a theme that runs throughout this memoir. Write a narrative piece that tells about the impact hope has played in your life.

2. Riva describes the "mountains of hair, the piles of shoes, clothing, and eyeglasses" that she sees in the camps. Read the poem and the journal entry on the next page. Each focuses on the shoes of the victims of the Holocaust. Write your own poem or personal narrative expressing the effect that the mountains of personal effects had on you.

3. The Gruber family, once good friends and neighbors of Riva and her family, have turned into perpetrators and bystanders. Imagine that you overheard a conversation the Grubers had that expresses their choice to become bystanders and perpetrators rather than rescuers. How might they have rationalized their decision?

4. Select one of the quotes from the book, analyze it, and write a personal response.

Researching the History

1. In the midst of the raids and chaos, Riva realizes that the books they have collected have survived and says, "Ideas cannot be killed. These books carry the ideas of freedom, justice and brotherhood. The Nazi perpetrators cannot destroy the spirit in these books." Research other quotes related to censorship and/or the burning of books during the Holocaust. Create an illustrated book of these quotes, using actual photographs when appropriate.

2. Research one of the following topics as it applies to Auschwitz or select a topic of your own choosing: *selection, food, clothing, shelter, work details, roll call, medical experiments, selection, kapos.*

3. Hope was a pervasive influence in survival. Research this phenomenon and its effect on human beings.

WHERE ARE THE CHILDREN?

The shoes
All those shoes
I've never seen so many shoes

Who were they?
Where are they?
Why are they so little?
Where are the children?

Who would kill so many little children?
Who would take such innocents?
Who were in these shoes?
Who was Julika? Her name is engraved on her shoes—
For me to know her

Where is that little ballerina now?
Does she cry for her lost dancing shoe?

I can see the laces and the buckles
And the bows—

But

I can't see the children…

Where are they?
Who are they?
Where are the children?

Miriam Klein Kassenoff

SHOES

Even now, months later, I can still see the shoes, thread-bare, ragged, and torn. There were three rooms of shoes, rooms twelve feet high, packed from floor to ceiling with nothing but shoes. A silent memorial.

They were the shoes of those who had nothing in common and yet everything in common. They were the shoes of the young wife who would never again know a tender touch; they were the shoes of the young boy who knew nothing of play and everything about fear and survival; they were the shoes of the mother who would never sing another lullaby or hear the laughter of her children; they were the shoes of the writer, the teacher, the doctor, the dreamer.

There was a mountain of shoes reaching to forever, the shoes of the millions who lived with hope, and died still believing in tomorrow. In the end, these shoes led to one place, a place with many different names— Treblinka; Auschwitz; Birkenau; Majdanek.

I remember the shoes, and I feel a deep emptiness and an overwhelming sadness for what might have been. I wonder what roads might have been traveled, what words might have been written, what pains might have been eased. And I wonder what dreams might have come true.

Anita Meyer Meinbach

Lessons for Today

Making Connections

1. With classmates, discuss the following: Why is it important to learn about and remember the Holocaust? What are the lessons of the Holocaust and how do they apply to all people everywhere? Write a letter to your school board to encourage members to support Holocaust education. In your letter include some of the ideas offered during your discussion.

2. Elie Wiesel was offered various pieces of advice about how to survive in the concentration camp. Debate the question "Do we survive best by ourselves or when we work together?" Use historical evidence and current events in your research.

3. The lessons of the Holocaust encourage people to never be *bystanders, victims,* or *perpetrators.* Select one contemporary event in which one or more of these lessons was illustrated and write a positive paper about the event so that the moral is evident.

Topic 8

The Power of Perseverance: Children Surviving the Holocaust

Now that we have survived, Miriam, you must do three things: always continue to learn, teach what you learn, and always do community service.

— Rabbi Maurice Klein
(father of Miriam Klein Kassenoff, co-author)

Child survivors are those children, ages 16 and younger, who were displaced, terrorized, or tyrannized during the Holocaust. Child survivors were in the ghettos, the camps, or "on the run to refuge" during the years 1933–1945. Child survivors who were hidden in attics, in the forests, in convents, and in homes of non-Jews are called "Hidden Children of the Holocaust." Today many of these children have memories of the past, however faded the images, and they know they that must transmit these memories. They are the last generation of Holocaust survivors, the last eyewitnesses to what was.

"Of all the crimes conceived in fanaticism and hatred, the war against the Jewish children will remain the worst, the most vicious, and the most implacable in recorded history. . . ." says Elie Wiesel. "We now know that Hitler's Germany made the Jewish child its principal target. In condemning our people's children to death, it sought to deprive us, as a people, of a future. For the children who did survive Hitler's Germany; laughter and joy were largely eliminated from their lives."

This chapter's topic includes many of the stories of child survivors and hidden children, their experiences, and their realities. Their tales reflect the hope that sustained the children and the questions that plague them, even to this day. Their stories are of a childhood lost and the quest to find themselves.

Film: *Let Memory Speak*

Written, produced, and directed by Batia Bettman

Source: United States Holocaust Memorial Museum Shop
100 Raoul Wallenberg Place SW
Washington, DC 20024-2150
(800) 259-9998

Recommended for: Middle and high school

Summary

This short but powerful documentary by Batia Bettman, a Holocaust survivor, author, and playwright, examines life in Europe for Jewish children. The film develops four stages in the lives of the children:

Before the war. This chronicles the very normal lives of the children, their school life and celebrations. As time passes into the mid and late 1930s the film describes the prejudice and discrimination that becomes widespread.

During the Holocaust. Often the first to be targeted as "useless" and killed, some Jewish children did survive.

At liberation. There was no normal life to which to return. Survivors were taken to displaced persons camps, and from there they immigrated to different countries. For children it was especially difficult; they were often alone.

50+ years later. This follows the lives of children who survived the Holocaust, rebuilding their lives, living with their memories.

The film is 27 minutes long.

Symposium: Critical Thinking and Discussion

1. What are the earliest memories of the children speaking in the opening of the film? In what ways were their experiences much like your own today?

2. What is the significance of oral history in understanding the Holocaust? The film uses direct quotes from the diaries of the children. Which quote(s) did you find most powerful? Which had the greatest impact on you? Explain.

3. Many of the children survived by being hidden, others "on the run" needed to find a safe place to hide. This involved trusting strangers. In a world gone mad, how could they trust a stranger with their lives?

4. What roles do self-expression and creativity have in spiritual resistance? Support your answer.

5. Discuss the significance of the documentary's title, *Let Memory Speak.*

Reflections in Writing

1. Often in discussing the Holocaust we use the word *tolerance*. Elie Wiesel prefers the term *respect*. Explore this issue; get feedback from friends and family. Which word do you prefer? Is there another word you can suggest? Write a paper that persuades the reader to use the word you think most appropriate.

2. The concept of faith enters into many conversations regarding the victims of the Holocaust. Many lost their faith, others looked for some kind of meaning, whereas others became even more religious. How is it possible to find meaning in life after surviving the Holocaust?

3. It has been said that in remembering the Holocaust, we are reflecting on what it means to be human. React to this statement from the film.

4. Create a poem written in tribute to the children of the Holocaust. You may wish to remember their dreams, their spirit, their loss, their hope.

5. At each stage described in the film, the children faced specific challenges. Select one of the stages and describe the challenges.

Researching the History

1. Two Nobel Prize winners are highlighted in the documentary, Nelly Sachs and Elie Wiesel. Who were they and how did their Holocaust experiences impact their lives and work?

2. Many survivors of the Holocaust had great difficulty in talking about their experiences. It has been said often that there is a "conspiracy of silence." Survivors believed for a long time, that anyone who didn't experience the Holocaust can't understand and that society in general doesn't want to hear about such horrors. Research this phenomenon to understand it more fully. Is it still true today?

3. Look through the local newspapers for a week. Record events involving prejudice, stereo-types, and persecution. What happened? What, if anything, was done to stand up to the perpetrators?

4. After liberation, several agencies like the United Nations Relief and Rehabilitation Agency, the Hebrew Immigration Aid Society (HIAS) and the American Jewish Joint Distribution Committee helped survivors. Research the work of one of these agencies to discover what they did to support the survivors and help them to begin their lives again.

5. Where are the child survivors today? Research the topic *child survivors* to gain a perspective about where they went after liberation, how they worked to rebuild their lives, what they accomplished, and the importance of memory.

Film: *The Power of Good*

Source: National Center for Jewish Film at Brandeis University (see Appendix, p. 180)
[(781) 899-7044; film may be purchased or rented]

Recommended for: Middle school, high school, and college

Summary

Nicholas Winton saved 669 Czech children from the fires of the Holocaust between March 13 and August 2, 1939, yet for half a century he never told his wife or anyone else about his heroic deeds. One day in 1998, his wife discovered an old scrapbook while cleaning the attic of their home in England. She discovered pictures and lists of names of children Winton had rescued from the Nazi regime. Writer-Director Matej Minac has made one of the most touching and spiritually uplifting documentaries that exist today based on the true story of how Winton accomplished this feat. The film highlights interviews with some of the children who are now adults. Winton speaks about how he planned and carried out the business of saving the lives of these children. This film illustrates how one person can make a difference in so many lives when one is determined not to be a bystander in the face of evil. The film is 64 minutes long.

Symposium: Critical Thinking and Discussion

1. The narrator in the film asks, "Why did he do it?" What do you think, from research on Winton, inspired him to risk his life and career to save the children of Czechoslovakia?

2. How did the mystery of Nicholas Winton's life come to light? Why do you think he never chose to talk about this chapter in his life?

3. One survivor explained that they were "more Czech than Jews." How did this philosophy make it possible to think that the Nazis would not harm the Jews of Czechoslovakia?

4. How do the images of Czechoslovakia reflect the very ordinary lives of its Jewish citizens? In what ways was it a good life before the Holocaust?

5. "There's nothing that can't be done if it's fundamentally reasonable," says Winton. Explain this and its significance to rescue efforts during the Holocaust.

6. From the 669 children Winton saved, there are now 5,000 (children and grandchildren). How does this exemplify the Talmudic quote "He who saves one life, saves the world entire." What else does this quote suggest?

Reflections in Writing

1. Imagine that you are at the train station as the children and their families say good-bye. Write a newspaper article that reflects the scene you are witnessing. Describe the final actions of various parents and children. Describe the emotions and the atmosphere.

2. Can you imagine making the decision that so many parents had to make in allowing their children to be taken from them in order to save their lives? Write a paper to express one parent's viewpoint in stream of consciousness style.

3. As the children crossed the English Channel on one ship, they sang the Czech national anthem, "Where Is My Home?" Create a stanza to the tune of one of your country's patriotic songs that relates to the experience of immigrants, especially the children.

4. What might a typical first night be like for a refugee child in a strange new country, in a strange new home, in a strange new bed? What questions and worries might this child have? List as many as you can and select one as the topic for a diary entry. (Do research for this by speaking with students in your class, school, or community who have immigrated from another country.)

5. Create a *This Is Your Life* program based on Nicholas Winton. Write a script and act it out for other classrooms. Include information that highlights not only his heroic deeds but the ways in which individual children were impacted.

Researching the History

1. Only two countries agreed to take in the children that Winton was attempting to rescue—Britain and Sweden. Research to learn what prevented other countries from doing the same.

2. Research Czechoslovakia before and after World War II. In what ways did the war's outcome affect the country's political climate?

3. Research the life of Nicholas Winton. What new information did you uncover that was not presented in the film?

4. How have the children Winton saved chosen to pay back the goodness he showed?

5. "All societies require ordinary human decency to survive," says the narrator of this film. What example of ordinary human decency do you encounter every day? Do you believe this is the exception or the rule? Explain.

Film: *Marion's Triumph*

Source: Seventh Art Releasing
7551 Sunset Blvd. Suite 104
Los Angeles, CA 90046
(323) 845-1455

Recommended for: Middle school and high school

Summary

In 1938, the Blumenthals began their journey to the United States as refugees from Nazi Germany. Just before they were scheduled to leave Holland, it was invaded by the Germans and they were trapped. What followed were six and a half years of horror in Hitler's camps and an incredible story of near escapes, dashed hopes, and tragedy. The family finally arrived in New York in 1948, using the tickets paid for a decade earlier.

This film is based on the memoir *Four Perfect Pebbles* by Lila Perl and Marion Blumenthal. Narrated from her point of view, *Marion's Triumph* includes the surviving members of her family and additional narration from the actress Debra Messing. Also included is a wealth of photos and some never-before-seen historic film footage.

Symposium: Critical Thinking and Discussion

1. Discuss the plan that Marion's family had to leave Germany and then the plan to leave Holland. What were the results of each plan?

2. Describe examples from Marion's life that exemplify the perseverance, faith, and hope that sustained her during the Holocaust.

3. Based on Marion's recollections, what conditions in the camps were the most difficult to endure? How did children find food? How did they survive?

4. Discuss Marion's return to Bergen-Belsen in 1995 and the tragic irony of this visit. Discuss her homecoming. What amazing events occurred? What would compel a person to return to places that hold such dark memories?

5. What was Marion's triumph? To what do you think the title refers?

Reflections in Writing

1. What message for living does this film inspire? Using a creative venue, share this message with others.

2. Create an illustrated time line of the Blumenthals' experiences from the time they left Germany to the time they arrived in New York City.

3. Using the Internet, obtain a picture taken at one of the concentration camps in which Marion Blumenthal was imprisoned. Make as many observations as you can from this photo and create a caption for it. Put it together into a collage with photos of the same concentration camp found by classmates and create a pictorial history of the camp. Include captions.

4. Based on all you have learned about the Blumenthal family from this film, to what do you attribute their survival? Write an essay that expresses your thoughts on this subject. Use support from the film.

5. Marion explains that "death was constant" while they were in the camps. How does this affect one's humanity and one's ability to go on in life?

Researching the History

1. Research the concentration camp of Westerbork in Holland. What were Marion's experiences there? What world-famous Jewish girl was also a prisoner there?

2. Research the concentration camp of Bergen-Belsen and compare it to Westerbork.

3. Read the book *Four Perfect Pebbles* by Lila Perl and Marion Blumenthal and compare to the film. Is one more powerful than the other? Why?

Memoir: *The Hidden Children: The Secret Survivors of the Holocaust*

Author: Jane Marks (1993)

Recommended for: High school and college

Summary

The Hidden Children of the Holocaust have been the least-talked-about subject in teaching about the Holocaust. Yet they are extremely important, for their stories are probably the best first-person testimony we have of the rescue and courage of non-Jews who saved Jewish children during those perilous times. In addition, the *hidden children* and *child survivors* are the last generation of witnesses to the Holocaust. As the older survivors are dying, it is imperative that these younger survivors tell their stories of how they were hidden by courageous gentiles during World War II.

In this excellent collection of first-person testimony by Jane Marks, you will read touching stories of children who coped, persevered, and survived in the homes, farms, barns, and convents throughout Europe at the youngest of ages. Each story in this collection is important, but four are developed with questions and activities specific to each story.

Into the Arms of Strangers (see chapter 6) as well as the film by the same title is also an excellent resource to use in a study of hidden children.

Before reading the selections in *The Hidden Children: The Secret Children of the Holocaust,* read the following excerpt from the essay "Revealing Evidence: Witnesses in and Out of Hiding," written by Dr. Ellen Fine. This selection carefully explains the term *hidden child* and gives the reader insight into the life of the hidden child, the challenges, and the way in which the past has affected all the days that have followed. As you read this selection, ask yourself these questions: To whom does the term *hidden child* refer? What types of experiences did the *hidden children* endure? What is the distinction between *in hiding* and *hidden*? What challenges did these children face, not only during the Holocaust but in all the years that have followed?

Dr. Ellen Fine is a well known scholar, historian, and expert on the subject of Elie Wiesel and his writings. Dr. Fine is Professor Emerita of French at City University of New York. We gratefully acknowledge and thank her for permission to reprint the following essay on "hidden children."

Excerpt from "Revealing Evidence: Witnesses In and Out of Hiding"

Evidence Obliterated

Before exploring the "new kind of secrecy" of the now adult-child-survivors who will be referred to as "hidden children," let us briefly examine general aspects of the hiding experience, which we can call *evidence obliterated,* or as one hidden child expressed it, "a way of life without life," (Dwork, 69). In *Children with a Star,* Deborah Dwork makes the distinction between in hiding and hidden, and "in hiding" and visible (68). "The essential problem," she states, "is to leave no evidence or sign of one's presence, to live without trace or vestige of existence" (71).

In hiding and hidden meant to vanish from the world, to cut all ties with one' s community, and with one' s family, although some families did manage to stay together, such as . . . Anne Frank's family in the secret annex. Hiding places ranged from attics, haylofts, closets, sewers, and bunkers to barrels, cellars, and graveyards. Emergency hiding places were set up during round-ups, and children were drilled to disappear within seconds (Dwork). Since they were small, they could fit into tiny spaces such as cupboards, ovens, or wardrobes where they were confined for hours in the dark without moving or speaking. "Silence became ingrained in all hidden children," says Nechama Tec, who herself was hidden in Poland, and is author of the memoir, *Dry Tears* (1984) and other books such as *When Light Pierced the Darkness: Christian Rescue of Jews in Nazi-Occupied Poland* (1986). Breaking the silence could mean denunciation or death. Young children had to learn not to cry nor to laugh, not to express their feelings, their needs; they had to become invisible.

The dilemma of leaving no evidence of one's presence is demonstrated throughout the oral histories in Jane Mark' s book, *The Hidden Children: The Secret Survivors of the Holocaust.* For example, Kristine Keren remembers how at the age of seven, in the ghetto of Lvov Poland, she and her brother of three and a half years sat for hours in a small empty space below the window of their apartment, camouflaged to look like a wall. Tears ran down her cheeks but she dared not make a sound. Terrified, she struggled for air, waiting for her father to let them out. As the danger became more imminent for the family, her father dug a tunnel from the basement of a nearby house into the sewer. The family lived in the sewer for fourteen months, surrunded by rats, often soaking wet, sick with dysentery. "All this time," Keren says, "nobody had to tell us to be quiet. I felt like an animal, ruled by instinct, I never spoke above a whisper." While other conditions were not as extreme, the problem was always the same: to eradicate all traces of one's existence.

For those children "in hiding" and visible, it was not a question of concealing their physical presence, but rather their Jewish identity. Separated fram their family, often abruptly and without understanding why, they felt a deep sense of loss, of being abandoned by parents who seemed to be punishing them by giving them away. Staying with non-Jewish families, on farms, in town, or with groups in Catholic convents, monasteries, orphanages, schools and institutions, they often had to be shunted from place to place in order to escape detection. They were given false papers and birth certificates, manufactured by the underground resistance movement, black market or even by priests. Obliged to rupture with the past, the children had to adopt false names, a new religion and new personalities; they acquired fictitious life histories, learning fabricated dates, places and names of family members in case of being questioned by the Nazis or by the local population. They were trained what to say, and what not to say. They had to invent, to lie, to lead double lives, in effect, to become someone else.

Saul Friedlander, for example, named Pavel in Prague where he grew up, became Paul when his parents escaped to Paris. At the Catholic boarding school of Montneuf, he was known as Paul-Henri after his baptism and communion. At first, he was unable to get accustomed to his new name: "I had crossed a line and was now on the other side. . . . Paul-Henri could be nothing but French and resolutely Catholic" (*When Memory Comes,* by Saul Fried-lander). Eventually he became so immersed in his role ("I had passed over to Catholicism, body and soul," 120) that he planned to become a Jesuit priest. It was only when the war was over and one of his Jesuit teachers explained to Paul-Henri that his parents had died in Auschwitz, that he began to vaguely feel Jewish. The uneasiness about the shifts in identity nonetheless persisted, demonstrated by his continuous change of name. Upon arriving in Israel, he became Shaul, and finally Saul. "It is impossible to know which name I am, and that in the final analysis seems to me sufficient expression of a real and profound confusion," he confesses (94).

The loss of one's name at times generated the fear of amnesia: not remembering one's authentic name could erase all signs of one's former life. Jana Levi, for example, was smuggled out of the Cracow ghetto in 1942 at the age of eight, and did extremely hard physical work on a farm, posing as a Catholic Pole under the name of Janina Lesiak. Yet, the obliterated evidence was never entirely obliterated; her unconscious would not let her forget. Nocturnal reminders of Jana's buried self surfaced to create deep anguish about becoming the perpetual "other," a non-person who risked disappearing into anonymity:

> I didn't remember anymore what my real name was. I only dreamt about it at night. When I woke up in the morning I wouldn't remember again.. .if my parents didn't know my name they couldn' t find me. They wouldn't know, nobody would know who I was. I had completely become someone else. . . (Dwork)

Evidence Revealed

The trauma of having a double identity continued to haunt hidden children in the postwar epoch. They were possessed by an overwhelming desire to resume normal lives, expressed over and over again in the oral histories in Jane Marks' important book, *The Hidden Children: The Secret Survivors of the Holocaust,* (Marks, 255, 264). Ann Shore, a hidden child from Zabno, Poland, acknowledges: "As soon as the war was finished. . . . I just wanted to be like everyone else. . . . For years and years I never wanted to talk or think about my experience—it brings up such pain" (Marks, 265). And Josie Martin, born in 1938 in a border town between France and Germany, sheltered in a Catholic girls' school in a small French village during the war, and reunited with her parents in August 1944, describes how when singled out by teachers in elementary school in Los Angeles because she spoke three languages but did not know English, she wanted to cry. "I hated being different," she confesses (Marks, 254–255).

Even when not singled out, many hidden children still saw themselves as observers, spectators, alienated, not belonging. "I'm always the outsider," admits Joseph Steiner who during the war hid in twenty-two places in Poland, including a warehouse filled with bales of rags, and the graveyard of a church. Born in Warsaw in 1934, he tells of a recurring dream—being in a burning ghetto but always managing to escape. "I'm always looking," he says. "The bad things are happening to other people." (Marks, 137–38). A psychiatrist friend of his confirms Steiner's problems of distancing: "You're always on the outside looking in. You're never really *there*" (138).

Accustomed to leading a secret existence, hidden children persisted in sealing the pain within. This willed oblivion became a burden unshared. We always have the feeling about this secret, that we should keep it inside," Aharon Appelfeld, a child survivor writer, tells us (*Dimensions,* 16). Saul Friedlander also preserves the fragments of his memories "in the very depths of myself. . . . like those shards of steel that survivors of great battles sometimes carry about inside their bodies" (110).

Selections from *The Hidden Children: The Secret Survivors of the Holocaust* by Jane Marks. Read the following stories and answer the following questions.

Nicole and David

1. Describe Nicole's life in hiding and the new adjustments she had to make while living with a Catholic family.

2. Of the family who hid her, Nicole said, "This family was good. They willingly risked their lives and they never took any money for keeping me." Frequently, she said, they reminded her to say her "Jewish prayers." How are qualities of "goodness" fostered through life? Why do some people exhibit this type of humanity while others turn their backs on suffering, and still others choose to inflict pain?

3. How did Nicole cope to make sense of life and deal with her separation from her family?

4. For a time, Nicole hid in a convent. Describe her situation there.

5. In 1987, Nicole discovered that *hidden children* share a common bond. Explain this bond.

6. Why are *hidden children* often afraid to talk about their experiences in the Holocaust? In what ways are so many *hidden children* of the Holocaust still in hiding?

Rina Kantor

1. "I was born in Berlin, Germany, in 1934. When I was five, my father was beaten to death in a concentration camp." Thus begins the memoir of Rina Kantor, today a professor of social sciences at a prestigious midwestern university. Discuss the defining moments in Rina's life in hiding.

2. "Buried feelings" seems to be a thread that is common to *Hidden Children*. Discuss this as a coping mechanism in young Holocaust survivors.

3. We learn in almost all the testimonies that getting false papers of identity was sometimes possible. Describe how this could be accomplished.

4. Rina's mother was so determined that they would live and not give in to the Nazis, she even defied wearing the yellow star and then decided that her family should succeed in passing themselves off as non-Jews. How was she able to accomplish this?

5. What happened to Leon? What guilt has haunted Rina to this day? Why do so many hidden children and child survivors harbor similar feelings of guilt?

6. Discuss the various hiding places that Rina and her family were subjected to and how they survived in each.

7. How did Rina eventually end up in a convent that was directly under the supervision of the Vatican?

8. In June 1944, Rome was liberated and Rina (then Elena) left the convent to rejoin her mother who had been in hiding elsewhere. By now, Rina was "a Catholic on the outside, but Jewish on the inside." Discuss this phenomenon.

9. Even in 1945, Rina and Tova were not free. After they were sent along with 500 other children to Palestine, they were detained on the island of Cyprus. Research this situation to learn why it was so difficult to immigrate to Palestine in 1945.

The Lessings (Carla and Ed)

First answer the following questions:

1. In 1940, the Germans occupied Holland. Describe how life immediately changed for 10-year-old Carla. What were the new restrictions against Jews?

2. When Carla was 12, she and her family went into hiding. How? Where? What part did the Catholic underground have in helping the family?

3. Describe the way in which fear lived in each of the children in hiding.

4. After the summons for Ed and his family to report to a work camp in Poland, Ed and his family went into hiding. Discuss his experiences in hiding. Why didn't Ed's rescuers allow him to stay for a longer time?

5. Discuss Ed's transformation from "city boy" to "farm boy" in hiding. What do you think would be the most difficult aspects of this transformation?

6. Research the Dutch Resistance efforts that helped people like Ed and his family.

7. Ed faced incredible obstacles in the years 1943–1945, yet he endured and survived them all. To what characteristics do you attribute this ability?

8. How did Ed meet Carla? How has Carla learned to heal in her new life in America?

9. What happened in the war years? What impacted you most about Ed's survival?

10. Today, Carla Lessing is a family psychotherapist and is responsible each year for the therapy support group workshops at the annual International Hidden Child and Child Survivor Conferences. Research the work of this organization.

11. Learn about the contributions of other child survivors and what they have accomplished in their lives.

Ann Shore

1. "It was confusing for a child to experience such brutality," begins Ann Shore's memoir. When Ann was 12 years old, a Nazi-trained policeman in Zabno, Poland, "stuck a gun to me and asked me where my father is." Discuss how this incident and the subsequent shooting of her father by the police would impact any child.

2. For 2½ years, Ann and her family hid in the barn of a widowed woman. How did they survive?

3. "We had to whisper—for 2½ years we never spoke above a whisper." Compare and contrast Ann Shore's experience hiding in the barn with that of Anne Frank, who hid in an attic.

4. After the war, Ann said she wanted to forget about the past, celebrate life, and "be like every other teenager." How do these feelings compare to teens today who have suffered traumatic experiences?

5. Ann admits that "our childhood experiences surely affected our children." Discuss the impact that the experiences of *hidden children* have had on their children and grandchildren, many of whom might be in your classroom today.

6. Discuss the importance of the *Hidden Child/Child Survivor and the Second Generation* (the children of Holocaust survivors) in countering those who deny the Holocaust because of anti-Semitism.

7. Today, Ann Shore is the president of the Hidden Child Foundation of the Anti-Defamation League in New York City. Research this organization to learn of its efforts.

Memoir: *A Scrap of Time and other Stories* Excerpt "The Tenth Man"

Author: Ida Fink (1987)

Recommended for: High school and college

Summary

Ida Fink has authored a haunting collection of stories about life in Poland during World War II and the Holocaust. These fictionalized accounts accurately reflect the lives of ordinary people as they are compelled to do the unimaginable: a couple who must decide what to do with their little daughter as Nazis come to liquidate their area; a young girl who must pay a grim price for an Aryan identity card; a young woman who must decide whether to be true to her heritage or hide her Jewish identity at the close of the war; and in "The Tenth Man," the way in which survivors cope with life after liberation.

The stories in this book acquaint the reader with rural and small-town life—and death—as experienced by Polish Jews during the Holocaust. Brief vignettes illustrate scraps of time.

Ida Fink was born in Poland in 1921. She was a music student in Lvov but was forced to stop her studies in 1941 when the war broke out between Nazi Germany and the Soviet Union. During the early years of the war she was interned in a ghetto, but later she escaped and was able to get Aryan papers and live with the false identify on the Aryan side. She survived the war and in 1957 immigrated to Israel. Since then she has written many short stories, a play, and a novel, which have been translated from Polish into various languages.

Following is the story "The Tenth Man," from *A Scrap of Time* by Ida Fink.

The Tenth Man

by Ida Fink (reprinted with permission)

The first to come back was Chaim the carpenter. He turned up one evening from the direction of the river and the woods; no one knew where he had been or with whom. Those who saw him walking along the riverbank didn't recognize him at first. How could they? He used to be tall and broad-shouldered; now he was shrunken and withered, his clothes were ragged, and, most important, he had no face. It was completely overgrown with a matted black thicket of hair. It's hard to say how they recognized him. They watched him from above, from the cliff above the river, watched him plod along until, nearing the first houses of the lower town, he stopped and began to sing. First they thought he had gone mad, but then one of the smarter ones guessed that it was not a song, but a Jewish prayer with a plaintive melody, like the songs that could be heard on Friday evenings in the old days, coming from the hundred-year-old synagogue, which the Germans had burned down. The synagogue was in the lower town; the whole lower town had always been Jewish—before the Germans came and during the occupation—and no one knew what it would be like, now that the Jews were gone. Chaim the carpenter was the first to come back.

A dark cloud from the burnt-out fire still lingered over the town, the stench still hung in the air, and gray clouds floated over the marketplace the Germans had burned.

In the evening, when the news had spread, a crowd gathered in front of Chaim's house. Some came to welcome him, others to watch, still others to see if it was true that someone had survived. The carpenter was sitting on the front steps in front of his house; the door of the house was nailed shut. He didn't respond to questions or greetings. Later, people said that his eyes had glittered emptily in the forest of his face, as if he were blind. He sat and stared straight ahead. A woman placed a bowl of potatoes in front of him, and in the morning she took it away untouched.

Four days later the next one came back. He was a tenant on a neighboring farm and had survived in the forest with the help of the farm manager. The manager brought the tenant back by wagon, in broad daylight. The old man was propped up, half reclining, on bundles of straw. His face, unlike the carpenter's, was as white as a communion wafer, which struck everyone as strange for a man who had lived so long in the open.

When the tenant got down from the wagon he swayed and fell face down on the ground, which people ascribed more to emotion than to weakness. In fact, it was possible to think he was kissing the threshold of his house, thanking God for saving him. The manager helped him up, and supporting him on his arm, led him into the entrance hall.

A week passed and no one came back. The town waited anxiously; people came up with all sorts of conjectures and calculations. The stench of burnt objects faded into the wind and the days became clear. Spring blossomed suddenly as befitted the first spring of freedom. The trees put forth buds. The storks returned.

Ten days later three more men came back; a dry goods merchant and two grain dealers. The arrival of the merchant upset the conjectures and calculations, since everyone knew that he had been taken away to the place from which there was no return. He looked just as he had before the war; he might even have put on some weight. When questioned, he smiled and explained patiently that he had jumped out of a transport to Belzec and hidden in a village. Who had hidden him, and in what village, he didn't want to say. He had the same smile on his face that he used to have before the war when he stood behind his counter and sold cretonnes and percales. That smile never left his face, and it astonished everyone, because no one from this man's family had survived.

For three days the grain dealers slept like logs. They lay on the floor near their door, which was left slightly ajar, as if sleep had felled them the moment they walked in. Their high-topped boots were caked with dried mud, their faces were swollen. The neighbors heard them screaming in their sleep at night.

The grain dealers were still asleep when the first woman returned. No one recognized her. Only when she reached the teacher's house and burst out sobbing did they understand that she was his wife. Even then, they didn't recognize her, so convincing was her beggar woman's disguise. She had begged in front of Catholic and Orthodox churches, had wandered from church fair to church fair and market to market, reading people's palms. Those were her hiding places. From beneath her plaid kerchief peered the drawn face of a peasant woman.

They asked in amazement: "Is it you?"

"It's me," she answered in her low voice. Only her voice was unchanged.

So there were six of them. The days passed, the gardens grew thick and green. They're being careful, people said, they're waiting for the front to move—it had been still for so long that an offensive seemed likely. But even when the offensive began and the front made a sudden jump to the west, only a few more came back.

A wagon brought the doctor back. He had lain for nine months in a hole underneath the cowshed of one of his patients, a peasant woman. He was still unable to walk. The accountant and his son and the barber and his wife returned from a bunker in the forest. The barber, who had once been known for his mane of red hair, was bald as a bowling ball.

Every day at dusk, the dry goods merchant left his house and walked towards the railway station. When asked where he was going, he explained, "My wife is coming back today." The trains were still not running.

The farmer, a pious man, spent more and more time by his window; he would stand there for hours on end. He was looking for a tenth man, so that the prayers for the murdered might be said as soon as possible in the ruins of the synagogue.

The days kept passing, fragrant and bright. The trains began to run. The people in the town no longer conjectured and calculated. The farmer's face, white as a communion wafer, shone less often in his window.

Only the dry goods merchant—he never stopped haunting the railway station. He would stand there patiently, smiling. After a while, no one noticed him anymore.

Symposium: Critical Thinking and Discussion

1. Discuss the major concepts in this short story: *survival, starting over, dealing with death and loss.*

2. What did all of the people returning to the town have in common? How was each impacted by the events of the Holocaust?

3. How did each deal with his or her own loss?

4. Why did the dry goods merchant have a constant smile on his face? Do you believe the dry goods merchant's wife will return to the village?

5. What does this story tell you about the nature of humanity?

Reflections in Writing

1. Select one of the survivors from the story. Write a monologue about his or her experiences upon returning to the village.

2. What symbolism is evident in this story? Write a paper that analyzes the symbolism and its impact on the story.

3. Imagine starting over, as these Holocaust survivors did. What challenges would be most difficult to face? Research the experiences of Holocaust survivors. Select one and write a short biography about the way in which this individual built a new life.

4. Select another story from the book. Write a review of this piece and how it affected your understanding of the way in which the Holocaust affected life.

Researching the History

1. Research the life of Ida Fink. In what ways did her life experiences impact her writing?

2. Most survivors did not return to their homes; there was nothing left to go back to—no family, no friends, no home. What options were open to survivors at the end of the war? Where could they go? What assistance was available?

Memoir: *My Bridges of Hope: Searching for Life and Love After Auschwitz*

Author: Livia Bitton-Jackson

Recommended for: Middle school and high school

Summary

Livia Bitton-Jackson describes the harrowing 6 years that she and her family endured in their journey to a safe haven, after liberation in the years following the Holocaust. It is a story of the time when, as the author writes, "we attempted to reclaim our lives while carrying the burden of the past." This is the story of triumph in the face of overwhelming odds, of extraordinary events in an extraordinary time. It is the story of one extraordinary individual.

Livia Bitton-Jackson was born Elli L. Friedman in Czechoslovakia. She was 13 when she, her mother, and her brother were taken to Auschwitz. They were liberated in 1945 and came to the United States on a refugee boat in 1951. She received a Ph.D. in Hebrew culture and Jewish history from New York University and is professor emerita of Judaic Studies at Herbert H. Lehman College of the City of New York. Dr. Bitton-Jackson is the author of *I Have Lived a Thousand Years* (1997), which received the Christopher Award and was named an American Library Association Best Book for Young Adults.

Symposium: Critical Thinking and Discussion

1. To what does the title *My Bridges of Hope* refer?

2. After liberation, the author returned to her home. She said that it was not just 1 year and 2 months that she'd been away, "it was an eternity." What changes, both in herself and her environment, created this feeling?

3. What was the Tattersall? Describe it and explain how it helped or hindered survivors' ability to become accustomed to their world after liberation?

4. Elli wonders why the British were keeping Jewish survivors from immigrating to Palestine, especially in view of the fact that the British were the Allies and their liberators. What was the reason behind the British decision to restrict immigration?

5. In the book, it mentions that the Talmud teaches that there are four kinds of students (page 159). Which kind are you? Explain.

6. Why was the establishment of Israel as a Jewish state such a significant event not only to the survivors, but to the Jewish community as a whole?

7. What was *Bricha*? What responsibilities did Elli have as a liaison for Bricha? How did it strengthen her confidence in humanity?

8. Trace the path Elli and her family followed in order to get a visa for the United States?

Reflections in Writing

1. Select one of the dilemmas or choices the author had to make. Describe the situation, the choices, and what action she took.

2. Elli and her mother voiced different dreams for the future soon after liberation. Elli spoke about immigrating to Palestine, whereas her mother wanted to go to New York. Write a dialogue between Elli and her mother that expresses the arguments each has for selecting her final destination. Read or perform the dialogue for the rest of the class.

3. How does the past affect your stand on immigration policy into the United States today? Write a letter to national leaders to let them know your stand on the issue and support it with what you learned.

4. The author has had a remarkable life. Write a short oral report based on the book *My Bridges of Hope* by researching stories of life after the Holocaust and on themes of hope and renewal.

5. Create a new cover for *My Bridges of Hope* to encourage others your age to read this remarkable book. Include information about the book and its author, as well as a creative illustration.

Researching the History

1. Miki and Elli discuss internment camps in Cyprus, Germany, and Austria, where Jews were kept after liberation. These camps became known as DP (displaced persons) camps. Research DP camps to understand that although the concentration camps had been liberated and the war was over, for the Jewish survivors the struggle continued. What were conditions like in these camps? Who was responsible for supplying the camp with food, clothing, and other essentials? What other types of help did the people in the DP camps receive?

2. After the Holocaust, young Jews registered to join the Haganah, the Israeli underground army, to be trained for combat. Their fear was that after the British left Palestine, the Arab nations would be poised to attack. Where they right? Research the wars in which Israel was involved after the establishment of the country in 1948.

3. Like so many other survivors, Livia Bitton-Jackson went on to accomplish herself in academics. Research the ways in which Holocaust survivors rebuilt their lives and learn about the accomplishments they have achieved. Create a "Who's Who" booklet or poster to reflect what you discovered. You may wish to read portions of the book *Against All Odds: Holocaust Survivors and the Successful Lives They Made in America* by William B. Helmreich (1992).

4. Although many survivors left Europe to begin their lives again in a new land, there were those who stayed and those who returned years later. Now, more than 50 years after the Jewish people of Europe came close to extinction in the Holocaust, Jewish identity in Central Europe is again taking root. The young are discovering their heritage and bringing back Judaism to their parents. Read the article in *Time* magazine, "More Than Remembrance," February 6, 1995, pages 36–40, to learn about the realities of being Jewish in Europe today and the way in which the Jewish people are rebuilding their world.

Memoir: *The Children of Buchenwald*

Authors: Judy Hemmendinger & Robert Krell (2000)
e-mail: gefenbooks@compuserve.com

Recommended for: Middle school, high school, and college

Summary

On April 11, 1945, American soldiers were astonished to find 1,000 children alive in Buchenwald's Barrack 66. All of them were survivors of the death march from Auschwitz and orphaned. Within 2 months, these children were admitted to France, Switzerland, and England. Of these, 426 children were brought to Ecouis, France, and approximately 90 were placed in a home in Taverny, near Paris, where Judith Hemmendinger of the OSE, a French Social Service agency, was in charge from 1945–1947, until it was shut down.

How did these children survive? How did they come back to life? How did they rebuild a life from their tragic pasts? Although a majority of the Buchenwald children kept silent throughout the years, 31 of them have offered their life stories in this book. Portraits include Nobel Prize winner Elie Wiesel, Chief Rabbi of Israel Meir Lau, and George Goldbloom, a founding member of the Holocaust Memorial, Miami Beach, Florida.

One chapter, highlighting Elie Wiesel, is included here.

Elie Wiesel

Excerpt from *The Children of Buchenwald.* Reprinted with permission.

Why single out one person of 426 for special consideration? We know from the struggles of every one of the children and adolescents (and young adults) who were on the convey to Ecouis, that each deserves special consideration. For have not the vast majority achieved a life of distinction, given such a brutal background of torment and loss? Have not the majority found gainful employment, become loving fathers and loving husbands, contributed to their communities and fought daily against disillusionment and despair?

Perhaps we must say something about Elie Wiesel, precisely because he is only one of 426 persons, in order to appreciate more deeply what was lost. We pay tribute not only to his talents and contributions but also reflect on the meaning of the murders of one and a half million Jewish children. If even only one in 500 children had the potential for extraordinary achievements, the world would have been enriched by 3,000 more intellectual giants.

It is no wonder that one sees in Elie Wiesel a sadness, the sadness of a persistent awareness of the missing. It may indeed be part of every young survivor's life: the silent presence of silenced family and companions of another time.

And what has Elie Wiesel contributed? In a sense, he has rescued religious faith from the ashes of Auschwitz. Had silence prevailed, the slaughter of Europe's Jews would surely have eroded faith like a growing cancer. The Nazi perpetrators and their henchmen, primarily Christians—and the victims, primarily Jewish—neither could have survived the fundamental assault on the religions involved in this tragic encounter.

Wiesel gave voice to what could not be spoken, believed, or understood. He struggled to break the silence and thereby inspired theologians to confront the Holocaust and provide an opportunity to re-examine the basic tenets of their faith. In a post-Holocaust world he surely expanded humanity's encounter with G-D and deepened faith and commitment.

Elie's insatiable intellectual curiosity was in evidence at Ambloy where he was a close friend of Daniel's who became a famous physicist. Elie mastered French within one year and after completing his studies, became the Paris correspondent for an Israeli newspaper. In his tiny apartment he worked for the newspaper and continued the study of Talmud with Mr. Shushani.

It was at Ambloy where Elie Wiesel wrote his first memories in a notebook in Yiddish. It was the original version of what was to become his book *Night*. Eight hundred pages long, it was first published in Yiddish in Buenos Aires, Argentina titled, *Und Die Welt Hot Geschwiegen (And the World Remained Silent)* in 1956.

During the 1950s, the French President, Pierre Mendes-France, was a popular figure, particularly after successfully ending the war in Indochina. The Israeli newspaper sought an interview with him, but he never granted interviews during his term in office. Elie instead approached Francois Mauriac, a fervent defender of the French President during his battle with critics and political enemies. Mauriac, a writer, agreed to see the young reporter.

Francois Mauriac's intellectual curiosity connected with the sympathy he felt for Wiesel, adding a personal dimension to their first conversation. The tragic experiences of the young man made a deep impression on Mauriac, but those experiences were connected by him to themes in Catholic spiritual life, such as suffering, forgiveness, and redemption. This was too much for Elie who stood up to leave, but was held back by Mauriac. Elie explained to him that he could not accept that the ordeals he had endured and which led to the murder of millions would be reduced to a divine mystery with moral implications. Francois Mauriac listened to him, asked questions, and encouraged him to inform the general public of his experiences. In short, he encouraged him to write a book, which appeared in 1958, as *Night*, with a foreword by Mauriac.

They remained friends and when Elie Wiesel was awarded the Prix Medicis honoring the best foreign author writing in French, the illustrious old man came to congratulate the younger man he considered a younger brother.

In the late 1950s Elie went to New York with no particular intention to settle there but he was hit by a taxi and seriously injured. During his long hospitalization and recovery, his French visa expired and he remained in the United States.

As a writer, journalist, lecturer, and professor, his influence grew widely. His works encompassed the complexity of Jewish destiny, strongly informed by his Hasadic background. He is deeply concerned about the fate of his people and is their champion everywhere, whether in Israel, the former USSR, or at the United Nations. His influential book *Jews of Silence*, helped breach the Iron curtain, which eventually led to the immigration of hundreds of thousands of Russian Jews to the free world. On awarding him a prize, then President of Israel Yitzhak Navon stated that Elie's travels take him around the globe and that his address is the universe.

Elie Wiesel's concerns are not only for his Jewish brethren. They extend to the oppressed, no matter where. He has been personally involved in American civil rights, in the fight against oppression in Latin America, in combating hunger in Cambodia, and drawing attention to the slaughters in Bosnia. Wherever he feels he can make a difference, he appears in order to plead for an end to indifference, for people to become involved and help to combat evil.

In 1986 he was awarded the Nobel Peace Prize. Elie Wiesel's activism has led to special relationships with American presidents and world leaders. President Jimmy Carter invited him to head the US Holocaust memorial Council which eventually led to the establishment of the US Holocaust Memorial Museum in Washington, DC.

In a conversation with one of us (J.H.) he said,

> Our persecution must never be forgotten. I have taken it upon myself to keep it in everyone's memory. Yet although I mention the camps during my lectures, I cannot describe what happened. For many years I could not utter the word 'Auschwitz.' I teach 'Knowledge of Humanity' at Boston University where more students sign up than there are places in my class. I always accept the children of my friends from Taverny, those who themselves are unable to speak of their past and therefore send them to me as students. I tell them about Hassidism and what the holy communities accomplished before being consumed by flames. The world was not worthy of their existence.

> I watched the movie 'Holocaust' on television. It was an insult to those of us who were there, for the reality of life in the concentration camps was falsified and distorted. It disturbs me deeply for I introduced the term 'Holocaust' in my writings. I am not pleased at all with that word and yet it has become adopted worldwise. The meaning of Holocaust is, in fact, consensual sacrifice, whereas we speak of a catastrophe (Shoah). A more precise term is genocide.

> I married late in life. For a long time I hesitated to bring a child into this world, a world about which I feel so pessimistic. Today, my child is my most precious possession. Watching him grow up reminded me of my relationship with my father. He spoke very little and I had to guess at his feelings and intentions. I talk a lot with my son and take him with me on my travels. He has received a traditional education at a Jewish school.

Elie Wiesel emphasizes that what he does, he does as a Jew. He writes, behaves, and leads with a keen awareness of his origins. With the strength derived from his Jewish identity and his Jewish experience, he is able to understand with compassion the tragedies and plight of others.

It is because all of us are in debt to him for assisting in our own struggle with faith, depression, hope, despair, pessimism, issues of life and death, grief and loss, that we pay particular attention to this survivor, one of the children of Buchenwald.

Symposium: Critical Thinking and Discussion

1. Robert Krell, the co-author of this book, is a child survivor. Today he is a world-renowned psychiatrist. In his piece "A Reflection," he explains that when the children first arrived in France they were viewed as "damaged beyond hope of repair, of recovery of normalcy." Why do you think that people at the time believed that these children would never have normal lives? How did the children defy the predictions forecast for them?

2. Robert Krell asks, "If these 'doomed' souls contributed so much, what might have been the contribution of the one and one-half million children who were robbed of their chance to live and dream?" After reading the piece about Elie Wiesel, how would you answer this question?

3. From where does Wiesel get his strength, and how does it help him empathize with the tragedies of others?

4. Wiesel is not pleased with the word *Holocaust*. Why does he feel this word should be replaced with either the Hebrew word *Shoah* or the word *genocide*? Which would you select? Why?

5. In your opinion, why was Wiesel chosen to receive one of the world's most prestigious awards, the Nobel Peace Prize?

Reflections in Writing

1. Look at a picture of Wiesel. How would you describe him? What do you see?

2. Write a character sketch of Wiesel based on the chapter.

3. Wiesel gave voice to what "could not be spoken, believed or understood." How would you portray the experiences of the Children of Buchenwald and the other victims of the Holocaust? Select an artistic medium to help others understand and remember.

4. In the Foreword to the book, Wiesel gives credit to Judith Hemmendinger for helping him as well as the other children to re-enter the world of the living. Write about a person who has inspired you. How did he or she accomplish this?

5. Of the 1,000 children who were found in Buchenwald, 426 went to Ecouis to begin rebuilding their lives. Many of these adolescents became rabbis, scholars, physicists and physicians, businessmen, and artists. How does a knowledge of the achievements against such overwhelming odds encourage you to live your life? Write a paper that reflects an examination of your own life, the obstacles you face, and your hopes for the future.

Researching the History

1. Elie Wiesel writes, "Our persecution must never be forgotten. I have taken it upon myself to keep it in everyone's memory." Read about Elie Wiesel. What are some of the things he has done to help us remember?

2. Research Wiesel's many accomplishments. Which impresses you most? Explain.

3. Read other chapters from *The Children of Buchenwald*. Give an oral presentation of one child's story before the Holocaust, during the Holocaust, and his life today.

4. The Oeuvre de Secours aux Enfants, or OSE, is the organization that sent Judith Hemmendinger in 1945 to help the Children of Buchenwald in their rehabilitation while in France. Research the life of Hemmendinger as well as the work of the OSE. What did they do that most helped these children?

Lessons for Today

Moral or Ethical Dilemma

A new student comes to your school, having immigrated to the United States a few years earlier. The student wears clothing that is nothing like you or your friends wear. Although this individual has learned English, it is spoken with a thick accent. The person tries to smile and fit in, but he or she is excluded from the group and eats lunch alone in the cafeteria. You would like to get to know this person, but you're afraid your friends will ridicule you or ignore you as well. What do you do?

Making Connections

1. "I realize the importance of talking about this to you, the last generation who will hear this story firsthand—let us build bridges and reach out to each other," says one Holocaust survivor when she speaks to students throughout the world. Author Livia Bitton-Jackson also mentions bridges in her book *My Bridges of Hope*. What bridges do you believe need to be made? What can you do to help build these bridges?

2. Invite a *hidden child* of the Holocaust to your classroom or connect with one by e-mail: holocaustchild@comcast.com. Ask him or her to speak or write on the topic of being one-self—not being afraid to show others who and what we are.

3. During one of her talks to schoolchildren, Ann Shore, whose testimony was included in the book *The Hidden Children* (Marks, 1993), was asked by one child, "What would you do if there was another Holocaust?" She replied: "You know what? It will have to be your job to see that it never happens again. That's why I'm here in your school today. We survivors can tell our stories of the past. What will happen in the future is up to you." Each survivor today is passing the torch to students all over the world. Think about what you can do to prevent such horrors from happening to anyone anywhere. Then, do it!

4. What have you learned about the "power of perseverance?" How can this quality enable you to fulfill your dreams for the future? Create an action plan for a future goal and include the steps that will help you achieve this goal. Then, do it!

Topic 9

The Holocaust, Human Rights, and Social Responsibility

Tikkun Olam: To Heal the World.

— A basic Jewish concept

"Together with the Jew, the image of man was destroyed," says Elie Wiesel. Since the Holocaust, our world has been plagued with acts of terror spawned by hatred. We have been witness to evil and the repression of human rights. Yet throughout the world, the lessons of the Holocaust are being shared and learned by a new generation that will hopefully be inspired to take a stand against injustice, take responsibility for one another, and no longer tolerate prejudice, hatred, and indifference.

It is up to this generation to stand on the shoulders of all those men and women of courage who came before, people whose choices were based on a foundation of moral behavior and a belief in a world of human decency. Creating such a world is not easy, but it is possible. Through education, we can bring people together so we can learn to understand, accept, and celebrate the differences that exist among us.

Today's world is being torn apart by terror and fanaticism. It often seems more divided than ever. We must first understand the roots of hatred so that we can put an end to the death and destruction it causes. In speaking to students, Nobel prize winner and Holocaust survivor Elie Wiesel has said:

> Do not make someone else pay the price for your pain. Do not see in someone else a scapegoat for your difficulties. Only a fanatic does that—not you, for you have learned to reject fanaticism. You know that fanaticism leads to hatred, and hatred is both destructive and self-destructive. . . . I speak to you, for I do not want my past to become your future.

This chapter's topic deals with the ideas and ideals of human rights and social responsibility and considers ways in which we can stop the hate, build bridges, and create a world of peace. The section begins with the aftermath of the Holocaust, the Nuremberg trials, and the implications in terms of moral right and wrong. It also deals into the issue of guilt and responsibility, not only regarding the Holocaust but in light of current world events. Finally, this chapter looks at ways in which people across the nation and across the continents have joined together in order to live together and work together.

Film: *Nuremberg* (TNT Version)

Source: Social Studies School Service
10200 Jefferson Boulevard
P.O. Box 802
Culver City, CA 90232-0802
800-421-4246

Recommended for: High school (mature students only) and college

Summary

After World War II ended, the question of how to punish those responsible for the atrocities committed was considered. U.S. Treasury Secretary Henry Morgenthau thought all captured Nazi leaders should be dealt with immediately without benefit of trial. U.S. Secretary of War Henry Stimson believed that this would violate everything America stood for, including the right to a trial. Finally, Army Colonel Murray Bernays suggested an international court to determine guilt and responsibility. Judges from the United States, Great Britain, France, and the Soviet Union, as well as four alternates, tried high-ranking Nazis deemed personally responsible for specific charges. This was the first time an international court would hold a government responsible for the way it treated its own citizens and citizens of other countries during war time.

This film focuses on the proceedings of the historical international trial held in Nuremberg, Germany, which brought 22 Nazi perpetrators to trial for their war crimes during the Holocaust. Archival film, including that of the liberation of a number of concentration camps, is used throughout this modern version of an earlier film to bring to life the events of the Holocaust as well as the legal proceedings and courtroom strategies of the Nuremberg International Military Tribunal. Alec Baldwin stars as chief prosecutor Robert Jackson.

This is an important film in that it brings to the forefront the concepts of morality, responsibility and culpability. As a result of the issues raised, this film is an excellent springboard for discussion and debate in the classroom. It is 3 hours long.

Symposium: Critical Thinking and Discussion

1. What was the main reason for conducting the Nuremberg trial? What is a "war crimes" trial?

2. The film largely focuses on the Nazi official Hermann Goering. How would you characterize him? What is his attitude toward his role in the Holocaust? What does the film convey to you about this individual and his guilt or responsibility? Cite specific instances in the film that support your answers.

3. Compare the treatment of German officials before and after the announcement of the trial. To what do you attribute these changes?

4. What is the symbolism in choosing the city of Nuremberg as the site for the trial?

5. Who were the people selected to prosecute and preside over the trial? Explain the background and importance of the proceeding.

6. Why is the arrival of the media so important in the history of the Nuremberg trial? Jackson mentions the "melancholy grandeur" of the trial. What oxymoron would you use to describe it?

7. In what ways did the prosecution humanize the victims of the Holocaust rather than talk just about the enormity of the tragedy? How effective was this?

8. What were the findings of the Nuremberg trial? Do you agree or disagree with the various verdicts and sentences? How have these verdicts affected later policy?

9. How did the film manage to show the devastation of the Holocaust while the trial takes place inside a courtroom? What image ends the film? Why do you think the filmmakers chose this image? What lines ended the film? What is your reaction to them?

10. "Some are guilty, all are responsible" is a famous quote concerning the Holocaust. Discuss it in relation to the film.

11. How does the film explore the concepts of *human rights, justice, ethics, fairness, responsibility,* and *guilt*?

12. What do you believe is the most significant legacy of the Nuremberg trial?

13. How will the lessons of the Holocaust impact your life? What have you learned? What will you try to change? What message will you pass on to others?

Reflections in Writing

1. After watching Hermann Goering and listening to his testimony and his conversations with the appointed psychologist, create a character sketch.

2. Imagine that you were a reporter at the time of the Nuremberg trial. Write an editorial that reflects your opinion concerning the significance of the trial to later generations.

3. Based on your knowledge of the Holocaust and the proceedings of the Nuremberg trial, write a paper to explore the principle of individual responsibility.

4. Explore the concept of "man's inhumanity to man."

5. The psychologist Gustav Gilbert defined evil as the "absence of empathy." Consider this and write your own definition of evil. Do you believe that there are individuals who are the personification of evil? Explain.

Researching the History

1. Research the facts of the historic Nuremberg trial on www.ushmm.org. Compare the facts you learned from the film to what you uncovered during your research.

2. Read the text of Jackson's opening statement. Which part(s) of it made the most impact upon you?

3. Since the Nuremberg trial there have been instances of others being accused of *crimes against humanity*. Research this topic and write a summary of one such instance.

4. In a discussion with Gilbert, Goering draws comparisons between racism in the United States in the early 20th century and anti-Semitism in Germany. What conclusions can you draw after researching this topic?

5. After researching the Nuremberg trial in greater depth, do you feel that in the end, it met its goal? Was justice done?

Film: *Not in Our Town*

Sources: California Working Group
P.O. Box 10326
Oakland, CA 94610
(510) 547-8484

Facing History and Ourselves National Foundation, Inc. (lending library)
16 Hurd Road
Brookline, MA 02445
(617) 232-1595

Recommended for: Middle school, high school, and college

Summary

When acts of prejudice and racism threatened to harm certain groups of citizens in Billings, Montana, in 1993, the population took action. Among other things, they organized committees, penned resolutions against hate groups, held rallies, and worked with law enforcement agencies. They let it be known that hate would not be tolerated in their town.

The resolve of the people of Billings, Montana, serves to inspire the viewer and makes each person aware of the dangers of indifference and apathy. Furthermore, the film conveys a powerful message, illustrating "the power of one." It is 26 minutes long.

Symposium: Critical Thinking and Discussion

1. What is a *hate crime* and how does it differ from other crimes? What hate crimes were committed in Billings, Montana? How did these crimes serve to rally the people to action?

2. What were some of the ways in which the community fought prejudice and hate? Which do you believe were most effective?

3. One of the citizens interviewed said that his biggest fear was indifference. Explain the dangers of indifference.

4. In what ways does racism affect everyone, not only those being targeted?

5. A former racist admits that he was once a white supremacist. What might have shaped his earlier views? What might have helped him to change his attitude and perceptions?

Reflections in Writing

1. The people of Billings created a resolution in 1993 that reflected the fact that there would be zero tolerance for hate groups or actions resulting from hate. Write a resolution for your community that takes aim at prejudice and hate.

2. Rallies were held in Billings to demonstrate the community's feelings about prejudice and hate. Create posters with clever captions and illustrations to combat hate. Post these in your school.

3. *Not in Our Town* has inspired other cities to take a stand against racism. For example, in Bloomington, Illinois, an official road sign was erected with a red circle with a slash over the word *racism* followed by the words *Not in Our Town*. The people of Bloomington signed a pledge against intolerance, and police officers wore "Not in Our Town" buttons. Help get your town involved in fighting hatred. Create an advertising campaign that not only encourages citizens to work together to fight racism and persecution but gives suggestions as to how this can be accomplished. With others in the class, create public service announcements— audio and video, and create a web site. Contact local radio and television stations and encourage them to air these pieces.

4. Write a letter to the people of Billings (send it to the editor of the Billings local newspaper) thanking them for their efforts as a community to fight hate.

5. Create a picture book for children in which a main character is involved in a situation that involves a bully. Make sure the book is age-appropriate. Send it to the media specialist of a local elementary school or local library so that it can be shared with children.

Researching the History

1. Surf the Internet to get more information about the events in Billings, Montana on December 12, 1993. What did you learn that adds to your knowledge of what happened there?

2. What other communities can you locate who have done something similar to the efforts of the people of Billings?

3. Research the ways in which hate crimes affect children who are targeted.

4. One of the citizens in the film said that it only takes a small group to do a lot of damage. Find examples in history to support this.

5. Locate organizations such as the Anti-Defamation League that fight prejudice and bigotry. Learn what you can do to support the efforts of one of these organizations, and then get involved.

Memoir: *The Sunflower*

Author: Simon Wiesenthal (1976)

Recommended for: High school and college

Summary

While imprisoned in a Nazi concentration camp, Simon Wiesenthal was taken from his work detail to the bedside of a dying Nazi soldier. The soldier wanted to confess to—and obtain forgiveness from—a Jew. Wiesenthal was faced with the choice between compassion and justice, silence and truth, and his decision haunts him to this day. He wonders if he did the right thing and what others would have done, faced with the same situation.

In *The Sunflower*, Wiesenthal discusses his dilemma and his choice and then poses a question to 53 men and women—theologians, political leaders, writers, jurists, psychiatrists, human rights activists, Holocaust survivors, and victims of other attempted genocides in Bosnia, Cambodia, China, and Tibet. "What would you have done?" he asks. Their responses are varied and thought provoking. *The Sunflower* challenges its readers to define their own beliefs.

Symposium: Critical Thinking and Discussion

1. Wiesenthal said, "There are many kinds of silence. Indeed it can be more eloquent than words, and it can be interpreted in many ways." Discuss the various kinds of silence as expressed in this book. What message did Wiesenthal's silence convey?

2. "In his confession there was true repentance," writes Wiesenthal. Do you believe as did Wiesenthal, or do you believe, as did some of the commentators, that Karl was just remorseful because he knew he was dying?

3. Can we or should we forgive a repentant criminal, no matter how horrible the crime? Are we in the position to forgive a crime committed against others? What do we owe the victims?

4. Most of the essayists agreed with Wiesenthal about not telling the Nazi officer's mother about her son's crimes. However, psychotherapist Andre Stein disagreed and said that it was Wiesenthal's responsibility to tell the truth. With whom do you agree and why?

5. Discuss the main points of the various essays. How do they compare? What similarities can you find? What differences in opinion do they pose?

Reflections in Writing

1. Many concepts are developed in this book: *survival and hope*; *responsibility and choice*; *denial*; *silence*; *forgiveness*; *remembrance*. Select one of these concepts and copy several quotes from the book that reflect it. Then write a paper that reflects your ideas about this concept, using support from the quotes.

2. The Nazi soldier's mother discussed the question of Germany's guilt and said, "In this district we always lived with the Jews in a very peaceful fashion. We are not responsible for their fate." Do you agree or disagree? Write a persuasive paper to convey your views.

3. Select one of the essays written to answer the question "What would you do?" Summarize the essay and then debate its main points with others who read the same essay.

4. Form groups with others who read different essays. Discuss each writer's answer and the reasons behind it. As a group, whose viewpoint most closely matches your own? Explain in a journal entry.

5. In the poem "Silence," Edgar Lee Masters writes about an array of "silences": "the silence of the stars and the sea . . . the silence of the sick . . . the silence of great hatred and the silence of great love…the silence of a spiritual crisis . . . the silence of defeat." Research this poem and write your own poem about the silences that exist in the world today.

Researching the History

1. Simon Wiesenthal was born in 1908 in Buczacz, Galicia, then part of the Austro-Hungarian Empire. He was working in an architectural office in Lvov when Poland was invaded by the Nazis. Research the life of this man before, during, and after the war. He has been honored with numerous awards for his work as well as with 16 honorary doctorates. To what extent do you believe that Wiesenthal's experience as a Nazi hunter was his response to the question posed in his book?

2. Research the work of the Simon Wiesenthal Center. What are its main objectives? How well has the center done in achieving its goals?

3. "The Heavy Burden of Being German" (*Miami Herald*, May 7, 1995) was written by a young German writer, Annette Wronka, who has worked for U.S. news organizations as a translator and researcher. Locate and read this article, in which she expresses the fact that she does not believe in *collective guilt* but she does believe in *collective responsibility*. Compare her feelings with those of essayists such as Dith Pran, who draws a moral line between followers and leaders. Research the concept of collective guilt and collective responsibility. What are your views on both?

Document: *The United Nations' Universal Declaration of Human Rights*

Source: United Nations, 1948

Recommended for: Middle school and high school

Summary

The United Nations' Universal Declaration of Human Rights was created in 1948 in direct response to the horrors of the Holocaust and the poverty of much of the world's population. Proclaimed by the United Nations General Assembly, the Declaration lists 30 important rights as a standard of achievement for all people and all nations. Although almost all countries promise to protect human rights, events are unfolding in our world every day in which these same rights are violated.

Following is the text of the Declaration:

UNIVERSAL DECLARATION OF HUMAN RIGHTS

Preamble

Whereas recognition of the inherent dignity and of the equal and inalienable rights of all members of the human family is the foundation of freedom, justice and peace in the world,

Whereas disregard and contempt for human rights have resulted in barbarous acts which have outraged the conscience of mankind, and the advent of a world in which human beings shall enjoy freedom of speech and belief and freedom from fear and want has been proclaimed as the highest aspiration of the common people,

Whereas it is essential, if man is not to be compelled to have recourse, as a last resort, to rebellion against tyranny and oppression, that human rights should be protected by the rule of law,

Whereas it is essential to promote the development of friendly relations between nations,

Whereas the peoples of the United Nations have in the Charter reaffirmed their faith in fundamental human rights, in the dignity and worth of the human person and in the equal rights of men and women and have determined to promote social progress and better standards of life in larger freedom,

Whereas Member States have pledged themselves to achieve, in co-operation with the United Nations, the promotion of universal respect for and observance of human rights and fundamental freedoms,

Whereas a common understanding of these rights and freedoms is of the greatest importance for the full realization of this pledge,

Now, therefore,

THE GENERAL ASSEMBLY

Proclaims this Universal Declaration of Human Rights as a common standard of achievement for all peoples and all nations, to the end that every individual and every organ of society, keeping this Declaration constantly in mind, shall strive by teaching and education to promote respect for these rights and freedoms and by progressive measures, national and international, to secure their universal and effective recognition and observance, both among the peoples of Member States themselves and among the peoples of territories under their jurisdiction.

Article 1

All human beings are born free and equal in dignity and rights. They are endowed with reason and conscience and should act towards one another in a spirit of brotherhood.

Article 2

Everyone is entitled to all the rights and freedoms set forth in this Declaration, without distinction of any kind, such as race, colour, sex, language, religion, political or other opinion, national or social origin, property, birth or other status.

Furthermore, no distinction shall be made on the basis of the political, jurisdictional or international status of the country or territory to which a person belongs, whether it be independent, trust, non-self-governing or under any other limitation of sovereignty.

Article 3

Everyone has the right to life, liberty and the security of person.

Article 4

No one shall be held in slavery or servitude; slavery and the slave trade shall be prohibited in all their forms.

Article 5

No one shall be subjected to torture or to cruel, inhuman or degrading treatment or punishment.

Article 6

Everyone has the right to recognition everywhere as a person before the law.

Article 7

All are equal before the law and are entitled without any discrimination to equal protection against any discrimination in violation of this Declaration and against any incitement to such discrimination.

Article 8

Everyone has the right to an effective remedy by the competent national tribunals for acts violating the fundamental rights granted him by the constitution or by law.

Article 9

No one shall be subjected to arbitrary arrest, detention or exile.

Article 10

Everyone is entitled in full equality to a fair, and public hearing by an independent and impartial tribunal, in the determination of his rights and obligations and of any criminal charge against him.

Article 11

1. Everyone charged with a penal offence has the right to be presumed innocent until proven guilty according to law in a public trial at which he has had all the guarantees necessary for his defence.
2. No one shall be held guilty of any penal offence on account of any act or omission which did not constitute a penal offence, under national or international law, at the time when it was committed. Nor shall a heavier penalty be imposed than the one that was applicable at the time the penal offence was committed.

Article 12

No one shall be subjected to arbitrary interference with his privacy, family, home or correspondence, nor to attacks upon his honour and reputation. Everyone has the right to the protection of the law against such interference or attacks.

Article 13

1. Everyone has the right to freedom of movement and residence within the borders of each State.

2. Everyone has the right to leave any country, including his own, and to return to his country.

Article 14

1. Everyone has the right to seek and to enjoy in other countries asylum from persecution.

2. This right may not be invoked in the case of prosecutions genuinely arising from non-political crimes or from acts contrary to the purposes and principles of the United Nations.

Article 15

1. Everyone has the right to a nationality.

2. No one shall be arbitrarily deprived of his nationality nor denied the right to change his nationality.

Article 16

1. Men and women of full age, without any limitation due to race, nationality or religion, have the right to marry and to found a family. They are entitled to equal rights as to marriage, during marriage and at its dissolution.

2. Marriage shall be entered into only with the free and full consent of the intending spouses.

3. The family is the natural and fundamental group unit of society and is entitled to protection by society and the State.

Article 17

1. Everyone has the right to own property alone as well as in association with others.

2. No one shall be arbitrarily deprived of his property.

Article 18

Everyone has the right to freedom of thought, conscience and religion; this right includes freedom to change his religion or belief, and freedom, either alone or in community with others and in public or private, to manifest his religion or belief in teaching, practice, worship and observance.

Article 19

Everyone has the right to freedom of opinion and expression; this right includes freedom to hold opinions without interference and to seek, receive and impart information and ideas through any media and regardless of frontiers.

Article 20

1. Everyone has the right to freedom of peaceful assembly and association.

2. No one may be compelled to belong to an association.

Article 21

1. Everyone has the right to take part in the government of his country, directly or through freely chosen representatives.

2. Everyone has the right of equal access to public service in his country.

3. The will of the people shall be the basis of the authority of government; this will shall be expressed in periodic and genuine elections which shall be by universal and equal suffrage and shall be held by secret vote or by equivalent free voting procedures.

Article 22

Everyone, as a member of society, has the right to social security and is entitled to realization, through national effort and international co-operation and in accordance with the organization and resources of each State, of the economic, social and cultural rights indispensable for his dignity and the free development of his personality.

Article 23

1. Everyone has the right to work, to free choice of employment, to just and favourable conditions of work and to protection against unemployment.

2. Everyone, without any discrimination, has the right to equal pay for equal work.

3. Everyone who works has the right to just and favourable remuneration ensuring for himself and his family an existence worthy of human dignity, and supplemented, if necessary, by other means of social protection.

4. Everyone has the right to form and to join trade unions for the protection of his interests.

Article 24

Everyone has the right to rest and leisure, including reasonable limitation of working hours and periodic holidays with pay.

Article 25

1. Everyone has the right to a standard of living adequate for the health and well-being of himself and of his family, including food, clothing, housing and medical care and necessary social services, and the right to security in the event of unemployment, sickness, disability, widowhood, old age or other lack of livelihood in circumstances beyond his control.

2. Motherhood and childhood are entitled to special care and assistance. All children, whether born in or out of wedlock, shall enjoy the same social protection.

Article 26

1. Everyone has the right to education. Education shall be free, at least in the elementary and fundamental stages. Elementary education shall be compulsory. Technical and professional education shall be made generally available and higher education shall be equally accessible to all on the basis of merit.

2. Education shall be directed to the full development of the human personality and to the strengthening of respect for human rights and fundamental freedoms. It shall promote understanding, tolerance and friendship among all nations, racial or religious groups, and shall further the activities of the United Nations for the maintenance of peace.

3. Parents have a prior right to choose the kind of education that shall be given to their children.

Article 27

1. Everyone has the right freely to participate in the cultural life of the community, to enjoy the arts and to share in scientific advancement and its benefits.

2. Everyone has the right to the protection of the moral and material interests resulting from any scientific, literary or artistic production of which he is the author.

Article 28

Everyone is entitled to a social and international order in which the rights and freedoms set forth in this Declaration can be fully realized.

Article 29

1. Everyone has duties to the community in which alone the free and full development of his personality is possible.

2. In the exercise of his rights and freedoms, everyone shall be subject only to such limitations as are determined by law solely for the purpose of securing due recognition and respect for the rights and freedoms of others and of meeting the just requirements of morality, public order and the general welfare in a democratic society.

3. These rights and freedoms may in no case be exercised contrary to the purposes and principles of the United Nations.

Article 30

Nothing in this Declaration may be interpreted as implying for any State, group or person any right to engage in any activity or to perform any act aimed at the destruction of any of the rights and freedoms set forth herein.

Symposium: Critical Thinking and Discussion

1. Which of these human rights were most often violated during the Holocaust? Select one of the human rights that was violated. From your study of the Holocaust, give specific examples of the ways in which this right was violated.

2. Of the rights listed in the Declaration, which, if violated, would most impact your own life? Explain.

3. The Declaration of Human Rights is not a treaty and lacks any enforcement provisions. It is a set of principles to which the member nations of the United Nations made a commitment. Discuss the ways in which our country does and does not adequately address certain economic and social rights mentioned in the Declaration.

4. Read the paragraphs preceding the articles. What ideas are presented about the positive and negative aspects of human nature?

5. Do you believe this Declaration of Human Rights makes a difference in the world today? Explain.

Reflections in Writing

1. Select one of the rights mentioned in number 3 above that you believe is not being addressed sufficiently by our government. Write a letter to national leaders to challenge them to fix what needs fixing and ensure that this right is guaranteed to all people in our nation.

2. The Declaration of Human Rights was written in 1948. Since that time, many events affecting human rights have surfaced. Create an additional right that would be relevant to today's world and explain why you think it is vital to add it to the Declaration.

3. Create a Web site dedicated to human rights education and issues. Encourage students to contribute any information dealing with human rights in our country and throughout the world. Disseminate information about this Web site to other schools in your county, district, or state.

4. Create a Universal Declaration of Students Rights that includes rights that will better enable you to learn, get along with peers, and respect individual differences. Make copies of this Declaration and post it around school and share it with the media.

Researching the History

1. Research the history of the United Nation's Universal Declaration of Human Rights.

2. What steps would be needed to amend the Declaration in order to add additional rights that have become apparent based on world events since 1948?

3. Research various human rights organizations such as Amnesty International and the Red Cross. Select the organization whose work you most admire and contact it to learn what you and your classmates can do to further its objectives.

Lessons for Today

Moral or Ethical Dilemma

Discuss and debate the following quote, "We are morally responsible for wrongs we have the power to prevent and fail to do so." Use support from past and current events.

Making Connections

1. The right to vote is one of the most important American rights. Discuss and debate this democratic process and the privileges and responsibilities that go with it.
   - Why is it important for citizens to understand the philosophy and platforms of the various candidates?
   - Why is it so important that each eligible citizen exercise his or her right to vote?
   - Why is it important that students your age understand the obligation of voting and become involved in the political process?

2. In what ways can you speak out today to bring attention to injustices in human rights?

3. We are constantly influenced by what we see and hear in the media. Select a speech from the past or present that has influenced the course of history. Listen to the speech and analyze it to see what about it made it so effective (e.g., Martin Luther King's "I Have a Dream" speech, The Gettysburg Address) Create a speech of your own to inspire others to right a wrong.

4. Rabbi Harold S. Kushner, author of *When Bad Things Happen to Good People*, composed a prayer for readers of *Parade* magazine (March 23, 2003, p. 5) entitled "Prayer for the World." In it he writes, "Let the rain come and wash away the ancient grudges, the bitter hatreds held and nurtured over generations." Write your own hope for the world.

5. We know what words can do to harm, but conversely, words can create joy and hope. A new Web site, "Words Can Heal," is part of a national campaign dedicated to bringing people together by combating verbal violence and gossip. Visit the Web site and learn what you can do to use words to heal rather than hurt: www.wordscanheal.org.

6. In the article "How Can We Understand Their Hatred? *(Parade* magazine, April 7, 2002, pp. 4–5), Elie Wiesel wrote that terrorism and hatred cannot be stemmed until we fight indifference. "Indifference to evil is the enemy of good, for indifference is the enemy of everything that exalts the honor of man. We fight indifference through education; we diminish it through compassion. The most efficient remedy? Memory."

How does memory help us to fight indifference? How does memory help us as we move from the Holocaust and from the genocides in Cambodia, Rwanda, and Bosnia? How does it help us to fight the terrorism that allowed 9/11 to occur? How does it help us to understand the tragedy of Columbine and ensure "Never again"? How does it help us to fight hate?

What will you do with your memories of these and other tragedies to make this world a better place? How will you fight hatred and indifference?

There are many possibilities. Check the Web site of Tolerance.org—www.tolerance.org—for 101 ideas and successful strategies that have worked for others, such as the following:

- Attend a play, listen to music, or go to a dance performed by artists whose race or ethnicity is different from you own.

- Volunteer at a local social service organization.

- Speak up when you hear slurs. Let people know that prejudiced speech is always unacceptable.

- Start a pen-pal program. Get in touch with people in different parts of the community or even the world.

- Sponsor a conflict resolution team.

Appendixes

Bibliography

Professional Bibliography

Videography

Webography

Resource Centers

Holocaust Training Programs

Appendix A

Bibliography

Note: The U.S. Holocaust Museum in Washington, D.C. has one of the finest bibliographies of books and videos: U.S. Holocaust Memorial Museum
100 Raoul Wallenberg Place SW
Washington, DC 20024-2150
(800) 259-9998
http://www.ushmm.org/

Copyright dates are given for original publication; however, subsequent paperback editions, in many instances, have been published!

I. History

Altshuler, David. (1978). *Hitler's War Against the Jews—the Holocaust: A Young Reader's Version of the War Against the Jews, 1933–1945 by Lucy Dawidowicz:* West Orange, NJ: Behrman House. (Middle school, high school, and up)

Arad, Yitzhak. (1982). *Ghetto in Flames.* New York: Holocaust. (High school and up)

Bachrach, Susan D. (1994). *Tell Them We Remember: The Story of the Holocaust.* Boston: Little, Brown. (Middle school, high school, and up)

Bachrach, Susan D. (2000). *The Nazi Olympics.* Boston: Little, Brown. (Middle school, high school, and up)

Bauer, Yehuda, & Keren, Nili. *A History of the Holocaust.* New York: Watts. (High school and up)

Chaikin, Miriam. (1987). *A Nightmare in History: The Holocaust, 1933–1945.* New York: Clarion. (Middle school and up)

Friedrich, Ono. (1994). *The Kingdom of Auschwitz.* New York: HarperCollins. (High school and up)

Friedman, Ina. R. (1990). *The Other Victims: First-Person Stories of Non-Jews Persecuted by the Nazis.* Boston: Houghton Mifflin. (Middle school, high school, and up)

Gilbert, Martin. (1986). *The Holocaust: A History of the Jews in Europe During the Second World War.* New York: Holt. (High school and up)

Grolier Encyclopedia. (1997). *The Holocaust.* 4 vols. Danbury, CT: Grolier Educational. (All levels)

Meltzer, Milton. (1997). *Never to Forget: The Jews of the Holocaust.* New York: Dell. (Middle school, high school, and up)

Opfermann, Charlotte G. (2002). *The Art of Darkness.* Houston, TX: University Trace Press. (High school and up)

Read, Anthony, & Fisher, David. (1989). *Kristallnacht: The Tragedy of the Nazi Night of Terror.* New York: Random House. (High school and up)

Rogasky, Barbara. (1988). *Smoke and Ashes: The Story of the Holocaust.* New York: Holiday. (Middle school, high school, and up)

II. Voices: Biography, Personal Accounts, Memoirs

Appleman-Jurman, Alicia. (1988). *Alicia: My Story.* New York: Bantam. (Middle school, high school, and up)

Auerbacher, Inge. (1987). *I Am a Star: Child of the Holocaust.* New York: Prentice-Hall. (Middle and high school)

Auerbacher, Inge. (1997). *Beyond the Yellow Star to America.* New York: Royal Fireworks Press. (Middle, high school)

Ayer, Eleanor, & Heck, Alfons. (1995). *Parallel Journeys.* New York: Aladdin. (Middle school, high school, and up)

Bitton-Jackson, Livia. (1997). *I Have Lived a Thousand Years: Growing Up in the Holocaust.* New York Scholastic. (Middle school and high school)

Bitton-Jackson, Livia. (2002). *Bridges of Hope: Searching for Life and Love After Auschwitz.* New York: Simon Pulse. (Middle school, high school, and up)

Boas, Jacob. (1995). *We Are Witnesses: Five Diaries of Teenagers Who Died in the Holocaust.* New York: Scholastic. (Middle school and high school)

Brown, Jean E., Stephens, Elaine C., & Rubin, Janet E. (1997). *Images of the Holocaust: A Literature Anthology.* Lincolnwood, IL: NTC. (High school and up)

Drucker, Olga Levy. (1992). *Kindertransport.* New York: Holt. (Middle school, high school, and up)

Eliach, Yaffa. (1982). *Hasidic Tales of the Holocaust.* New York: Random House. (Middle school, high school, and up)

Eliach, Yaffa. (1990). *We Were Children Just Like You.* Brooklyn, New York: Center for Holocaust Studies Documentation and Research Center. (High school and up)

Filpovic, Zlata. (1995). *Zlata's Diary: A Child's Life in Sarajevo.* New York: Penguin. (Middle school and high school)

Fox, Anne L., & Abraham-Podietz, Eva. (1998). *Ten Thousand Children: True Stories Told by Children Who Escaped the Holocaust on the Kindertransport.* Berhman House. (Middle school and high school)

Frank, Otto, & Pressler, Mirjam. (Eds.). (1995). *Anne Frank: The Diary of a Young Girl.* New York: Bantam Doubleday. (Middle school, high school, and up)

Friedman, Ina. (1990). *The Other Victims: First-Person Stories of Non-Jews Persecuted by the Nazis.* Boston: Houghton Mifflin. (Upper elementary school and middle school)

Gies, Miep. (1988). *Anne Frank Remembered: The Story of the Woman Who Helped to Hide the Frank Family.* New York: Simon and Schuster. (High school and up)

Gold, Ruth. (1996). *Ruth's Journey.* University Press of Florida. (High school and up)

Helmreich, William B. (1992). *Against All Odds: Holocaust Survivors and the Successful Lives They Made in America.* New York: Simon and Schuster. (High school and up)

Hemmendinger, Judith, & Krell, Robert. (2000). *The Children of Buchenwald.* New York: Geffen. (Middle school and up)

Isaacman, Clara, & Grossman, Joan. (1984). *Clara's Story.* Philadelphia: Jewish Publication Society. (Upper elementary and middle school)

Klein, Gerda Weissmann. (1995). *All But My Life.* New York: Hill and Wang. (High School and up)

Leitner, Isabella. (1983). *Fragments of Isabella: A Memoir of Auschwitz.* New York: Dell. (High school and up)

Leitner, Isabela. (1992). *The Big Lie: A True Story.* New York: Scholastic. (Upper elementary school and middle school)

Levi, Primo. (1987). *Survival in Auschwitz.* New York: Macmillan. (High school and up)

Lobel, Anita. (1998). *No Pretty Pictures: A Child of War.* New York: Greenwillow. (Middle school and high school)

Marks, Jane. (1993). *The Hidden Children: The Secret Survivors of the Holocaust.* New York: Ballantine. (High school and up)

Mayer, Bernard. (1994). *Entombed.* Ojus, FL: Aleric Press. (Upper elementary school, middle school, high school, and up)

Perl, Lila, & Blumenthal, Marion. (1996). *Four Perfect Pebbles.* New York: Greeenwillow. (Middle school and high school)

Reiss, Johanna. (1990). *The Upstairs Room.* New York: HarperCollins. (Upper elementary and middle school)

Roth-Hano, Renee. (1989). *Touch Wood: A Girlhood in Occupied France.* New York: Puffin Books. (Upper elementary and middle school)

Sender, Ruth. (1986). *The Cage.* New York: Macmillan. (Middle school and high school)

Sendyk, Helen. (2000a). *The End of Days: A Memoir of the Holocaust.* Syracuse, NY: Syracuse University Press. (High school and up)

Sendyk, Helen. (2000b). *New Dawn: The Triumph of Life After the Holocaust.* Syracuse, NY: Syracuse University Press. (High school and up)

Siegal, Aranka. (1985). *Grace in the Wilderness*. New York: Farrar, Straus, and Giroux. (Middle school and high school)

Siegal, Aranka. (1994). *Upon the Head of the Goat: A Childhood in Hungary, 1939–1944*. New York: Puffin Books. (Middle school and high school)

Stagg, Sophal Leng. (1998). *Hear Me Now: Tragedy in Cambodia*. Tampa, FL: Mancorp. (High school and up)

Szpilman, Wladyslaw. (1999). *The Pianist*. New York: Picador. (High school and up)

Tec, Nechama. (1984). *Dry Tears: The Story of a Lost Childhood*. New York: Oxford University Press. (High school and up)

Tec, Nechama. (2003). *Resilience and Courage: Women, Men and the Holocaust*: New Haven, CT: Yale University Press. (High school and up)

Toll, Nelly. (1993). *Behind the Secret Window*: *A Memoir of a Hidden Childhood During World War II*. New York: Dial Books. (Middle school and high school)

Van der Rol, Ruud, & Verhoeven, Rian. (1993). *Anne Frank: Beyond the Diary*. New York: Viking. (Upper elementary school and middle school)

Wiesel, Elie. (1982). *Night*. New York: Bantam. (High school and up)

Wiesel, Elie. (1995). *All the Rivers Run to the Sea*. New York: Schocken. (High school and up)

Wiesenthal, Simon. (1976). *The Sunflower: On the Possibilities and Limits of Forgiveness*. New York: Schocken. (High school and up)

Wygoda, Hermann. (1998). *In the Shadow of the Swastika*. Urbana: University of Illinois Press. (High school and up)

Zapruder, Alexandra. (2002). *Salvaged Pages: Young Writers' Diaries of the Holocaust*. New Haven, CT: Yale University Press. (High school and up)

III. Historical Fiction

Ackerman, Karen. (1993). *The Night Crossing*. New York: Knopf. (Elementary school)

Applefeld, Aharon. (1986). *To the Land of the Cattails*. New York: Weidenfeld and Nicolson. (High school and up)

Bunting, Eve. (1989). *Terrible Things: An Allegory of the Holocaust*. Philadelphia: Jewish Publication Society. (All levels)

Fink, Ida. (1987). *A Scrap of Time and Other Stories*. New York: Pantheon Books. (High school and up)

Hesse, Karen. (1992). *Letters From Rifka*. New York: Puffin Books. (Upper elementary school and middle school)

Hoestlandt, Jo. (1995). *Star of Fear, Star of Hope*. New York: Walker. (Elementary school)

Innocenti, Roberto. (1991). *Rose Blanche*. New York: Steward Tabori and Chang. (Upper elementary school)

Lowry, Lois. (1989). *Number the Stars.* Boston: Houghton Mifflin. (Upper elementary school and middle school)

Matas, Carol. (1989). *Lisa's War.* New York: Scribner's. (Upper elementary and middle school)

Matas, Carol. (1993). *Daniel's Story.* New York: Scholastic. (Upper elementary school and middle school)

Oppenheim, Shulamith Levey. (1992). *The Lily Cupboard: A Story of the Holocaust.* New York: HarperCollins. (Elementary School)

Orlev, Uri. (1981). *The Island on Bird Street.* Boston: Houghton Mifflin. (Middle school and high school)

Orlev, Uri. (1991). *The Man From the Other Side.* Boston: Houghton Mifflin. (Middle school and high school)

Ozick, Cynthia. (1990). *The Shawl.* New York: Random House. (High school and up)

Richter, Hans. (1987). *Friedrich.* New York: Puffin Books. (Upper elementary school and middle school)

Schnur, Steven. (1994). *The Shadow Children.* New York: Morrow. (Middle school)

Uris, Leon. (1962). *Mila 18.* New York: Bantam Books. (High school)

Yolen, Jane. (1988). *The Devil's Arithmetic.* New York: Viking. (Upper elementary school and middle school)

IV. Resistance and Rescue

Atkinson, Linda. (1992). *In Kindling Flame: The Story of Hannah Senesh, 1921–1944.* New York: Morrow. (Middle school, high school, and up)

Bierman, John. (1981). *Righteous Gentile: The Story of Raoul Wallenberg, Missing Hero of the Holocaust.* New York: Viking. (High school)

Block, Gay, & Drucker, Malka. (1992). *Rescuers: Portraits of Moral Courage in the Holocaust.* New York: Holmes and Meier. (Middle school and high school)

Friedman, Phillip. (1978). *Their Brothers' Keepers: The Christian Heroes and Heroines Who Helped the Oppressed Escape the Nazi Terror.* New York: Anti-Defamation League. (High school and up)

Fremon, David K. (1998). *The Holocaust Heroes.* New York: Enslow. (Middle school and high school)

Harris, Mark Jonathan, & Oppenheimer, Deborah. (2000). *Into the Arms of Strangers: Stories of the Kindertransport.* New York: Bloomsbury. (High school and up)

Hilberg, Raul. (1985). *The Destruction of the European Jews.* New York: Holmes and Meier. (High school and up)

Keneally, Thomas. (1992). *Schindler's List.* New York: Simon and Schuster. (High school and up)

Lifton, Betty Jean. (1989). *The King of Children: A Portrait of Janusz Korczak.* New York: Schocken. (High school and up)

Meed, Vladka. (1979). *On Both Sides of the Wall.* New York: Holocaust. (High school and up)

Meltzer, Milton. (1991). *Rescue: The Story of How Gentiles Saved Jews in the Holocaust.* New York: HarperCollins. (All levels)

Mochizuki, Ken. (1997). *Passage to Freedom: The Sugihara Story.* Lee & Low. (Upper elementary school and middle school)

Rittner, Carol, and Meyers, (Eds.). (1989). *The Courage to Care: Rescuers of Jews During the Holocaust.* New York: New York University Press. (High school and up)

Scholl, Inge. (1983). *The White Rose: Munich, 1942–43.* Hanover, NH: University Press of New England. (High school and up)

Schur, Maxine. (1986). *Hannah Szenes: A Song of Light.* Philadelphia: Jewish Publication Society. (Middle school and high school)

Stadtler, Bea. (1975). *The Holocaust: A History of Courage and Resistance.* West Orange, NJ: Behrman House. (All levels)

Ten Boom, Corrie. (1986). *The Hiding Place.* New York: Macmillan. (Upper elementary and middle school)

Vinke, Hermann. (1980). *The Short Life of Sophie Scholl.* New York: Harper & Row. (Middle school and high school)

V. Poetry, Art, Photographs

Abells, Chana Byers. (1983). *The Children We Remember.* New York: Greenwillow. (All levels)

Bernbaum, Israel. (1985). *My Brother's Keeper: The Holocaust Through the Eyes of an Artist.* New York: Putnam. (Middle school and high school)

Blatter, Janet, & Milton, Sybil (Eds.) (1981). *Art of the Holocaust.* New York: Rutledge Press. (High school and up)

Langer, Lawrence L. (1995). *Art From the Ashes: A Holocaust Anthology.* New York: Oxford University Press. (High school and up)

Schiff, Hilda. (1995). *Holocaust Poetry.* New York: St. Martin's Griffin. (Middle school and high school)

Silten, R. Gabriele. (1991). *High Tower Crumbling.* Santa Barbara, CA: Fithian Press. (Middle school and high school)

Toll, Nelly. (1975). *Without Surrender: Art of the Holocaust.* Philadelphia: Running Press. (Middle school and high school)

Volavkova, Hana. (Ed.). (1993). *I Never Saw Another Butterfly: Children's Drawings and Poems From Terezin Concentration Camp, 1942–1944.* New York: Schocken. (All levels)

Appendix B

Professional Bibliography

Arad, Yitzhak, Gutman, Israel, & Margaliot, Abraham (Eds.). (1996). *Documents on the Holocaust.* Jerusalem: Yad Vashem.

Bauer, Yehuda. (2001). *A History of the Holocaust.* New York: Watts.

Bauer, Yehuda. (2001). *Rethinking the Holocaust.* New Haven, CT: Yale University Press.

Berenbaum, Michael. (1993). *The World Must Know: A History of the Holocaust as Told in the United States Holocaust Memorial Museum.* Boston: Little, Brown.

Berger, Alan, & Berger Naomi. (Eds.). (2001). *Second Generation Voices: Reflections by Children of Holocaust Survivors and Perpetrators,* Syracuse, NY: Syracuse University Press.

Berger, James. (1999). *After the End.* Minneapolis: University of Minnesota Press.

Black, Edwin. (2001). *IBM and the Holocaust.* New York: Crown.

Blatter, Janet, & Milton, Sybil. (1981). *Art of the Holocaust.* New York: Routledge Press.

Brown, Jean E., Stephens, Elaine C., & Rubin, Janet E. (1997). *Images from the Holocaust: A Literature Anthology.* Lincolnwood, IL. NTC.

Browning, Christopher. (1992). *Ordinary Men: Reserve Battalion 101 and the Final Solution in Poland.* New York: HarperCollins.

Cargas, Harry James. (1981). *A Christian Response to the Holocaust.* Denver, CO: Stonehenge.

Davidowicz, Lucy. (1976). *A Holocaust Reader.* West Orange, NJ: Behrman House.

Davidowicz, Lucy. (1986). *The War Against the Jews, 1933–1945.* New York: Bantam.

Dwork, Deborah. (1991). *Children with a Star: Jewish Youth in Nazi Europe.* New Haven, CT: Yale University Press.

Dwork, Deborah, & Van Pelt, Robert. (2002). *Holocaust: A History.* New York: Norton.

Eliach, Yaffa. (1999). *There Once Was a World.* Boston: Little, Brown.

Epstein, Helen. (1988). *Children of the Holocaust.* New York: Viking Penguin.

Feinstein, Stephen. (1994). *Witness and Legacy: Contemporary Art About the Holocaust.* Minneapolis, MN: Lerner.

Fink, Ida. (1984). *A Scrap of Time and Other Stories.* Evanston, IL: Northwestern University Press.

Fleming, Gerald. (1982): *Hitler and the Final Solution.* Berkeley: University of California Press.

Fogelman, Eva. (1994). *Conscience and Courage: Rescuers of Jews During the Holocaust.* New York: Anchor Books.

Fry, Varian. (1992). *Assignment Rescue.* New York: Scholastic.

Gilbert, Martin. (1988). *Atlas of the Holocaust.* New York: Pergamon Press.

Gilbert, Martin. (1997). *Holocaust Journey: Traveling in Search of the Past.* New York: Columbia University Press.

Goldhagen, Daniel. (1996). *Hitler's Willing Executioners.* New York: Knopf.

Goldsmith, Martin. (2000). *The Inextinguishable Symphony.* New York: Wiley.

Gurewitsch, Bonnie. (1998). *Mothers, Sisters, and Resisters: Oral Histories of Women Who Survived the Holocaust.* University of Alabama Press.

Gutman, Israel. (1990). *Encyclopedia of the Holocaust.* New York: Macmillan.

Gutman, Israel, & Berenbaum, Michael. (Eds.). (1994). *Anatomy of the Auschwitz Death Camp.* Bloomington: Indiana University Press.

Helmreich, William B. (1992). *Against All Odds: Holocaust Survivors and the Successful Lives They Made in America.* New York: Simon and Schuster.

Hemmendinger, Judith, & Krell, Robert. (2000). *The Children of Buchenwald.* New York: Geffen.

Heyen, William. (1984). *Erika: Poems of the Holocaust.* New York: Vanguard Press.

Hilberg, Raul. (1985). *The Destruction of the European Jews* (3 vols). New York: Holmes and Meier.

Jackal, Eberhard. (1990). *Hitler in History.* University Press of New England.

Kaplan, Marian. (1988). *Between Dignity and Despair: Jewish Life in Nazi Germany.* New York: Oxford University.

Kershaw, Ian. (1991). *Profiles in Power—Hitler.* London: Longman.

Langer, Lawrence (Ed.). (1995). *Art From the Ashes.* New York: Oxford University Press.

Levi, Primo. (1986). *The Drowned and the Saved.* New York: Summit Books.

Lifton, Betty Jean. (1997) *The King of Children: The Life and Death of Janusz Korczak.* New York: St. Martin's.

Lipstadt, Deborah. (1993). *Denying the Holocaust.* New York: Free Press.

Littel, Marcia Sachs, & Gutman, Sharon Weissman. (1991). *Liturgies on the Holocaust.* Valley Forge, PA: Trinity Press.

Lozowick, Yaakow. (2002). *Hitler's Bureaucrats. The Nazi Security Police and the Banality of Evil.* New York: Continuum.

Marrus, Michael. (1987). *The Holocaust in History.* New York: Penguin.

Meed, Vladka. (1979). *On Both Sides of the Wall.* New York: Holocaust.

Melson, Robert. (2000). *False Papers: Deception and Survival in the Holocaust.* Chicago: University of Illinois.

Milton, Sybil. (1984). *Women and the Holocaust—The Case of German and German-Jewish Women.* Monthly Review Press.

Nicholas, Lynn. (1995). *The Rape of Europa: The Fate of Europe's Treasures in the Third Reich.* Vintage Books.

Novick, Peter. (1999). *The Holocaust in American Life.* Boston: Houghton Mifflin.

Ofer, Dalia, & Weitzman, Lenore J. (Eds). (1998). *Women in the Holocaust.* New Haven, CT: Yale University Press.

Paldiel, Mordecai. (2000). *Saving the Jews.* Rockville, MD: Schreiber.

Rapaport, Lynn. (1997). *Jews in Germany After the Holocaust.* Cambridge, UK: Cambridge University Press.

Ringelblum, Emmanuel. (1974). *Notes From the Warsaw Ghetto: The Journal of Emmanuel Ringelblum.* New York: Schocken.

Rittner, Carol. (1989). *The Courage to Care: Rescuers of Jews During the Holocaust.* New York: University Press.

Ritvo, Roger, & Plotkin, Diane. (1998). *Sisters in Sorrow.* College Station, TX: A&M University Press.

Rosenbaum, Ronald. (1999). *Explaining Hitler: The Search for the Origins of His Evil.* New York: HarperCollins.

Roth, John, & Berenbaum, Michael. (Eds.). (1991). *Holocaust Religious and Philosophical Implications.* New York: Praeger.

Saidel, Rochelle G. (2004). *The Jewish Women of Ravensbruck Concentration Camp.* Madison: University of Wisconsin Press.

Shulman, William. (2002). *Where Have All the Children Gone? Jewish Refugee Children During the Holocaust.* New York: City University of New York.

Tec, Nechama. (1984). *Dry Tears: The Story of a Lost Childhood.* New York: Oxford University Press.

Tec, Nechama. (1987). *When Light Pierced the Darkness: Christian Rescue of Jews in Nazi Occupied Poland.* New York: Oxford University Press.

Tec, Nechama. (1993). *Defiance: The Bielsky Partisans.* New York: Oxford University Press.

Tec, Nechama. (2003). *Resilience and Courage: Women, Men and the Holocaust.* New Haven, CT: Yale University Press.

Teichman, Milton, & Leder, Sharon. (1994). *Truth and Lamentations: Stories and Poems on the Holocaust.* University of Illinois Press.

Wiesel, Elie. (1982). *Night.* New York: Bantam.

Wiesel, Elie. (1995). *All Rivers Run to the Sea.* New York: Knopf.

Wiesel, Elie. (1999). *The Sea Is Never Full.* New York: Knopf.

Wyman, David S. (1986). *The Abandonment of the Jews.* New York: Pantheon.

Curriculum Resources

Meinbach, Anita Meyer, & Kassenoff, Miriam Klein. (1997). *The Holocaust: A Grolier Student Educational Encyclopedia for Upper Elementary, Middle and High School Students.* Danbury, CT: Grolier Educational.

Meinbach, Anita, & Kassenoff, Miriam Klein. (2003). *Memories of Night: A Study of the Holocaust.* Norwood, MA: Christopher-Gordon.

Shawn, Karen. (1994). What should they read and when should they read it? A selective review of Holocaust literature for students in grades 2–12. *Dimensions: A Journal of Holocaust Studies, 8.*

Strom, Margot Stern. (1994). *Facing History and Ourselves: Holocaust and Human Behavior.* Brookline, MA: Facing History and Ourselves National Foundation.

Totten, Samuel. (Ed.). (2001). *Teaching Holocaust Literature.* Boston: Allyn & Bacon.

Totten, Samuel, & Feinberg, Stephen. (Eds.) (2001). *Teaching and Studying the Holocaust,* Boston: Allyn & Bacon.

Appendix C

Videography

Note: For each film, grade levels are suggested: JMS—Junior/Middle School; HS—High School; HS+—Appropriate for college level

For ease in access, the vendors and their addresses are listed below. Many of the videos can be borrowed from Facing History and Ourselves and from the National Center for Jewish Film at Brandeis University.

Atlantis Productions
1252 La Granada Drive
Thousand Oaks, CA 91362
(805) 495-2790

Anti-Defamation League
823 United Nations Plaza
New York, NY 10017
(212) 885-7951
catalog@adl.org

California Working Group
P.O. Box 10326
Oakland, CA 94610
(510) 547-8484

Documentaries International
1880 K Street NW
Suite 1120
Washington, DC 20006

ERGO Media
P.O. Box 2037
Teaneck, NJ 07666-1437
info@jewishvideo.com
(800) 695-3746

Facing History and Ourselves
16 Hurd Road
Brookline, MA 02445
(617) 232-1595
www.facinghistory.org (click on "resources")

First Run Features
153 Waverly Place
New York, NY 10014
(212) 243-0600

Impact America Foundation
9100 Keystone at the Crossing, Suite 390
Indianapolis, IN 46240-2158

National Center for Jewish Film
Brandeis University
Lown #102
Waltham, MA 02254
(781) 899-7044
www.jewishfilm.org

PBS Video
13220 Braddock Place
Alexandria, VA 22314

Seventh Art Releasing
7551 Sunset Boulevard
Los Angeles, CA 90046
(323) 845-1455

Simon Wiesenthal Center
9760 West Pico Boulevard
Los Angeles, CA 90035
(310) 553-9036
information@wiesenthal.net

Social Studies School Service
10200 Jefferson Boulevard
P.O. Box 802
Culver City, CA 90232-0802
(800) 421-4246
www.socialstudies.com

U.S. Holocaust Memorial Museum Shop
100 Raoul Wallenberg Place SW
Washington, DC 20024-2150
(800) 259-9998
http://www.ushmm.org/

Women Make Movies, Inc.
462 Broadway, Suite 500
New York, NY 10013
(212) 925-0606

Zeitgeist Films
247 Centre Street
New York, NY 10013
(212) 274-1989

We gratefully acknowledge Dr. William Shulman, president of the **Associated Holocaust Organizations** (AHO) for this extensive annotated list of films and documentaries.

Act of Faith   28 min / BW / JHS+ / VHS Film (F 12-100)
This dramatic story of the heroic Danish resistance movement against Hitler was originally presented on CBS-TV. Filmed in Denmark, it is a firsthand account of the role played by the Danish people in saving their Jewish compatriots from Nazi extermination.
Subject(s): Resistance; Denmark
Vendor: Anti-Defamation League

Ambulance   9 min / BW / HS+ / VHS
This short film, with minimal dialogue, gives a powerful and perceptive view of the nature of the extermination process, although there are no scenes of horror in it. It shows a group of children, with their teacher, being held in a barbed wire enclosure just prior to being forced into an extermination van. The attitudes of the children, their teacher, and their guards and murderers will stimulate classroom discussion.
Subject(s): Nazi Atrocities; Children
Vendor: Facing History and Ourselves — www.facinghistory.org

America and the Holocaust: Deceit and Indifference   87 min / Color & BW / HS+ / VHS
This video explores the painful and difficult story of America's response to the murder of six million Jews by the Nazis and their collaborators. Using interviews, archival photos and documents, and home movies and film from the time, the program traces the tragic story of America's inaction on two levels: through the experiences of Kurt Klein, a Jewish refugee trying to save his parents, and through documented evidence of the U.S. government's official policy.
Subject(s): America; Survivor
Vendor: PBS Video

Anne Frank Remembered   117 minutes / Color / General Audience / VHS
This is a documentary film using archival photos and documents to present the life of Anne Frank and her family from her years in Frankfurt through her final years in Amsterdam.
Subject(s): Anne Frank; Nazi Persecution
Vendor: Social Science School Service

The Armenian Case   43 min / Color / HS+ / VHS
Survivors of Turkish atrocities and European and American eyewitness accounts recall the chilling historical events that were to shape the destiny of the Armenian people. The film includes notable sequences on World War I, President Wilson, the battle of Sardarabad, the establishment of the Republic of Armenia, and the rebuilding of Armenian life in the worldwide diaspora.
Subject(s): Genocide; Armenians
Vendor: Atlantis Productions

The Armenian Genocide   26 minutes / Color & BW / HS+ / VHS
This documentary raises questions about ethnic and racial discrimination by using the 1915–1923 annihilation by the Ottoman Empire as a case example.
Subject(s): Armenian Genocide
Vendor: Social Studies School Service

Assignment Rescue   26 minutes / BW & Color / General Audience / VHS
A documentary about the heroic efforts of Varian Fry, the American editor of *Living Age* magazine, in rescuing 200 famous intellectual refugees from the hands of the Nazis in 1940.
Subject(s): Varian Fry; Rescue
Vendor: Social Studies School Service

Au Revoir Les Enfants   103 min / Color / JHS+ / VHS
Based on filmmaker Louis Malle's experiences at boarding school during the Nazi occupation of France, this film documents the story of a Catholic schoolboy and his Jewish friend who is being sheltered at the school by a courageous French priest. After an act of betrayal, the Gestapo deports the Jewish youngster and the priest to Auschwitz.
Subject(s): Righteous Gentiles; France; Docudrama
Vendor: Social Studies School Service

Auschwitz: If You Cried, You Died   28 minutes / JHS + / VHS
A documentary video chronicling the journey of two Holocaust survivors as they revisit the Auschwitz concentration camp.
Subject(s): Survivors; Auschwitz
Vendor: Impact America Foundation

The Avenue of the Just   58 min / Color / JHS+ / VHS Film
The title refers to the tree-lined walk at Yad Vashem, Israel's Holocaust memorial honoring righteous gentiles who saved Jewish lives. There are interviews with men and women who sacrificed for others, and with some of the people they saved.
Subject(s): Righteous Gentiles
Vendor: Anti-Defamation League

The Boat Is Full   104 min / Color / JHS+ / VHS
This is the haunting story of a group of Jewish refugees who escape from Nazi Germany and seek asylum in Switzerland. Soon the village in which they are hiding becomes aware of their true identity, and their deportation seems imminent. They are forced back to the German border not by the Nazis but by ordinary Swiss civilians who are indifferent to the plight of refugees. Switzerland's immigration policies were so stringent that by 1942 the country was declared a full lifeboat. The struggle of those who sought freedom is explored in depth and with compassion.
Subject(s): Jewish Refugees in Switzerland; Escape Attempts; Fiction
Vendor: Social Studies School Service

Bound for Nowhere: The *St. Louis* Episode   9 min / BW / JHS+ / VHS
This tape contains extraordinary authentic film of the historic voyage of the 937 Jewish refugees who set sail from Hamburg, Germany, on May 13, 1939, for Cuba. Denied entry into Cuba and refused landing in the United States, the ship wandered the high seas for 5 weeks until forced to return to Europe. The role of the Jewish Joint Distribution Committee in helping the passengers to find a haven in Holland, Belgium, England, and France is recounted.
Subject(s): The *St. Louis* Voyage; Emigration
Vendor: National Center for Jewish Film

The Camera of My Family   18 min / Color & BW / JHS+ / VHS Filmstrip
Four generations of a German Jewish family are brought to life with material dating from 1845–1945. One of the best teaching tools available, this film, though gentle in its approach, easily leads to discussions about the attitudes of German Jews, their sense of national identity, their intense patriotism, and their inability to grasp what was happening.
Subject(s): Rise of Nazism in Germany; Anti-Semitism; Prejudice
Vendor: Anti-Defamation League

Conspiracy   96 minutes / Color / JHS+ / VHS and DVD
On January 20,1942, SS Chief of Reich Security Reinhard Heydrich met with 14 other high-ranking Nazis. Over appetizers and wine, they calmly discussed the murder of Europe's Jews. Based on notes meticulously kept by Adolf Eichmann, the film re-creates the infamous Wannsee Conference.
Subject(s): Perpetrators, Genocide
Vendor: Social Studies Film Service

Courage to Care   28 min / Color / HS+ / VHS 16mm
An unforgettable encounter with ordinary people who refused to succumb to Nazi tyranny. These people followed their conscience while others followed orders. They fed strangers, kept secrets, and provided hiding places. Their actions were exceptional in an era marked by apathy and complicity.
Subject(s): Righteous Gentiles
Vendor: Anti-Defamation League, Social Studies School Service

The Cross and the Star   55 min / Color / JHS +/ VHS
This video boldly examines the Christian anti-Semitism that paved the way for the Holocaust. It argues that the ideological seeds that developed into the Nuremberg laws and then the death camps was sown into Christian dogma many centuries prior to the rise of the Third Reich. The video questions the silence of foreign governments, institutional churches, and Christian neighbors while the Nazi atrocities were being committed. Director Michalczyk, a former Jesuit priest, utilizes archival footage of

Nazi Germany and interviews more than 30 Holocaust survivors, scholars, and Protestant, Catholic, and Jewish clergy.
Subject(s): Anti-Semitism; Christianity
Vendor: First Run Films

The Danish Resistance: The Power of Conscience & the Rescue of the Jews   55 minutes / Color / General Audience / VHS
The video features the testimony of prisoners and saboteurs, the rescuers and the rescued, to tell the story of the Danish people who refused to cooperate with the Nazis, and who rescued almost the entire Danish-Jewish community of 7,000 from the hands of the Nazis.
Subject(s): Denmark; Resistance
Vendor: Social Studies School Service

Daring to Resist   57 minutes / Color and BW / JHS+ / VHS
The story of three Jewish teenage girls: Faye Schulman, a photographer and partisan fighter in the forests of eastern Poland; Barbara Bodbell, a ballerina in Amsterdam who delivered underground newspapers as well as secured food and aid for Jews in hiding; and Schulamit Lack, who acquired false papers and a safe house for Jews attempting to flee Hungary.
Subject(s) Women in the Holocaust; Resistance
Vendor: Women Make Movies, Inc.

Debt to Honor   29 min, 35 sec / Color / General Audience / VHS
A video documentary that tells the compelling stories of ordinary individuals whose personal acts of courage resulted in the rescue of thousands of Jews after the Nazi occupation of Italy in 1943.
Subject(s): Rescue; Italy; Righteous Gentiles
Vendor: Documentaries International Film & Video Foundation

The Devil's Arithmetic   95 minutes / Color / HS+ / VHS
This powerful 1999 drama is based on the young adult novel of the same title by Jane Yolen and approaches the Holocaust from a unique angle. Hannah Stern is a modern teen of the 1990s who is apathetic toward Judaism and can't relate to the Holocaust experiences of her relatives. At a family Passover seder, Hannah mysteriously finds herself transported back in time to 1940s Poland and experiences the events and the horrors of the Holocaust.
Subject(s) Concentration Camps, Resistance
Vendor: Social Studies School Service

The Diary of Anne Frank   150 min / BW / JHS+ / VHS
Anne Frank and her family take refuge in an attic hideaway for two years in order to escape Nazi persecution. The film attempts to capture their struggle to preserve a civilized life under increasingly desperate circumstances.
Subject(s): Holland; Righteous Gentiles; Anne Frank; Fiction
Vendor: Social Studies School Service

Diplomats for the Damned   43 minutes / Color and BW / JHS+ / VHS
Profiles of four diplomats who sacrificed their careers to save the lives of thousands of Jews and other citizens: Aristedes de Sousa Mendes, Portuguese consul in Bordeaux; Harry Bingham, American vice-consul in Mareilles; Carl Lutz, Swiss diplomat in Hungary; and George Duckwitz, German attaché to Denmark.
Subject: Rescue, Righteous Gentiles
Vendor: Social Studies School Service

The Doomed Voyage of the *St. Louis*   50 minutes / Color / General Audience / VHS
A documentary about the passage of the German ocean liner *St. Louis* from Hamburg to Havana in 1939. The ship carried refugee Jewish passengers fleeing Nazi Germany with visas for Cuba. The Cuban denial of entry to these passengers and their forced return to Europe after being refused U.S. entry is the focus of this video.
Subject(s): Nazi Persecution; Survivors
Vendor: Social Studies School Service

Escape From Sobibor   149 min / Color / HS+ / VHS
Sobibor was a Nazi death camp in Poland, where more than a quarter of a million Jews were annihilated. It was also the site of the largest prisoner escape of WWII.
Subject(s): Extermination Camps; Resistance; Docudrama
Vendor: Social Studies School Service

Elie Wiesel: Witness to the Holocaust Nobel Peace Prize, 1986   20 min / Color / JKS+ / VHS
Cited by the Nobel Committee as a spiritual leader and guide in an age characterized by violence, repression and racism, Wiesel has devoted his life to the cause of peace. A Holocaust survivor who has written extensively about his experiences, Wiesel has based his literary career on the concept of the writer as witness. (Student notebook and teacher resource book are available.)
Subject(s): Holocaust Survivors
Vendor: United States Holocaust Museum Bookstore

Escape to Shanghai   25 min / Color / & BW / HS+ / VHS
This tape tells the story of the Jewish community of Shanghai, China, one of the most interesting of the Holocaust. Thousands of Jews came from Germany, Russia, and Eastern Europe to this open port, where no passport or visa was required, and lived out the war years, the majority of them under Japanese occupation. Although Germany was pressuring the Japanese to formulate an extermination policy similar to that which was in effect in Europe, Japan resisted.
Subject(s): Shanghai; Emigration; Japan
Vendor: Simon Wiesenthal Center

Eyes From the Ashes   12 min / BW / Adult / VHS
Many Jews brought personal photographs with them when they were deported to Auschwitz, not knowing their fate. The photographs were confiscated and 2,400 of them had been pasted into ledger books. The photos remained in Auschwitz until several years ago, when Ann Weiss, a photojournalist, found them. This video shows many of the faces, most unnamed. As viewers have seen these pictures, some of those unknown faces have been recognized.
Subject(s): Auschwitz; Prewar; Photographs
Vendor: e-mail the director, Ann Weiss at: thelastalbum@yahoo.com

The Forgotten Genocide   28 min / Color / HS+ / VHS
A classic and definitive film about the first genocide of the 20th century told for the first time by eyewitness accounts of Armenian survivors and rare archival film footage.
Subject(s): Genocide; Armenians
Vendor: Atlantis Productions

A Friendship in Vienna   94 minutes / Color / General Audience / VHS
Feature film about the friendship of two school girls, one Jewish, one Christian, in Vienna at the time of the Anschluss of 1938.
Subject(s): Fiction; Nazi Persecution; Austria; Vienna
Vendor: Social Studies School Service

Genocide   52 min / Color / & BW / MS+ / VHS
A documentary film that tells the inhumane story of Hitler's Final Solution. Set within the historical frame of 1920–1945, this film exposes the methodical insanity of the Nazi era. There are interviews with death camp survivors as well as Germans who were directly involved in implementing the Final Solution. (Part of the *World at War* series.)
Subject(s): Final Solution; Survivors
Vendor: Anti-Defamation League

The Hangman   12 minutes / Color / MS+ / VHS
A haunting animated short illustrating the poem by Maurice Ogden on the responsibility of the silent bystander.
Subject(s): Bystander
Vendor: Social Studies School Service

Hannah's War   148 minutes / Color / General Audience / VHS
This film, featuring Ellen Burstyn and Anthony Andrews, reenacts the story of Hannah Senesh, the Haganah heroine who parachuted into Nazi-occupied Hungary during World War to rescue Jews, losing her own life at the hands of the Nazis.
Subject(s): Hannah Senesh; Nazi Genocide; Hungary; Docu-drama
Vendor: Social Studies School Service

Heil Hitler! Confessions of Hitler Youth   30 min / Color & BW / JHS+ / VHS
A shocking true story based on the book by Alfons Heck, recalling how he became a high-ranking member of the Hitler Youth during World War II. Along with eight million other German children, he pledged his life to Hitler as an impressionable 10-year-old. Could it happen today? Of course, says Heck.
Subject(s): Hitler Youth; Nazism
Vendor: Social Studies School Service

Heritage: Civilization and the Jews   9 hours / Color and BW / JHS+ / VHS and DVD
A profoundly moving and important documentary that chronicles the history of the Jewish people from biblical times through the 20th century. The film, hosted by Abba Eban, former foreign minister of Israel and Israeli ambassador to the United Nations, uses paintings, artifacts, and modern cinematography of ancient sites, readings, and music.
Subject(s): History of the Jewish People, Anti-Semitism, Survival, Contributions of the Jewish People
Vendor: Available through Amazon.com and Video Stores

The Holocaust   7 hours 30 minutes / Color / MS+ / VHS
This 1978 Emmy Award–winning television epic follows the lives of two families, one Jewish and one Nazi, living in Nazi Germany during 1935–1945. The Weiss family is deprived of rights until their very survival is threatened, while the Dorfs join the German war effort and rise to affluence. The film stars Meryl Steep and James Woods. *Note:* Teachers may wish to use individual segments to highlight such events as Kristallnacht or the Warsaw Ghetto Uprising.
Subject(s): Nazi Persecution, Resistance
Vendor: Social Studies School Service

The Holocaust: In Memory of Millions   90 minutes / Color / JHS+ / VHS
This overall history of the Holocaust, hosted by Walter Cronkite, introduces viewers to the Holocaust Memorial Museum by tracing the gradually escalating horror of being Jewish under the Nazis.
Subject(s): Holocaust; Nazi Persecution
Vendor: Social Studies School Service

The Holocaust Through Our Own Eyes   58 min / HS+ / VHS
This documentary is edited from personal interviews with nearly 50 eyewitnesses—refugees, camp survivors, individuals in hiding, non-Jewish citizens of Nazi-occupied Europe, and liberators—who recount their painful experiences and chronicle the history of the Holocaust through their firsthand accounts.
Subject(s): Survivors; Liberation; Testimony
Vendor: Midwest Center for Holocaust Education, Inc., 5801 West 115 St. Suite 106
Shawnee Mission, KS 66211-1800, (913) 327-8190

Image Before My Eyes   90 min / Color / & BW / HS+ / VHS
This film re-creates Jewish life in Poland from the late 19th century through the 1930s, a unique and now vanished era. Through rare films, photographs, memorabilia, music, and interviews with survivors of the lost culture, the film brings to life the full range of the Jewish experience in the years before the disaster.
Subject(s): Jewish Life in Poland Pre-World War II
Vendor: Social Studies School Service

In Our Hands: The Hidden Story of the Jewish Brigade in World War II   60 min / Color /
General Audience / VHS
A documentary about the heroic work of this unit in the closing years of World War II and of its rescue work with Jewish survivors of the Holocaust.
Subject(s): Rescue; Survivors
Vendor: National Center for Jewish Film

In Their Words   30 min / Color & BW / JHS+ / VHS
This award-winning tape was produced by the Southeastern Florida Holocaust Memorial Center and contains excerpts from interviews of Holocaust survivors and American soldiers who participated in the liberation of the extermination camps in Europe during World War II.
Subject(s): Liberators; Survivors
Vendor: S.E. Florida Holocaust Memorial Center

Jakob the Liar   96 minutes / color / HS+ / VHS

This drama is based on the novel by Jurek Becker and is about Jakob Heym, a Jew in a Polish ghetto who hears news of the Russian army's advancement when he is detained in Gestapo headquarters after curfew. Jacob passes the good news and people believe he owns a radio. They press him for further news, and finally Jacob begins to invent stories of the progress of the Allies. Seeing the positive impact good news has, Jacob becomes a reluctant hero, able to bring hope but powerless to change the fate of those in the ghetto.

Subject(s): Resistance, Ghetto Life

Vendor: Social Studies School Service

Jehovah's Witnesses Stand Firm Against Nazi Assault   78 minutes / Color / JHS + / VHS

A documentary film featuring 10 historians from Europe and North America and more than 20 Jehovah's Witness survivors that tells the story of the persecution of the Witnesses by the Nazi regime.

Subject(s): Jehovah's Witnesses; Nazi Persecution

Vendor: Watch Tower Bible and Tract Society of New York, Inc., 25 Columbia Heights, Brooklyn NY 11201, (718) 625-3600

The Journey of Butterfly   62 minutes / Color / General Audience / VHS

Documenting a legacy of creativity that blossomed under the harshest conditions, this powerful program weaves together music, art, poetry, and personal histories of children imprisoned in the camp at Terezin. The American Boychoir sings the poetry of the children of Terezin.

Subject(s) Terezin (Theresienstadt); Art and Poetry of the Holocaust

Vendor: Social Studies School Service

Judgment at Nuremberg   187 minutes (2 cassettes) / BW/ HS + / VHS

This is the thought-provoking all-star film centered around the post–World War II Nuremberg trial of German judges who upheld the Nazi laws involving horrendous abuses of basic human rights. The juxtaposition of the pressures the defendants claimed they were under, with that imposed on the American judge at the trials, form the basis of the conflict in this powerful film, which features Spencer Tracy, Judy Garland, and Burt Lancaster.

Subject(s): Nazi War Crimes; Nuremberg Trial

Vendor: Social Studies School Service

Kitty Returns to Auschwitz   82 minutes / HS + / VHS

Kitty Hart was a teenager as an inmate in Auschwitz-Birkenau. Thirty-four years after her liberation, Kitty remembers and talks about her experience. As she returns to the camp, she relates what it was like to be a young girl in this horrific place.

Subject (s): Concentration Camps

Vendor: Social Studies School Services

Korczak   118 min / Color / HS+ / VHS

This video tells the true story of Janusz Korczak, a renowned physician and author, who ran a home for Jewish orphans in 1930s Warsaw. After the German invasion of Poland, friends urge Korczak to flee the country, but Korczak refuses to abandon his children and so must move his orphanage into the

Warsaw Ghetto. As the war continues, it becomes plain that despite Korczak's tireless efforts, the children will be deported to concentration camps. Yet Korczak vows to remain with them until the end. In Polish, with English subtitles.
Subject(s): Warsaw; Children; Poland; Fiction
Vendor: US Holocaust Memorial Museum

Kovno Ghetto: A Buried History   100 minutes / Color / HS+ / VHS
The video pieces together the story of the Jews of Kovno, Lithuania, from the first stirrings of World War II to the annihilation of the ghetto just days before the city's liberation.
Subject(s): Ghettos; Nazi Genocide; Lithuania
Vendor: Social Studies School Service

The Last Days   87 Minutes / Color and BW / HS+ Warning: Some graphic footage / VHS
This excellent video nominated for an Academy Award follows the lives and experiences of five Holocaust survivors from Hungary and how they survived the Holocaust. A Steven Spielberg production.
Subject(s): Survivors, the Holocaust
Vendor: Social Studies School Service

Let Memory Speak   Color / JHS+ / VHS
This documentary portrays the lives of children who were hidden during the Holocaust. Written, produced, and directed by Batia Bettman.
Subject(s): Rescue, Hidden Children
Vendor: U.S. Holocaust Memorial Museum

Life Is Beautiful   116 minutes / Color / HS+ / VHS
This 1997 acclaimed Holocaust film was nominated for seven Academy Awards. Italian actor Roberto Benigni stars as Guido in this film that breaks your heart while it makes you laugh. When Guido and his family are transported to a concentration camp he tries to protect his son by pretending that what is happening in the camp is all a game.

Note: This film was met with some controversy. Some feel it is about a father's overwhelming love and self-sacrifice under the most dire circumstances; others feel that the Holocaust is not a matter for humor or joking of any kind and that the film makes light of one of the most horrifying events in human history. Preview before using.
Subject: Concentration Camps, Survival
Vendor: Libraries and video stores in Italian with subtitles or dubbed in English.

The Longest Hatred   150 minutes / Color / HS+ / VHS
Uses images from art, vintage film clips, and a variety of voices to evoke the madness of anti-Semitism. The film explains the ancient roots of anti-Jewish prejudice and looks at the hatred engendered by religious antagonism from the Middle Ages through 1945.
Subject(s): Anti-Semitism; Jewish Life
Vendor: Social Studies School Service

Marion's Triumph: Surviving History's Nightmare   60 minutes / General Audience / VHS
Debra Messing narrates this compelling documentary of the Blumenthal family and how they began their journey to the United States in 1938. Marion Blumenthal relives the past as she explains how she

and her family survived Westerbork and Bergen-Belsen over a period of 6½ years. The documentary is based on Marion Blumenthal's memoir *Four Perfect Pebbles,* which is in its 11th printing and taught in schools worldwide.
Subject(s): Survival, Concentration Camps
Vendor: Seventh Art Releasing

Miracle at Midnight   88 minutes / Color / JHS+ / VHS
On October 1, 1943, Nazi authorities launched a lightning strike to round up more than 7,000 Danish Jews and transport them to Theresienstadt concentration camp. The raid was a failure, thanks to the Danes who learned of the plan and were able to help all but a few hundred of their neighbors flee to Sweden. *Miracle at Midnight* tells the true story of one rescuing family, the Kosters, who hide a Jewish family and get them on boats under the very noses of the Gestapo. The film stars Mia Farrow and Sam Waterston.
Subject: Rescue
Vendor: Social Studies School Service

The Murderers Among Us: The Simon Wiesenthal Story   HS+ / 160 minutes / Color / General Audience / VHS
This is a 1988 film production featuring Ben Kingsley and based on the career of Nazi hunter Simon Wiesenthal.
Subject(s): Simon Wiesenthal; Nazi War Crimes; Nazi hunters; Docu-drama
Vendor: Social Studies School Service

The Music Box   126 minutes / JHS+ / VHS
A Chicago attorney agrees to defend her beloved Hungarian immigrant father, who is accused of committing heinous war crimes as a Nazi. During the trial, she has trouble—both legally and personally—trying to prove his innocence. The film stars Jessica Lange.
Subject(s): Perpetrators; War Crimes
Vendor: Video stores

The Nazi Officer's Wife   96 min / HS +
Based on the memoir by the same title, this is the story of a Jewish woman, Edith Hahn Beer, who survived the Holocaust posing as a German housewife.
Subject: Surviving the Holocaust
Vendor: National Center for Jewish Film at Brandeis University

Not in Our Town   26 minutes / JHS, HS, HS+ / VHS
When acts of prejudice and racism threatened to harm certain groups of citizens in Billings, Montana, the population took action. The resolve of the people of Billings serves to inspire the viewer and makes each aware of the dangers of indifference and apathy.
Subjects(s): Perpetrators, Resistance, "the Power of One"
Vendor: California Working Group

Nowhere in Africa   178 minutes
Based on the best-selling autobiographical novel by Stefanie Zweig, *Nowhere in Africa* is the extraordinary true story of a Jewish family who flees the Nazi regime in 1938 for a remote farm in Kenya. Each member must deal with the harsh realities of the new life as war breaks out in Europe. Winner of

the 2002 Academy Award for Best Foreign Language Film.
Subject(s): Resistance, Rescue, fleeing Nazi terror
Vendor: Zeitgeist Films

Number the Stars   15 minutes / Color / Upper Elementary, JHS / VHS
This PBS video is based on Lois Lowry's book centering on a Danish Christian family who saves a Jewish family from the Nazis in 1943.
Subject(s): Fiction; Righteous Gentiles; Denmark
Vendor: Social Studies School Service

Nuremberg   3 hours / Color / HS+
This film focuses on the proceedings of the historic international trial held in Nuremberg, Germany, which brought 22 Nazi perpetrators to trial for their war crimes during the Holocaust. Archival film included.
Subject(s): Nazi War Crimes, Nuremberg Trial
Vendor: Social Studies School Service

One Survivor Remembers   39 Minutes / Color / General Audience
The United States Holocaust Memorial Museum and Home Box Office present this special tribute in commemoration of the 50th anniversary of the end of the Holocaust and the Second World War. Through a series of interviews, photographs, and footage shot in the actual locations of her memories, Gerda Weissmann Klein takes us on a journey of survival through one of the most devastating events in the history of humanity.
Subject(s): Survivors
Vendor: Social Studies School Service

The Optimists   80 minutes / color / HS+ / VHS
A compelling and unique film on the Bulgarian Jews and how they were saved by their compassionate Christian neighbors. The film was produced and directed by Jacky Comforty, the son of Bulgarian Holocaust survivors, and was released in 2002 at all the major film festivals, where it won numerous awards.
Subject(s): Rescue
Vendor: Comforty@comforty.com

The Pianist   120 minutes (approx.) / Color / HS+ / VHS
This tells the extraordinary true story of Wladyslaw Szpilman, a pianist living in Warsaw. Although he lost his entire family, he survived the Holocaust in hiding. In the end, his life was saved by a German officer who heard him play a Chopin nocturne on a piano found among the rubble. It is based on the book by the same title, written by Szpilman shortly after the war and suppressed for decades. This 2003 film has been recognized as one of the finest movies dealing with the Holocaust.
Subject(s): Warsaw Ghetto, Survival, Rescue
Vendor: Video stores

The Power of Good   64 minutes / JHS+ / VHS

This is the true story of Nicholas Winton, who personally rescued 669 children from Nazi-occupied Czechoslovakia. It is a compelling and inspiring film that demonstrates how one person can truly make a difference.

Subjects: Righteous Gentiles, Rescue

Vendor: National Center for Jewish Film

Raoul Wallenberg: Between the Lines   85 minutes / HS+ / Color and BW / VHS

Raoul Wallenberg, a Swedish diplomat, was responsible for saving thousands of lives. Friends, family, and former members of his staff describe his efforts to confront the Nazi destruction of Hungarian Jewry. The video also examines the controversy surrounding his arrest and imprisonment in 1945 by the Soviets.

Subject(s): Rescue

Vendor: Social Studies School Service

Rescuers: Stories of Courage   109 minutes / Color / JHS+ / VHS

These are the compelling true stories of two couples who selflessly risked their own lives to provide safe homes and passage to Jewish refugees during the Holocaust. Stars Dana Delany, Martin Donovan, Linda Hamilton, and Alfred Molina.

Subject(s): Rescue

Vendor: United States Holocaust Memorial Museum

Schindler's List   197 minutes / Color / HS+ contains graphic violence, strong language, and nudity, rated R / VHS

Directed by Steven Spielberg, this Oscar-winning 1993 film tells the story of German industrialist Oskar Schindler, a high-ranking Nazi Party member who risked his life and personal fortune to save more than 1,000 Jewish workers from deportation and death. Adapted from Thomas Keneally's novelization of a true story. Stars Liam Neeson, Ben Kingsley, and Ralph Finnes.

Subject(s): Rescue; Concentration Camps

Vendor: Social Studies School Service

Secret Lives: Hidden Children and Their Rescuers During World War II   72 min HS +

This film tells the story of Jewish children hidden by Christians in German-occupied countries. It pays tribute to the people who risked their lives to offer refuge.

Subject: Rescue

Vendor: National Center for Jewish Film at Brandeis University

Shanghai Ghetto   95 minutes HS+

This documentary tells the story of the approximately 20,000 Jews who left Europe for China in 1939. These once-affluent German Jews remember the years they spent as children living in extreme poverty in China's most European city. The Shanghai Jews feel fortunate to have been saved in Shanghai and never felt discrimination from the Chinese.

Subject(s): Rescue

Vendor: National Center for Jewish Film at Brandeis University

Shoah   10 hours / Color / HS+ / VHS
An important film for any serious student of the Holocaust. It is a comprehensive overview of the events that led to the Holocaust in Poland and includes eyewitness Holocaust testimonies. Segments of this film can be selected based on classroom objectives.
Subject(s): Events of the Holocaust; Survivor testimony
Vendor: Social Studies School Service

Sugihara: Conspiracy of Kindness
The true story of the Japanese consul to Lithuania who went against his governments' orders and wrote visas for Jews trying to flee persecution, thereby saving the lives of thousands.
Subject: Rescue, heroism
Vendor: National Center for Jewish Film at Brandeis University

Swing Kids   120 minutes (approx.) / color / JHS+ / VHS
Excellent view of life in Germany right after the Nuremberg Laws. The film focuses on teenagers who were frustrated by the restrictions of banned music in the club they frequented and contrasts the attitudes of the Nazi youth and those who resisted.
Subject(s): Resistance, Censorship
Vendor: Video stores

There Once Was a Town   90 minutes / JHS+ / Color / VHS
Based on Yaffa Eliach's book, which chronicles 900 years of Jewish life in the shtetl of Eishyshok.
Subject(s): Jewish Life in Eastern Europe
Vendor: United States Holocaust Memorial Museum

Triumph of the Will   110 min / BW / JHS+ / VHS
Leni Riefenstahl's film of the Sixth Nazi Party Congress at Nuremberg in 1934. A masterpiece of Nazi propaganda, it provides a fascinating psychological study of the Nazi leaders in action. Told visually with very little dialogue. Speeches by Hitler and others are in German with no subtitles.
Subject(s): Nazi Propaganda
Vendor: Social Studies School Service

Uprising   177 minutes / JHS / Color / VHS and DVD
"Can a moral man maintain his moral code in an immoral world? " asks Mordecai Anielewicz (Hank Azaria), soon to be leader of the Jewish resistance in the Warsaw Ghetto. This docudrama depicts life and death in the ghetto, mass deportations by train, including the orphans under the care of Dr. Janus Korczak, and the organization of armed resistance, culminating in the famed uprising of April 1943.
Subject(s): Resistance, Ghetto Life
Vendor: Social Studies School Service

The Voyage of the *St. Louis*   52 minutes / BW / General Audience / VHS
A documentary about the German ocean liner that carried 917 Jewish refugees from Nazi Germany to Cuba in May 1939. The story of the revoking of their entry visas by the Cuban dictator, the subsequent denial of the U.S. to grant them asylum, and the eventual death of three-quarters of the passengers in Nazi death camps make this a compelling historical account.
Subject(s): Rescue; Refugees; United States; Cuba
Vendor: United States Holocaust Memorial Museum; The National Center for Jewish Film

Weapons of the Spirit   38 minutes / color (classroom version) / JHS+ / VHS
This is the original version of the film by Pierre Sauvage about the French village of Le Chambon—a remote village in southeastern France—and its rescue of more than 5,000 Jews during the Holocaust. The Huguenot Protestant villagers sheltered the Jews, and not one villager informed the authorities. The film uses interviews with the rescuers and survivors, newsreel footage, photographs, and historical accounts.
Subject(s): Rescue
Vendor: Social Studies School Service

Appendix D

Webography

http://www.ushmm.org
http://www.ushmm.org/outreach (for the Student Outreach Site—authorization required)

The United States Holocaust Memorial Museum homepage. Includes information about background history and statistics of the U.S. Holocaust Memorial Museum, how to plan a visit to the museum, museum membership, community programs, films and lectures conferences for educators, guidelines for teaching about the Holocaust, historical summaries, a videography for teachers, answers to five frequently asked questions about the Holocaust, Holocaust Resource Centers nationwide, and a searchable database of the Research Institute's archives and library.

http://www.holocaust-trc.org

Holocaust Education Foundation includes lesson plans, guest lectures lists, and curriculum resources.

http://www.chgs.umn.edu

An excellent site from the University of Minnesota Holocaust and Genocide Studies Center.

http://www.yadvashem.org.il

Yad Vashem. Homepage for Israel's Museum and Memorial to the victims of the Holocaust, contains primarily general information, some photographs and excerpts from survivor testimony transcripts. There are educational materials available in Hebrew.

http://www.wiesenthal.com

The Simon Wiesenthal Center homepage. Headquartered in Los Angeles, the Simon Wiesenthal Center is an international center for Holocaust remembrance and the defense of human rights and the Jewish people. Contains answers to 36 frequently asked questions about the Holocaust, biographies of children who experienced the Holocaust, updates on current events, information on hate groups on the

Internet, and information about the center and the Museum of Tolerance. Much of this information is available in several languages, including Spanish, German, and Italian.

http://web.acc.qcc.cuny.edu/hrca

This is the website for the Associated Holocaust Organizations (AHO). It includes a comprehensive listing of all Holocaust centers nationally and internationally. In order to find a center close to your area go to "Links," then "Associated Holocaust Organization," then to "Member Directory."

http://www.facinghistory.org

Facing History and Ourselves homepage. Facing History and Ourselves is a national educational and professional development organization whose mission is to engage students of diverse backgrounds in an examination of racism, prejudice, and anti-Semitism in order to promote the development of a more humane and informed citizenry. At the present time, its homepage offers basic information about its programs and resources.

http://www.remember.org

Homepage of the Cybrary of the Holocaust. The Cybrary is probably the largest Web site on the Holocaust. It contains a collection of encyclopedic information, answers to frequently asked questions, curriculum outlines (including a lesson plan on Anne Frank), excerpts from survivor testimony, transcripts of Nazi speeches and official documents, artifact photos, historical photos, artwork, poetry, books written by survivors, links to other Holocaust sites, and more. Both audio clips and transcripts of survivor testimony and interviews with scholars are available. Some of the recent additions to this site include photo tours of Auschwitz, genealogy tracing information, and online chats with scholars.

http://www.vhf.org

Survivors of the Shoah: The Visual History Foundation created by Steven Spielberg has recorded 50,000 videotaped interviews with Holocaust survivors. These are being recorded electronically for computer distribution to museums, CD-ROMs, and other sites.

http://www.historyplace.com

The perfect site for learning about almost any historical event. Includes a comprehensive timeline of the Holocaust.

http://www.annefrank.com

Anne Frank Online. This site is dedicated to everything about the Nazis' most famous victim.

http://www.interlog.com

This is one of the few and best sites available on the topic of women in the Holocaust. It includes memoirs, diaries, and scholarly essays written about the special role of women during the Holocaust.

http://www.yahoo.com\Arts\Humanities\History\20th_Century\Holocaust_The\

Yahoo's Holocaust listings, which offer links to many resources.

http://www.holocaustchronicle.org

Includes more than 800 pages of historical text on the Holocaust.

http://www.wfjcsh.org

Website for the World Federation of Jewish Child Survivors of the Holocaust.

http://www.fcit.usf.edu/Holocaust

A Teacher's Guide to the Holocaust: An Overview for Teachers, which includes a timeline, people, the arts, student activities, and teacher resources.

http://www.splcenter.org/teachingtolerance.html

The Southern Poverty Law Center Teaching Tolerance project started in 1991 in response to an alarming increase in hate crime among youth. Offers free or low-cost resources to educators at all levels.

http://www.hatewatch.org

Hate Watch is a Web-based organization that monitors the growing and evolving threat of hate-group activity on the Internet.

http://www.mol.org

Official website of the March of the Living.

http://www.hrusa.org

Human Rights USA suggests ideas and tools for advocating and protecting human rights. Encourages community-based actions.

http://www.adl.org

The Anti-Defamation League is an organization founded in 1913 to fight anti-Semitism through programs and services that counteract hatred, prejudice, and bigotry. The mission of the ADL is "to stop the defamation of Jewish people, to secure justice and fair treatment for all citizens alike."

http://www.historychannel.com

The History Channel.

http://www.annefrank.nl

The Anne Frank House in Amsterdam.

http://www.gfh.org.il

Ghetto Fighters' House. The Holocaust and Jewish Resistance Heritage Museum in Israel.

http://www.ellisisland.org

Ellis Island Home Page.

http://www.socialstudies.com

Social Studies School Service. An on-line catalog.

http://www.iearn.org/hgp

IEARN Holocaust/Genocide Project is an international nonprofit telecommunications project focusing on the study of the Holocaust and other genocides. Involves participating schools around the world.

http://www.library.yale.edu/testimonies/homepage.html

Fortunoff Video Archive for Holocaust Testimonies. Contains general information about the archive and how to use it, as well as audio and video clips of several testimonies from survivors, liberators, rescuers, and bystanders.

http://www.hatewatch.org

Hate Watch is a Web-based organization that monitors the growing and evolving threat of hate group activity on the Internet.

http://www.hrusa.org

Human Rights USA suggests ideas and tools for advocating and protecting human rights. Encourages community-based action.

Appendix E

Resource Centers

For an up-to-date list of Holocaust Centers, national and international, contact:

AHO (Associated Holocaust Organizations)
Holocaust Resource Center and Archives
Queensborough Community College
222-05 56th Avenue
Bayside, NY 11364-1497
Dr. William L. Shulman, president and founder
Sara Roberts, director

(718) 281-5770

http://web.acc.qcc.cuny.edu/hrca (go to "Links," then "Associated Holocaust Organizations," then to "Member Directory")

Appendix F

Teacher Training Institutes,
Community Programs,
and Seminars

For resource information and presentations on this book for your school, district, or community, please contact Dr. Miriam Klein Kassenoff.

Dr. Miriam Klein Kassenoff
Director of the Teacher's Institute on Holocaust Studies, University of Miami, Coral Gables, Florida
Education Director, Holocaust Memorial, Miami Beach, Florida
5700 Collins Avenue, Suite 3G
(305) 868-5127
e-mail: MiriamK10@aol.com
www.Holocaust-trc.org/kassenoff.htm
www.Christopher-Gordon.com

About the Authors

Miriam Klein Kassenoff fled Nazi Europe as a small child in 1941, along with her parents and infant brother. Dr. Klein Kassenoff has studied at *Yad Vashem,* the International Center for Holocaust Studies in Jerusalem, Israel and co-authored *Memories of the Night: A Study of the Holocaust,* with Dr. Anita Meyer Meinbach. Dr. Klein Kassenoff is the Education Director at the Holocaust Memorial in Miami Beach, Florida, the Director of the Teacher Institute on Holocaust Studies at the University of Miami, and a graduate of the prestigious international *Vladka Meed Holocaust Teacher's Program.*

As the Education Specialist for Holocaust Studies for Miami-Dade County Public Schools, she is responsible for all staff development/teacher training on teaching the Holocaust. Dr. Klein Kassenoff is an appointee to the Florida Governor's Task Force on Holocaust Education, an active member of Associated Holocaust Organizations (AHO), a member of the *Federation of Jewish Child Survivors/Hidden Children of the Holocaust,* and serves as the Educational Consultant on the forthcoming film, *Destination Lisbon: Escape from the Nazis,* by the award-winning film director, Jacky Comforty.

Dr. Klein Kassenoff was honored as *Israel Bonds Woman of the Year Honoree 2000,* in Miami, Florida and was also named as one of the *Women of the Year 2002,* by the Miami City Commission. Currently, Dr. Klein Kassenoff also serves as the Education Consultant for the Holocaust Teacher Institute in Boone, North Carolina, and is an adjunct lecturer at the University of Miami in Florida. She is a frequent speaker and presenter on Holocaust Education at conferences and workshops nationwide.

Anita Meyer Meinbach has been with the Miami-Dade County Public Schools for the past 20 years in various capacities and was honored as the county's "2003 Teacher of the Year." She has been a teacher, curriculum writer, and teacher trainer, providing seminars and guidance in curriculum development. As an adjunct professor at the University of Miami she has taught courses in language arts, reading, and children's literature and is currently a consultant to the university's School of Education as well as the co-director at the University of Miami's Summer Institute for Holocaust studies. Dr. Meinbach is the author/coauthor of several textbooks and numerous resource books in reading and language arts. A frequent speaker at workshops and professional conferences, she speaks on a variety of topics dealing with Holocaust education, children's literature, and curriculum development.

Among the numerous honors and recognition she has received, Dr. Meinbach was selected by *U.S.A. Today* for their "2002 All-USA Teacher Team," one of only twenty teachers selected nationwide.

Index

Allies, 8, 9–10, 112, 152–154; *see also names of four countries*

American Jewish Joint Distribution Committee, 131

Amnesty International, 110, 163

Anielewicz, Mordecai, 79–80

Anti-Defamation League, 155

Antisemitism
  history of, 29
  political, 3
  postwar, 10
  religious, 3

Attenborough, Lord Richard, 101, 102

Austria,
  displaced person camps in, 10

Ayer, Eleanor, 39–40

Babi Yar, 6

Bachrach, Susan, 38–39

Belgium,
  German conquest of, 6
  and Jewish refugees, 50

Berenbaum, Michael, xi–xiii, 36

Bermuda Conference, of 1943, 52

Bernays, Murray, 152

Bernbaum, Israel, 78

Bettman, Batia, 130

Bierman, Wolf, 70

Billings, Montana, 110, 154–155

Bingham, Harry (Hiram), 96, 97

Bitton-Jackson, Livia, 24–25, 143–145

Block, Gay, 98

Bloomington, Illinois, 155

Blumenthal, Lila Perl and Marion, 133–134

Britain; *see also* Allies
  army of, 10
  and Jewish refugees, 5, 8, 10, 50, 144, 145
  Kindertransport to, 101–102

Bulgaria,
  war crimes trials in, 9

Burke, Edmund, 58

Bystanders, 8

Cain and Abel, story of, 31

Camps, 111–128
  administrators of, 9
  Auschwitz-Birkenau, 3, 7, 28, 29, 37, 81, 112, 115–119, 120, 143
    death march from, 145
  Belzec, 7, 112
  Bergen-Belsen, 8, 82–83, 134
  Buchenwald, 112, 120, 145–149
  Chelmno, 7, 111
  Dachau, 5, 9, 112, 113
  deportations to, 7
  DP; *see* "Displaced persons"
  eastern Poland chosen for, 30
  Ebensee, 112
  Kovno Ghetto declared as one, 69
  liberation of, 8, 112, 115, 131
  Majdanek, 7, 111
  Ohrdruf, 112
  shoes from, 127
  slave labor in, 125
  Sobibor, 7, 81, 111
  survivors of, 10
  system of, 6, 111–112
  Terezin, 75, 84–89
  Treblinka, 3, 7, 60, 61, 81, 111
  Westerbork, 134

Canada,
  and Jewish refugees, 5

Chagall, Marc, 97

Chelmno, 3

Children, 127, 129–149
  of Buchenwald, 145–148
  hidden, 99, 104–105, 135–138

"Choiceless choices," 72
Christianity,
    anti-Jewish prejudice in, 3
    hidden children and, 139
    Nazi plan to wipe out, 40
    reaction to Nazism by, 50, 98
Cohen, Judy, 77
Collaborators, 8
Columbine, 164
Corman, Cis, 97
Cuba,
    and Jewish refugees, 50, 51

Death marches, 8
Denmark,
    German conquest of, 6
    resistance in, 8, 96, 103
"Displaced persons," 9, 10, 130, 138, 144
Displaced Persons Act, 10
Documents
    "Extract from Written Evidence of Rudolf Höss,
        Commander of the Auschwitz Extermination
        Camp," 37
    "First Regulation to the Reich Citizenship Law," 22
    "Nuremberg Law for the Protection of German
        Blood and German Honor, September 15, 1935,"
        22
    "UN Declaration of Children's Rights," 67
    "UN Universal Declaration of Human Rights, 1948,"
        158–162
Drawings
    I Never Saw Another Butterfly, 84–89
    political cartoons, 35
Drucker, Malka, 98
Duba, Ursula, 41–43
Duckwitz, George, 96

Eichmann, Adolf, 35, 96
Einsatzgruppen, 3, 6, 9, 111
Eliach, Yaffa, 25, 106, 121–124
Erban, Arno, 84–88, 117–119
Evian Conference of 1938, 52, 96
Exodus, 4–7, 10

Facing History and Ourselves Foundation, xxii
Feng-Shan Ho, 97
Films and videos
    Act of Faith, 179
    Ambulance, 179
    America and the Holocaust: Deceit and Indifference,
        179
    Anne Frank Remembered, 180
    The Armenian Case, 180
    The Armenian Genocide, 180

    Assignment Rescue, 180
    Au Revoir, Les Enfants, 180
    Auschwitz: If You Cried, You Died, 180
    The Avenue of the Just, 180
    The Boat Is Full, 181
    Bound for Nowhere: The St. Louis Episode, 181
    *The Camera of My Family: Four Generations in
        Germany, 1845–1945*, 20–23, 181
    Conspiracy, 35–37, 181
    *The Courage to Care: Rescuers of Jews During the
        Holocaust*, 99–100, 181
    The Cross and the Star, 181–182
    The Danish Resistance, 182
    Daring to Resist, 182
    Debt to Honor, 182
    The Devil's Arithmetic, 182
    The Diary of Anne Frank, 182
    Diplomats for the Damned, 96–97, 183
    The Doomed Voyage of the St. Louis, 50–51, 183
    The Double Crossing: The Voyage of the St. Louis,
        50
    *Elie Wiesel: Witness to the Holocaust Nobel Peace
        Prize, 1986*, 183
    Escape From Sobibor, 183
    Escape to Shanghai, 183
    Eyes From the Ashes, 183
    The Forgotten Genocide, 184
    A Friendship in Vienna, 184
    Genocide, 1941–1945, 102–115, 184
    The Hangman, 46–50, 184
    Heil Hitler! Confessions of a Hitler Youth, 34, 184
    Heritage: Civilization and the Jews, 184
    The Holocaust, 185
    The Holocaust: In Memory of Millions, 185
    The Holocaust Through Our Own Eyes, 185
    Image Before My Eyes, 185
    *In Our Hands: The Hidden Story of the Jewish Bri-
        gade in World War II*, 185
    In Their Words, 185
    Jakob the Liar, 186
    *Jehovah's Witnesses Stand Firm Against Nazi As-
        sault*, 186
    The Journey of Butterfly, 186
    Judgment at Nuremberg, 186
    Kitty Returns to Auschwitz, 186
    Korczak, 60–67, 186–187
    Kovno Ghetto: A Buried History, 68–69, 187
    The Last Days, 187
    Let Memory Speak, 130–131, 187
    Life Is Beautiful, 187
    The Longest Hatred, 187
    Marion's Triumph: Surviving History's Nightmare,
        133–134, 187–188
    Miracle at Midnight, 188

The Murderers Among Us: The Simon Wiesenthal Story, 188
The Music Box, 188
The Nazi Officer's Wife, 188
Not in Our Town, 110, 154–155, 188
Nowhere in Africa, 188–189
Number the Stars, 189
Nuremberg, 152–154, 189
One Survivor Remembers, 23–24, 189
The Optimists, 189
The Pianist, 69–71, 189
The Power of Good, 102, 132–133, 190
Raoul Wallenberg: Between the Lines, 190
Rescuers: Stories of Courage‹Two Couples, 97–98, 190
Schindler's List, 115–116, 190
Secret Lives: Hidden Children and Their Rescuers During World War II, 190
Shanghai Ghetto, 190
Shoah, 191
Sugihara: Conspiracy of Kindness, 191
Swing Kids, 191
There Once Was a Town, 191
Triumph of the Will, 191
Uprising, 78–81, 191
The Voyage of the St. Louis, 50–52
Weapons of the Spirit, 192
"Final Solution to the Jewish Question," 3, 37, 39, 111, 113; *see also* Wannsee Conference
Fine, Ellen, 135–137
Fink, Ida, 140–143
Fort Ontario, 8
France; *see also* Allies
   German conquest of, 6
   and Jewish refugees, 5, 50, 145, 148
Frank, Anne, 8, 75, 82–83, 93; *see also* Memoirs, Anne Frank
Frank, Otto, 82
Frankfurt Trial of Auschwitz camp personnel, 9
Fry, Varian, 97

Genocides, other, 114, 156, 164
Germany,
   army of, 9
   displaced person camps in, 10
   Interior Ministry of, 33
   Nazi; *see* Nazi Germany
   West (Federal Republic of), 9
Gettysburg Address, 163
Ghettos, 27, 59–74
   Bedzin, 81
   Bialystok, 81
   Czestochowa, 81
   Jewish Councils of the, 60, 68, 69, 72, 73, 78, 90

Kovno, 68–69
Krakow, 81
Lodz, 7, 27, 59, 72, 124–125
Minsk, 81
Sosnowiec, 81
Tarnow, 81
Vilna, 27, 73
Warsaw, 7, 27, 54, 57, 59–64, 71–74, 78, 89–93
   uprising, 8, 78–81
Gies, Miep, 83
Gilbert, Gustav, 153, 154
Glick, Hersh, 81
Goering, Hermann, 153, 154, 155
Goldbloom, George, 145
Greece,
   German conquest of, 6
Gypsies, 4, 5, 6, 7, 11, 13

Hamburg-Amerika Line, 51
Handicapped, the, 11; *see also* Nazi Party, euthanasia program of
Hate crimes, 154–155
Heck, Alfons, 34–35, 39–40
Helmreich, William B., 144
Hemmendinger, Judith, 145, 149
Henie, Sonja, 38
Heydrich, Reinhard (SS Lt. Gen.), 3, 36
Hilberg, Raul, 45
Himmler, Heinrich, 37, 112, 114
History Place, The, xx, 114
Hitler, Adolf, 11
   rise to power of, 4
Hitler Youth, 34–35, 39–40, 52
Holland. *See* Netherlands
Holocaust,
   bystanders, 45–58, 98
   context of, in European history, 13
   definition of, 11, 148
   and faith, 131
   historical overview of, 3–15
   perpetrators, 33–43
   refugees, 5, 8, 10, 50–52, 96–97
   rescuers, 95–110
   resisters; *see* Partisans; Resistance
   righteous gentiles; *see* Resistance, by gentiles
   and social responsibility, 151–164
   survivors, 10, 58, 89, 100, 130, 131, 142; *see also names of individuals*
   victims, 19–31
Holocaust education,
   components of, xvi–xix, xx–xxi
   guidelines for, xx–xxii
   methodological considerations in, 11–15
   Nazi paraphernalia and, 14

pitfalls to avoid in, 14–15
reasons for, xv–xvi
sources for, xix–xx, 167–199
Homosexuals, 11
Höss, Rudolf, 9, 37
Hull, Cordell, 8
Hungary,
    alliance with Germany, 28
    righteous gentiles in, 76
    war crimes trials in, 9

Internet, 30, 77, 155
Israel,
    as haven for Jews, 10, 144
Italy,
    displaced person camps in, 10

Jackson, Robert, 152, 153
Jehovah's Witnesses, 5, 11
Jewish Brigade Group, 10
Jews,
    Austrian, 4, 5, 156–157
    complicity by; *see* Ghettos, Jewish Councils of the
    Czechoslovakian, 24–27, 84–89, 132–133, 143–145
    Dutch, 82–83, 139
    emigration of, 5; *see also* St. Louis
    German, 4, 5, 20–22, 50–52, 133–134, 138
    German economy and, 4
    Hasidic, 121–125
    Hungarian, 7, 8
    Nazi definition of, 22
    Polish, 6–7, 23–24, 104–106, 115–119, 120–125, 140–143; *see also* Ghettos, Warsaw
    population of, 4, 113
    roundups of, 5
    Rumanian, 27–29, 120–121
    Russian; *see* Ghettos
Judenrat. *See* Ghettos, Jewish Councils of the

Kantor, Rita, 138
Keneally, Thomas, 116
Killing centers. *See* Camps
King, Martin Luther, 163
Klein, Gerda Weissmann, 23–24
Klein family, vii
Korczak, Janusz, 60–67
Krell, Robert, 148
Kristallnacht, 4, 5, 21, 34, 96
Kushner, Rabbi Harold S., 163

Lack, Shulamit, 76
Langer, Lawrence, 89
Latin America,
    Jewish emigration to, 5

Lau, Chief Rabbi Meir, 145
League of German Girls, 35; *see also* Hitler Youth
Lessing, Carla and Ed, 139
Levi, Primo, 45, 53, 71
Lifton, Betty Jean, 63, 67
Lithuania, 68, 69
Lutz, Carl, 96
Luxembourg,
    German conquest of, 6

Mann, Thomas, 97
Masters, Edgar Lee, 157
Meed, Vladka, 75, 89–93
Meltzer, Milton, 103
Memoirs
    All the Rivers Run to the Sea, 28–30
    Anne Frank: The Diary of a Young Girl, 82–83
    "Auschwitz," 117–119
    The Cage, 125–126
    The Children of Buchenwald, 145–148
    Dry Tears: The Story of a Lost Childhood, 104–106
    The Hidden Children, 135–138
    I Have Lived a Thousand Years, 24–27
    I Never Saw Another Butterfly, 84–89, 93
    Images of the Holocaust: A Literature Anthology, 71–72
    In the Shadow of the Swastika, 54–57
    Into the Arms of Strangers: Stories of the Kindertransport, 101–102, 135
    "The Last March," 63–67
    My Bridges of Hope: Searching for Life and Love After Auschwitz, 143–145
    The Nazi Olympics, 368–39
    Night, 27–30, 120–121
    On Both Sides of the Wall, 89–90
    Parallel Journeys, 39–40
    The Pianist, 69–71
    Rescue: The Stories of How Gentiles Saved the Jews During the Holocaust, 102–104
    "Stars," 121–124
    The Sunflower, 156–157
    "The Tenth Man," 141–142
    "Volunteers," 91–93
Mengele, Josef, 124
Messing, Debra, 134
Minac, Matej, 132
Morgenthau, Henry, 152
Mueller, Heinrich, 35

National Center for Jewish Film (Brandeis U.), xxii
National Socialist German Workers Party; *see also* Nazi Germany
    judged to be a criminal organization (Nuremberg), 9

Nazi Germany. *See also names of individual men*
   African-Americans and, 38
   African-Germans and, 5
   anti-Jewish measures of, 21–23
   decrees of, 22–23
   Enabling Act of 1933, 4
   euthanasia program of, 6, 6
   Gestapo, 3, 4, 9, 35
   Jews as central victims of, 13, 22, 76
   and neo-Darwinism, 114
   and 1936 Olympics, 38–39
   physicians of, 9
   racial ideology of, 3, 4–5, 22, 38, 114
   SA (stormtroopers), 4
   SS, 8, 9
   sterilization programs of, 5
   war criminals of, 9–10, 152–154; *see also*
     Nuremberg, International Military Tribunal
Netherlands,
   German conquest of, 6, 139
   and Jewish refugees, 50
   righteous gentiles in, 76, 83
Niemoller, Martin, 53
Night of Broken Glass. *See* Kristallnacht
9/11, 164
Noren, Catherine Hanf, 20
Norway,
   German conquest of, 6
Novels, historical
   Friedrich, 52–54
Nuremberg,
   International Military Tribunal, 9, 33, 35, 151, 152–
     154
   Laws, 21–22, 38, 50

Ogden, Maurice, 46–48
Opdike, Irene, 99, 100
Owens, Jesse, 38, 39

Pagis, Dan, 30
Palestine,
   Jewish emigration to, 5, 10, 142, 144, 145
   UN partition of, 10
Partisans, 8, 54, 76–78
   song, 77, 81
Poetry
   "The Hangman," 46–48
   I Never Saw Another Butterfly, 84–88, 89
   "Sara and Lili," v–vi
   "We Were Children Just Like You," 26
   "Words," 42–43
   "Written in Pencil in the Sealed Railway-Car," 31
Poland,
   German invasion of, 5–6, 59, 69, 157

Russian liberation of, 104–105
   war crimes trials in, 9
Poles,
   in the camps, 7, 11
Political dissidents, in camps, 11
Pran, Dith, 157
Pritchard, Marion, 100

Racism, 154–155
Red Cross, 163
Refugee Relief Act, 10
Resistance, 12, 75; *see also* Partisans
   by gentiles, 71, 76–77, 82–83, 95–110, 136; *see also*
     Children, hidden
   by Jews, 76–77, 82–83
     in camps and ghettos, 8, 54, 78–80, 84–92
Richter, Hans, 52–54
Rodbell, Barbara, 77
Roma. *See* Gypsies
Romania,
   war crimes trials in, 9
Roosevelt, Eleanor, 82
Roosevelt, Franklin Delano, 8
Rumkowski, Chaim, 72–73
Russia. *See* Soviet Union

Sachs, Nelly, 131
St. Louis, 50–52
Schindler, Oskar, 95, 115–119
Schulman, Faye, 77
Sender, Ruth, 125–126
Shanghai, Japan,
   Jewish emigration to, 5
Shore, Ann, 139, 144
Sinta. *See* Gypsies
Social Studies School Service, xxii
deSousa Mendes, Aristedes, 906
Soviet Union; *see also* Allies
   German invasion of, 6
   POWs in the camps, 7, 11
   and Raoul Wallenberg, 110
   war crimes trials in, 9
Speeches, 73
Spielberg, Steven, 115, 116
Stein, Andre, 156
Stimson, Henry, 152
Stories
   "The Merit of a Young Priest," 107–109
Streisand, Barbra, 97
Sugihara, Chiune, 68, 97
Switzerland,
   and Jewish refugees, 145
Szpilman, Wladyslaw, 69–71

Tec, Nechama, 104–105
Trocme, Magda, 99

Umschlagplatz, 69
United Nations, 67, 131, 158–162
United States; *see also* Allies
    Congress, 10, 67
    decision not to bomb Auschwitz of, 30
    Holocaust Memorial Museum, xix, xxii, 52, 83, 110,
        153
    and Jewish refugees, 5, 8, 102
    soldiers, 114
    State Department, 8, 152
    Treasury Department, 8, 152
    War Refugee Board, 8
    white supremacists in, 154–155
Uris, Leon, 93

Van Binsbergen, Marion P., 99
Versailles, Treaty of, 11, 21
Visual History Foundation, xx

Wallenberg, Raoul, 8, 95, 103, 110
Wannsee Conference, 3, 35–36, 111
Weimar Republic, 11
White Rose, 58, 77–78, 102–103
Wiesel, Elie, 3, 28–30, 74, 90, 97, 99, 120–121, 128,
    131, 146–148, 149, 163
Wiesenthal, Simon, 71, 156–157
Winton, Nicholas, 102, 132–133
World War I, 21
World War II, 60, 69, 77, 103, 110, 133, 140, 152
Wronka, Annette, 157
Wygoda, Hermann, 54–56

Yad Vashem, xvi, 71, 100, 103
Yugoslavia,
    German conquest of, 6
    war crimes trials in, 9